Praise for *Addicted to Drama*

"*Addicted to Drama* is an incredible resource of tools for transformation. Whether you're looking to find more peace and intimacy in your relationships, become more resilient and thrive under stress, or break free of cycles that keep you in pain and suffering, this is the book to help set you free."

—SHELEANA AIYANA, Rising Woman, author of *Becoming The One*

"*Addicted to Drama* is a must-read for anyone caught up in this vicious circle. As the founder and president of Cancer Schmancer Movement, identifying dis-ease in one's life and gain the tools to distance yourself from unhealthy habits is the beginning of living your best life in optimal health. This journey we all begin at birth is a learning experience and a constant quest to become more refined, present, and mindful."

—FRAN DRESCHER, actor, health activist,
and author of *Cancer Schmancer*

ADDICTED TO
DRAMA

ADDICTED TO
DRAMA

Healing Dependency
on Crisis and Chaos
in Yourself and Others

DR. SCOTT LYONS

hachette
BOOKS

NEW YORK

Hachette Go, an imprint of Hachette Books
Hachette Book Group
1290 Avenue of the Americas
New York, NY 10104
HachetteGo.com
Facebook.com/HachetteGo
Instagram.com/HachetteGo

First Edition: May 2023

Hachette Books is a division of Hachette Book Group, Inc.

The Hachette Go and Hachette Books name and logos are trademarks of Hachette Book Group, Inc.

The publisher is not responsible for websites (or their content) that are not owned by the publisher.

Print book interior design by Linda Mark

Library of Congress Cataloging-in-Publication Data
Names: Lyons, Scott, author.
Title: Addicted to drama : healing dependency on crisis and chaos in yourself and others / Scott Lyons, PhD.
Description: First edition. | New York : Hachette Books, 2023. | Includes bibliographical references and index.
Identifiers: LCCN 2022050892 | ISBN 9780306925832 (hardcover) | ISBN 9780306925849 (ebook)
Subjects: LCSH: Dependency (Psychology) | Interpersonal relations. | Psychic trauma.
Classification: LCC BF575.D34 L96 2023 | DDC 158.2--dc23/eng/20221102
LC record available at https://lccn.loc.gov/2022050892

ISBNs: 978-0-306-92583-2 (hardcover); 978-0-306-92584-9 (ebook)

Printed in the United States of America

LSC-C

Printing 1, 2023

Author's Note

All names and identifying details have been changed; in some instances, some examples are composites.

Contents

Preface

FOR MOST OF MY LIFE, I ASSUMED THAT BAD THINGS JUST HAPPENED TO ME. Things never seemed to work out. My days felt like a constant series of breakups, betrayals, disappointments, and losses. I was forever saying, "That's the story of my life."

While no one ever called me a drama queen to my face, Lord knows they were all thinking it. And to be honest . . . they were right. I thought that drama just knew where to find me. I assumed it was normal to need intense situations and high-impact exercise to find a single moment of settling or rest. But in reality I was chasing the emotional high, creating conflicts and clashes, and drumming up drama at every opportunity. People may have assumed it was for attention, but as I came to realize, the truth is drama was my way of surviving.

I came into the world with a bang, rupturing two of my mother's vertebral disks as I was born, leaving her in the hospital for months. Generations of abuse and addiction to alcohol, drugs, and gambling set the stage for a chaotic childhood where slaps were given as freely as hugs. The inconsistent environment veered between tenderness and chaos, and I came to expect the unexpected. Love was shown through subversive humor. To love and be loved meant to be funny and entertaining, and I learned to perform for all to see. I spent my childhood disconnected from my body—I refer to myself in those years as *the walking ghost*—chasing after moments where it felt okay to come home to myself. Those moments were far and few between.

At school, I was bullied by both students and teachers who had no tolerance for a young, gay child with a severe learning disability. On many afternoons I was shoved into a locker like the underdog in a coming-of-age movie. I felt trapped, nowhere to run, and needing to get far away. So, at the age of thirteen, I actually faked my own suicide—I meticulously set the stage: tossing pills around, carefully composing the room by placing the bottle just centimeters from my fingers, and writing a good-bye letter. I wanted to punish my parents, my classmates, my teacher for causing so much pain or for not seeing it, not protecting or helping me. I wanted someone to rescue me and sweep me away from the chaos and hurt. I was looking for a deep reset, like restarting a computer gone haywire.

I spent months in and out of the hospital. Every time they let me out, I created a way to get myself readmitted. The hospital felt like stable ground. There was room to be big and expressive. In music therapy, I got to play Tori Amos songs and talk about how they related to my life, sometimes accompanied by an interpretive dance. This sparked the next chapter in my life—channeling that flair for the dramatic.

Drama was my life. After high school, I even made it my profession. Working as a professional actor, director, and choreographer, I was always under stress. My work was a constant resource for drama.

Meanwhile, I met a partner who triggered all my deeply buried pain and dysfunction and brought it to the surface. I always thought I was good at handling stress—what I didn't realize was that I was using it to thrive. My tolerance for dysfunction, crisis, and chaos was being pushed to the limits and was soon well beyond my ability to cope.

I started developing migraines and transient ischemic attacks (TIAs) due to the pervasive stress—I was even losing my ability to coordinate my body. I must have tried to end the relationship a hundred times, and as much as I wanted to, there was a greater force that kept pulling me back into it.

That force—although I didn't realize it until much later—was my hunger, my need for that endless source of crisis.

After my then-partner ended our relationship, I withdrew completely, both from my career and my social life. This was followed by inexplicable, severe health issues (fainting, blackouts, anxiety, depression, tightness in my chest, a racing heart, and spontaneous hypothyroidism).

In the beginning, I thought this was me purging from a toxic situation, but it soon became clear that these intense symptoms were actually signs of withdrawal from prolonged stress. I noticed that the symptoms were relieved for a brief time when I was involved in other people's crises—listening to gossip, watching high-action violent movies, or venting about my ex or other people who had wronged me. I manufactured conflicts with people around me.

I was *creating conditions* that I now understand as one aspect of addiction to drama: seeking sensation through conflict and creating stories that stirred up an emotional charge—which felt oddly soothing because of its familiarity. As a kid, I would escape into daydreams about sharing terrible news that wasn't necessarily true. Imagining involving others in the drama offered some strange satisfaction, as if it settled me.

It was like the worse things got, the more I was reaching for a fix of drama, to the point where my body couldn't take any more. Finally, at the peak of this episode, I went into cardiac distress, resulting in a week of hospitalization.

This crisis finally opened my eyes and I knew something had to change. In the months after the cardiac distress, I began meditating and practicing yoga every day, reading every self-help book I could get my hands on, recognizing my desire for drama, and living through the discomfort of not giving in to the cravings. This was incredibly difficult. I never realized how creative I was with the infinite ways of distracting myself with drama. I lost track of how many times a day I caught myself trying to stir things up and having to talk myself out of doing it. It was also boring as hell. It was like taking out the sugar and spice from a doughnut or all the salt from the popcorn at the movies. It tasted bland. When the spice of my life—drama—was eliminated, everything else seemed unexciting and uninspiring.

After wading through months of the dangerous monotony of spaciousness and quietude, I was able to unearth the historic trauma that had seemingly been protected by the pattern of drama I had constantly created or found myself in.

In *resisting the urges for drama and processing the underlying trauma*, things started to shift. I began to open to a richer and more multidimensional emotional life. I can best describe it as slowly waking up and feeling myself more present and responsive. I felt alive in a way that was different from the buzz I had gotten from riding the emotional roller coaster of a crisis. I was shocked how subtly and quickly my emotions could move through me—compared to when I would intensify every feeling and cling to every emotion, refusing to let them go as they piled up one on top of the other. For once, I didn't feel that life was constantly going wrong, and if something didn't work out, it wasn't a big deal. At the time, I was concerned that my friends would find me unentertaining (or that my therapist would find me boring). But the truth is, it didn't matter if they did, because something healthier was emerging.

In this journey of getting in touch with the past and the ways I negotiated life to manage it, I accessed a deeper sense of self. I developed the ability to relate with other people without having to use drama to connect. Conflict no longer felt like passion, and when things felt good, it no longer meant that something bad was around the corner.

After the dust had settled and the urges to kick the dust back up had become less frequent, I started searching for books or articles unpacking this dependency on chaos and crisis. I was shocked that as commonly as the term *addiction to drama* was thrown around, that there was no science on the subject, no program (twelve-step or otherwise), and no books to guide people through an understanding of what addiction to drama encompasses, how it comes about, and how to heal from it—not just for those with an addiction to drama, but also for the people around them. I decided there and then that I would dedicate myself to finding these missing links, to research, and to fill in the gaps between a firsthand experience of an addiction to drama and the science and psychology of it.

My hope is this book provides a deeper understanding and path to healing an addiction to drama, and a way to cope for those who are in relationship with someone who suffers with it.

PART ONE

WHAT IS ADDICTION TO DRAMA?

CHAPTER 1

The Storm Chaser; the Storm Creator: Identifying Someone Who Is Addicted to Drama

A N ADDICTION TO DRAMA IS FAR MORE COMPLEX, LAYERED, AND PERVASIVE than simply an extravagantly loud cry for attention. It's a way of trying to exist in a world you are constantly out of sync with—chasing sensation to feel alive and seeking crisis as a way of validating an unidentifiable and insatiable discomfort. Being addicted to drama is like driving on life's highway aiming for a place of peace, yet accompanied by an invisible force that seizes control of the wheel and never allows you to take the right exit. Instead of moving you toward peace, it pulls you farther away—leaving destruction in your wake. Living in drama is like getting caught in a storm that's searching for a grounding rod and consequently pulling everything into its vortex—while destroying the ground on which it so desperately wishes to land. This nuanced phenomenon, which many of us are caught in, is no different than dependence on a drug that you might ingest, inhale, or shoot up. Except the "drug," drama, isn't something that you can tangibly hold; you can only seek it or manufacture it.

Drama is the stirring, the excitement, the exaggeration, the eruption, the unrest, and the battle to feel alive in relation to the numbing of the internal and external world around you.

CHASING THE STORM

History is littered with people who thrived in extreme situations. Harry Houdini escaping his shackles in the belly of an embalmed whale. Amelia Earhart attempting to circumnavigate the globe in an early airplane. Evel Knievel trying to jump over Snake River Canyon on a rocket-powered cycle. Tightrope walkers, high-profile athletes, race car drivers, soldiers on battle-fields—whatever their reason, some people are more inclined than others to go where the excitement is sure to follow.

In the mid-1950s, after a particularly strong storm left a trail of de-struction in his hometown of Bismarck, North Dakota, David Hoadley became one of the early pioneers of the storm-chasing world. Storm chas-ing was once the domain of people who were trying to better understand meteorological phenomena, but they no doubt also got caught up in the excitement and the unpredictability of storms. Storm chasing requires heightened senses, an intuitive knack for finding the epicenter of meteoro-logical chaos, and a willingness to leave the safer and more mundane aspects of life. Since Hoadley's day, chasing storms has only grown in popularity, but the risks can outweigh the benefits. Every summer, there are stories of people who get too close to the unpredictable reach of thunderstorms, flash floods, and tornadoes and end up seriously injured or killed.

It's not hard to imagine drama as its own type of storm. The damage it can cause can vary widely and the toll it takes isn't always known until well after the actual incident has occurred. A person might find themself in the middle of the storm by circumstance, but much like Hoadley and his contemporaries, people addicted to drama can also seek it out by engaging, following it, and chasing it down. It can rain where we are or we can go where it is raining. A person suffering from addiction to drama can always find or *create* drama.

Many people say they "feel alive" during thunderstorms. In author Adam Silvera's novel *History Is All You Left Me*, one character remarks,

Storms can suck when they're knocking out power and ripping apart houses, no doubt. But other times the thunder is a soundtrack to something unpredictable, something that gets our hearts racing and wakes us up. If someone had warned me about the weather, I might have freaked out and stayed inside.

But I didn't.

It's not unexpected that people would "feel alive" with drama. In the moment it makes all other worries pale in comparison. Who can be worried about the mundane when the possibility of all-out catastrophe is so close? For some people, this escape can come in the form of watching the storm on film (videos, documentaries, or movies such as *Twister*); others need to experience the real thing firsthand, and like Hoadley, they go out in the world in search of it.

The same can be true of those addicted to drama. "You have to be in crisis all the time or you'll become compliant," says Marline, a self-identified drama addict. "Crisis is the place where action happens. Drama is an inner coil that needs to be wound up and stay that way so it can react."

IDENTIFYING PATTERNS AND CHARACTERISTICS

"How many of you know someone who is addicted to drama?"

When lecturing on this topic, I always begin by asking the audience this question. Nearly everyone raises their hand. Some people even raise both hands.

"And how many of you are addicted to drama?" At my follow-up question, few hands, if any, are raised. This became a continual pattern both when I was lecturing to large groups of people and in one-to-one interviews. Nearly everyone I speak with can identify others as addicted to drama and yet few identify themselves as such. This is the case for most addictions, with those with an addiction the last to self-identify. People who are addicted to drama often are not able to recognize themselves as the origin of the conflict that they unknowingly seek or create.

To help identify patterns in the expression of drama, I gathered stories and observations from a wide group of people and looked for the commonalities between them. This included stories from those who are addicted to drama, those around them, and clinicians who have worked with them. Through my roles as researcher, clinical psychologist, and therapy workshop facilitator, I have been able to work with thousands of individuals to evolve and develop that initial self-exploration. While their stories are subjective and can't possibly paint a complete picture of an addiction to drama—there's a lot of nuance to cover, and every individual is different—this information allowed me to create a profile of the person addicted to drama. Drama addiction is a multilayered pattern with feedback loops surrounding a core internal experience that often manifests in the following ways:

- Feeling out of control, both in themselves and their environment (the speed, pressure, and challenges of the world around them)
- Perceiving the world in extreme or intense terms and sometimes engaging in extreme activity
- Living with a pervasive sense of isolation, betrayal, abandonment, and uneasiness
- Feeling numb much of the time, and trying to remedy it by seeking a feeling of aliveness
- Having a sense of self that fluctuates and disperses, often becoming unanchored
- Making a situation bigger than the circumstance warrants
- Impaired or exaggerated self-esteem
- Having problems with engaging with other people and communicating needs and feelings
- Feeling an underlying current of agitation or something being "wrong"
- Being hypersensitive to stressors, resulting in impulsive, extreme reactions
- Having tunnel vision, tending to focus on the negative with little ability to shift attention
- Feeling a deep and unmet desire to be seen and heard
- Being intolerant, or unable to recognize interpersonal connection and offer or accept empathy
- Seeking, creating, or finding oneself the victim of crisis

Instead of focusing on their own feelings and unmet needs, a person dealing with an addiction to drama will instead focus on an outside stimulus (e.g., situations, events, people, etc.). They may also often feel anxious or bored when things are calm, and feel more alive or thrive under pressure—perhaps filling their schedule to the brim, and then becoming overwhelmed by it. They may pull others into their whirlwind and play out a scenario or interaction over and over again, even adding variations of the original situation. They may live in the past and the future rather than the present—through compulsive worry, repetitive thoughts, stories, reenactments of the past or projected future, and may keep grudges and find it hard to forgive.

(By the way, if this sounds like all of us, basically, Chapter 9 touches on what could be considered a drama epidemic. We'll explore how, in our urgent, go-go-go culture and always-on-display social media world, addiction to drama is actually a daily occurrence for many of us.)

A person who is addicted to drama may be preoccupied with fixing things, space out, or have their attention wander in conversation. They may feel a sense of agency or control during intense situations, or seem to "take all the air out of the room."

They may become reactive or feel exaggerated emotions without clear reasons, and sense that another person or the world conspires against them, and wonder, "Why me?" They may think that others don't understand or validate them and become more critical the closer people get to them. They may retell the same emotional story to different audiences—making the rounds between people—so that they can vent continually. They may be consumed by what's happening in the lives of other people, constantly scanning social media for news or information.

Finally, they may express love or affection through intensity. Intimacy is often replaced with extremes. This could show up as experiencing connection through debating, arguing, big adventures, or falling in love fast and furious.

Some of these characteristics—the intense reactions, exaggerated emotions, unease, agitation, numbness, and dissociation—are also associated with chronic stress, which hint at the genuine, though hidden, cost of addiction to drama.

A LOOK AT THE MONSTER IN THE CLOSET

Drama is the monster in the closet that everyone knows about, but few can put their finger on exactly on what it is.

In surveying individuals who self-identify with addiction to drama, those who identify others in their life with the propensity for being addicted to drama, and clinical psychologists who work with such people, I began to notice familiar comments and themes:

- Drama can be defined as the "unnecessary" turmoil and chaos in one's life or the world.
- It's easy to recognize dramatic behavior but harder to **define** drama.
- Drama is dissonance between an incoming stimulus and the response it produces. A mismatch and exaggeration between external circumstances and internal reactions.

Drama, when used as an adjective (*dramatic*) has been described as a whirlwind—internal for the dramatic person and external for those around this person. For the person craving or creating drama, there is a sense of intensity that feels like an inner warfare. This whirlwind and inner warfare is the world dramatic people live in, and how they perceive and engage in the outer world. It is an internal experience of—and need for—extreme experience. Something is either hot or cold, black or white. *No middle ground exists*.

Drama, as a noun, is more amorphous and poorly defined. It is defined by external circumstances, interpersonal interactions, and the perception of and response to the combination of circumstances and interactions. One participant in my research study defined drama as "life-changing things that I have to deal with all by myself." For yet another person, drama was "the big things that have happened in life in which everybody drops everything and they shout at each other."

But we all react to stressful or difficult situations, so how does one determine the line between a normal response and a dramatic reaction that may suggest an addiction to drama? We humans have evolved to be responsive to internal and external stimuli, but if the dramatic intensity is habitual rather than short term or adaptive, and if chaos and crisis appear to dominate the person's life, an affinity for drama is likely.

- - - - -

BLOWING A BIRTHDAY CANDLE OUT WITH A FIRE HOSE

Drama is a dissonance between what's happening and your response to it. It can also be a way of avoiding oneself. Let's look at Shawn, for example. He experiences life as generally overwhelming, filled to the brim with unending demands that build a tense pressure, like heavy logs sitting on his shoulders and chest. Shawn's calendar is overscheduled—his workday starts at eight a.m. and ends at six or seven p.m., with his evenings full of phone calls and social events. He can never sit still—his days off are occupied with seemingly endless errands, chores, seeing his family and friends, and the work that didn't get done during the week; there's always some project on the horizon before the last one could be completed. When he temporarily unloads his plate of those demands he feels a quietness—and *that quietness leads to an uncomfortable emptiness.* Shawn promptly begins to fill his plate back up until it is sufficiently full and overwhelming once again. He has a "hunger for his neurons to fire." More honestly, he craves and needs the overload to avoid the emptiness lying beneath the surface.

People intoxicated by drama show increased emotional intensity that generally exceeds what we would call a "normal" or expected response, like diving into a hurricane shelter during a light mist or blowing a birthday candle out with a fire hose. Jen, for example, was waiting in line at the pharmacy; when the clerk excused himself to take a short break when it was her turn, Jen essentially "blew up." She went from zero to a hundred in a blink of an eye, demanding to speak to the manager about why they didn't respect her time and why as a paying customer she was being cast aside.

When a person is experiencing a need for drama, they gravitate toward extreme thought, language, habits, behaviors, expression of feelings, and even relationships. Around them nothing is bland or boring. Their emotional life is marked by incessant volatility beyond sudden change or surprise or unexpected emotions. (This can seem attractive to others—at first.)

Habitual drama can be a protective mechanism to defend against experiencing our feelings: a form of suppression and self-medicating. Liz, for example, while she doesn't realize it at the time, is always on the lookout for actions and faults of others that will keep her from feeling her own feelings, such as sadness and rejection. What this strategy does, however, is create numbness to the subtle, deeper, and richer experience of what's happening within her and the world around her.

So, who are these individuals? Before I begin to answer that question, I'd like to turn it to you. Who are these individuals in your life? Mom? Dad? Sister? Brother? Partner? Friend? Stranger at the grocery store? You?

You'll find a section at the end of this chapter to help identify the person with an addiction to drama, whether it is someone else or perhaps yourself.

SO, NOW WHAT?

Maybe you're reading this book because you've been directly involved with people who are addicted to drama. At times you have found being around them exciting and interesting. But eventually (if not automatically) they are simply exhausting, as if they are a vacuum and you are constantly sucked into their emotional whirlwind, one crisis after the next, and nothing you do or say can de-escalate the intensity.

Or maybe you're reading this book because someone assumes you are addicted to drama and bought it for you. If that's the case, I would encourage you to come at this with a sense of humor and an open mind. Maybe, just maybe, there's something you can get out of this book—even if you never agree with the person who gave it to you.

Maybe you're reading this book because you're wondering if you are addicted to drama. Stress seems to always find its way to you, things feel bigger than they are, you are always in the midst of some crisis, and at some point you may notice that a tumultuous home or work environment fuels you—or your friends or loved ones point this out. Even though you might profess a desire for peace or calm, the lack of "noise" of all kinds gives you a sense of unease or anxiety.

You say you want peace and calm, but when you get it, the quietness may feel uncomfortable, or far away and foreign. As you reflect, you realize that your life has revolved in a tight, repetitive rhythm of intense ups and downs that eventually became the baseline of your own tempo. When you are not matching that intense rhythm, you feel alone in the world, like you're out of sync with it.

By the time you reach the end of this book, you may recognize yourself in all three categories. So, do take both of the following assessments, even if you think you already know the answers. I suggest taking them right now as you're reading the book, and again at least a week later, after you've finished reading, learned to identify the signs of addiction to drama, and observed how present they might be in your or a friend's or relative's life. What you learn may surprise you.

If you feel upset or disturbed by your results on these quizzes, take heart. Anyone can change and heal—and achieving self-awareness is the first step on the path to freedom. The final part of this book offers healing practices, regardless of where you sit and how you identify on the spectrum of drama.

IS SOMEONE YOU KNOW ADDICTED TO DRAMA?

Here you'll find two sets of questions. The first will help you pinpoint these characteristics in another person, while the second will guide you to see if you may be addicted to drama.

If any of these questions feel familiar to either something you've experienced about yourself or something someone has told you about yourself (whether you agree or disagree with it), or these questions make you think of one or more people you know in your life . . . then, this is the book for you.

Assessment #1:
Does someone I know have an addiction to drama?

Read the following statements and then rate them on how accurately they represent your experience of them: Never / Seldom / Sometimes / Frequently / Always.

While this assessment is not meant to help create a formal diagnosis of an addiction to drama, it can begin to illuminate just how present the traits and behaviors of an addiction to drama are in someone's life. Again, I suggest taking this now as you're reading the book, and again at least a week later, after you've read through these qualities and observed how present they might be in your friend's life. Tally up the amount of times you circled "Sometimes,"

"Frequently," and "Always." If you circled those responses sixteen times or more, your friend is in good company of the many people who have some propensity for drama. If your responses are more often "Sometimes," the propensity is milder, and if you responded "Frequently" or "Always" then the addiction to drama is more prevalent.

If it seems clear your friend has a propensity for drama, a gentle reminder as you will see throughout the book: they are still an incredible human being who for many reasons adapted this way of surviving.

1. They feel anxious or bored when things are calm.
   Never / Seldom / Sometimes / Frequently / Always

2. Intensity is their language of love.
   Never / Seldom / Sometimes / Frequently / Always

3. They seem to need pain, pleasure, or intense sensations to be in relation to their body.
   Never / Seldom / Sometimes / Frequently / Always

4. Compliments and/or validation are difficult for them to receive.
   Never / Seldom / Sometimes / Frequently / Always

5. They feel more alive or thrive under pressure.
   Never / Seldom / Sometimes / Frequently / Always

6. They recruit others to their state of being, pulling people into their whirlwind.
   Never / Seldom / Sometimes / Frequently / Always

7. They are preoccupied with fixing things.
   Never / Seldom / Sometimes / Frequently / Always

8. They play out a scenario or interaction over and over again—even adding variations of the original situation.
   Never / Seldom / Sometimes / Frequently / Always

9. They find it hard to forgive.
   Never / Seldom / Sometimes / Frequently / Always

10. They hold a grudge.
    Never / Seldom / Sometimes / Frequently / Always

11. They frequently space out or their attention wanders in conversation.
    Never / Seldom / Sometimes / Frequently / Always

12. During intense situations, they feel a sense of agency or control.
    Never / Seldom / Sometimes / Frequently / Always

13. They live in the past and the future rather than the present—through compulsive worry, repetitive thoughts, stories, projecting trouble in the future.
    Never / Seldom / Sometimes / Frequently / Always

14. They sense that another person or the world conspires against them, and they wonder, "Why me?"
Never / Seldom / Sometimes / Frequently / Always

15. They express that others don't understand or validate them.
Never / Seldom / Sometimes / Frequently / Always

16. They feel uncomfortable or restless when a situation is silent, still, or peaceful.
Never / Seldom / Sometimes / Frequently / Always

17. They fill their schedule to the brim and then feel overwhelmed by it.
Never / Seldom / Sometimes / Frequently / Always

18. They are consumed by what's happening in the lives of other people, constantly scanning social media for news or information.
Never / Seldom / Sometimes / Frequently / Always

19. They enjoy being provocative.
Never / Seldom / Sometimes / Frequently / Always

20. They seem to not want things to work out so they have something to talk about later.
Never / Seldom / Sometimes / Frequently / Always

21. They retell the same emotional story to different audiences—making the rounds between people—so that they can vent continually.
Never / Seldom / Sometimes / Frequently / Always

22. They become reactive or feel exaggerated emotions without clear reasons.
Never / Seldom / Sometimes / Frequently / Always

23. The closer people get to them, the more critical they become.
Never / Seldom / Sometimes / Frequently / Always

24. They feel abandoned by others.
Never / Seldom / Sometimes / Frequently / Always

25. They feel closest to people when things are exciting or activating.
Never / Seldom / Sometimes / Frequently / Always

26. When things are going well, they focus on the negative and find something that will make them agitated.
Never / Seldom / Sometimes / Frequently / Always

27. They think about past events or conversations on a loop—reliving them as if they could say something or do something different.
Never / Seldom / Sometimes / Frequently / Always

28. Sitting still or taking time off can be difficult; they feel unrest in rest.
Never / Seldom / Sometimes / Frequently / Always

29. Their presence has at times taken the air out of the room; there's no space for others to talk, share, or hold attention.
Never / Seldom / Sometimes / Frequently / Always

30. Their response to a situation feels bigger than the situation.
   Never / Seldom / Sometimes / Frequently / Always

31. Even when things are going good, they're focusing on problems.
   Never / Seldom / Sometimes / Frequently / Always

32. They "crisis hop"—focusing or jumping from one hardship or challenge to the next.
   Never / Seldom / Sometimes / Frequently / Always

Assessment #2:
Do I have a propensity for drama?

Review and then rate the following statements on how accurately they represent your experience of yourself: Never / Seldom / Sometimes / Frequently / Always.

As with the first assessment, while this assessment is not meant to help create a formal diagnosis of an addiction to drama, it can begin to illuminate just how present the traits and behaviors of an addiction to drama are in your life. While you may say to yourself, "I'll take this later," or avoid this self-analysis, I suggest taking this now as you're reading the book, and again at least a week later, after you've read through these qualities and observed how present they might be in your life. Tally up the amount of times you circled "Sometimes," "Frequently," and "Always." If these are your responses to sixteen or more questions, you are in good company of the many people who have some propensity for drama. If your responses are more often "Sometimes," the propensity is milder, and if you responded "Frequently" or "Always" then the addiction to drama is more prevalent.

And the same gentle reminder holds true here: If you discovered that you have a propensity for drama, as you will see throughout the book, you are still an incredible human being, who for many reasons adapted this way of surviving.

1. I feel anxious or bored when things are calm.
   Never / Seldom / Sometimes / Frequently / Always

2. Intensity is my language of love.
   Never / Seldom / Sometimes / Frequently / Always

3. I need pain, pleasure, or intense sensations to be in relation to my body.
   Never / Seldom / Sometimes / Frequently / Always

4. Compliments and/or validation are difficult for me to receive.
   Never / Seldom / Sometimes / Frequently / Always

5. I feel more alive or thrive under pressure.
   Never / Seldom / Sometimes / Frequently / Always

6. I recruit others to my state of being, pulling them into my whirlwind.
   Never / Seldom / Sometimes / Frequently / Always

7. I am preoccupied with fixing things.
   Never / Seldom / Sometimes / Frequently / Always

8. I play out a scenario or interaction over and over again—even adding variations of the original situation.
   Never / Seldom / Sometimes / Frequently / Always

9. I find it hard to forgive.
   Never / Seldom / Sometimes / Frequently / Always

10. I hold a grudge.
    Never / Seldom / Sometimes / Frequently / Always

11. I tend to space out or my attention wanders in conversation.
    Never / Seldom / Sometimes / Frequently / Always

12. During intense situations I feel a sense of agency or control.
    Never / Seldom / Sometimes / Frequently / Always

13. I live in the past and the future rather than the present—through compulsive worry, repetitive thoughts, stories, or projecting trouble in the future.
    Never / Seldom / Sometimes / Frequently / Always

14. I sense that another person or the world conspires against me, and I wonder, "Why me?"
    Never / Seldom / Sometimes / Frequently / Always

15. Others don't understand or validate me.
    Never / Seldom / Sometimes / Frequently / Always

16. I feel uncomfortable or restless when a situation is silent, still, or peaceful.
    Never / Seldom / Sometimes / Frequently / Always

17. I fill my schedule to the brim and then feel overwhelmed by it.
    Never / Seldom / Sometimes / Frequently / Always

18. I get caught up in an emotional whirlwind and feel hung over afterward.
    Never / Seldom / Sometimes / Frequently / Always

19. I am consumed by what's happening in the lives of other people, constantly scanning social media for news or information.
    Never / Seldom / Sometimes / Frequently / Always

20. I enjoy being provocative.
    Never / Seldom / Sometimes / Frequently / Always

21. I secretly don't want things to work out so I can talk about it later.
    Never / Seldom / Sometimes / Frequently / Always

22. I retell the same emotional story to different audiences—making the rounds between people—so that I can vent continually.
Never / Seldom / Sometimes / Frequently / Always

23. I become reactive or feel exaggerated emotions without clear reasons.
Never / Seldom / Sometimes / Frequently / Always

24. I am most critical of the people closest to me.
Never / Seldom / Sometimes / Frequently / Always

25. I feel abandoned by others.
Never / Seldom / Sometimes / Frequently / Always

26. I feel closest to people when things are exciting or activating.
Never / Seldom / Sometimes / Frequently / Always

27. When things are going well, I focus on the negative and find something that will make me agitated.
Never / Seldom / Sometimes / Frequently / Always

28. I think about past events or conversations on a loop—reliving them as if I could say something or do something different.
Never / Seldom / Sometimes / Frequently / Always

29. Sitting still or taking time off can be hard for me; I feel unrest in rest.
Never / Seldom / Sometimes / Frequently / Always

30. I prefer to be the center of attention in social situations.
Never / Seldom / Sometimes / Frequently / Always

31. My response to a situation feels bigger than the situation.
Never / Seldom / Sometimes / Frequently / Always

32. Even when things are going good, I am focusing on problems or what's going bad.
Never / Seldom / Sometimes / Frequently / Always

33. I tend to "crisis hop"—focusing or jumping from one hardship or challenge to the next.
Never / Seldom / Sometimes / Frequently / Always

KEY TAKEAWAYS

- Drama can be defined as the unnecessary turmoil and chaos in oneself and/or the world. It shows up in someone's responses, behaviors, interactions, or events that surround them.
- An addiction to drama is far more than a desire for "attention." It is a reflection of navigating the world through layers of numbness, discomfort, and internalized chaos.

- Drama is not something people want; it is something they need—and it is something that can be found or created.
- For someone with an addiction to drama, intensity, overwhelm, and heightened feelings, like anxiety, are tools to take the focus away from an internal emptiness or void, and the accompanying emotions that are stirring underneath that void.

Two Sides of the Coin: How We See People Addicted to Drama—and How They See Themselves

THE ASSESSMENTS IN THE PREVIOUS CHAPTER MAY HAVE CONFIRMED WHAT you've been suspecting; you may have had that flash of recognition about a friend or family member, or a sudden awareness or even confirmation about yourself. Many of us know someone who seems to create drama, crave attention, or cause issues where none seemed to exist.

To get an "outside-in" view of someone addicted to drama, I asked small groups of people three questions:

- Do you know a person addicted to drama?
- How would you describe a person addicted to drama?
- What is it like to be around such a person, or what effect does he or she have on you?

All the participants said *yes* to the first question—they all knew someone addicted to drama, usually someone in their circle of friends or family, but sometimes public figures.

BREAKING IT DOWN: THE EXTERNAL VIEW
OF PEOPLE ADDICTED TO DRAMA

The people I talked with shared their stories without hesitation. Listening to them highlighted what I had been thinking and formulating about common themes and traits (some of which we touched on in Chapter 1): overreaction to life events, a need to be the center of attention, preoccupation with their own story, and being in perpetual crisis. Let's take a closer look at how the people closest to those with an addiction to drama view their behavior.

1. "Their world seems painful": they overreact to life events.

People addicted to drama blow things out of proportion. One interviewee noted they have a tendency toward extreme language—"You never hear the words *good, okay,* or *fine* out of [their] mouths," he says. Another interviewee who is an astrologer says that a person addicted to drama can't just say "I'm sick" or "I'm ill"—it's "I'm dying." And, he notes, to "make sure you're paying attention, they perform it with dramatic gestures and facial expressions. It's like they are always on stage."

Tesha's Story

Tesha knows people addicted to drama and lives with one, and she finds herself needing to manage the relationship for her own sanity. "I'm always translating his language, tuning it down to a calmer mode. When he tells me he's in tremendous pain, I think, *Oh, he's hurt.* When it's an emergency, I think, *Well, an emergency for him is simply mild trouble or a small challenge for anyone else.*" Tesha admits that she sometimes responds, even if she knows the issue is exaggerated. For example, "If he complains about being desperately ill, I will say, 'Well, perhaps you should go to the ER.' That usually stops him short because he doesn't really want to see the consequences of his drama, he doesn't want to put it into the context of how others feel."

Tesha thinks that the world the person addicted to drama lives in "seems pretty painful." She points out, "Emergencies lose all their meaning because the drama is chronic, ongoing. If everything is urgent then nothing is urgent. And there's a real danger in that. Because if everyone around the drama addict stops taking the complaints seriously, then what happens when there is an actual emergency, when they really do need to go to the ER?"

2. "It's like being in a cult": they need to be the center of attention.

People with a tendency toward drama rarely stay in the background or on the sidelines. In the event they are able to suppress their urge to be the center of attention, they don't do it for long. Being the center of larger-than-life action seems to confer importance or significance, which, as one interview participant said, "is better than being a meaningless speck in the universe."

Belinda's Story

Belinda says her friend who seems to be addicted to drama always casts things as a crisis so she can be the center of attention. It seems that something is always wrong with her physically: an ache, a pain, an injury, that she focuses on and often exaggerates to others, seemingly to keep the focus always on her. And the urgency of things that others would describe as a "3" her friend treats as a "10." Belinda believes that people addicted to drama are insecure and need much attention, and they get what they need by making scenes and exaggerating stories to make them sound more interesting. Being friends with someone like this, she says, is like being in a cult with that person—and being expected to always agree with them to avoid even more drama.

3. "They are exhausting to be around": they are preoccupied with, and stuck in, their own story.

Like any star of the show, the person addicted to drama needs the one-way interaction of an audience—people whose only role is to bear witness to the drama. That is, except for those who are also expected to play the role of silent costars. The star of the show also likes to assign roles to the rest of the cast. And if cast mates don't deliver the right lines to their cues, then there's trouble. However, as one participant noted, "They have zero interest in your story," especially if it doesn't involve them.

Carter's Story

Carter was easily able to identify several people addicted to drama: "Some public figures, but people I know. My own circle." Carter said that they have a "heightened sense of reality," and points out that the drama is a self-fulfilling prophecy with its own continuous loop. "There's never an end to the cycle; there's always something new to throw into the drama machine to get dramatic about."

Carter guesses that the person addicted to drama "feels more alive, more valuable in some way." But he finds it exhausting to be around someone with this issue, and difficult not to get sucked in. He wonders how he can "detach or be detached without appearing detached," while retaining some semblance of friendship. He adds, "It's a challenge to figure out how I can stay in a relationship with someone without being part of their drama"— and admits that sometimes it's too much work. He has ended at least one friendship over this.

4. "They are always on the prowl": they live in perpetual crisis or chaos.

People addicted to drama seem to always be in crisis, although many people believe the crises are primarily self-manufactured and exaggerated. Some observations from interviewees:

- "Something is always wrong in their lives, and they seem rarely able to view things in a different way or in a positive light."
- "It is a self-fulfilling prophecy."
- "Always busy, always overscheduled," and then "complains about the competing demands."
- "Drama is like rolling down a hill, picking up speed, and unable to stop or slow down the intensity—continually fueled by the stories they tell, the extremeness of their thoughts (especially negative ones), and the bigness of their feelings. Whether they threw themselves down

the hill or fell is less relevant than the fact that once they're rolling down the hill of drama, it just feels unstoppable."

Perhaps the most common theme reported is that it feels terrible to be swept into the storm of the person addicted to drama, and it can be difficult to empathize with the one who has created it. Those interviewed recognized that the chaos in the life of someone addicted to drama feels real to the person suffering from it, but being sympathetic became difficult as the emotional toll grew heavier.

Zack's Story

Zack says it took less than five seconds to think of someone he considers addicted to drama, and then he quickly thought of more. Zack says addiction to drama isn't the same as strong feelings or intense emotions, which he points out that everyone has at times. A key difference, he says, is that "the addict is always on the prowl for material." Zack describes a person addicted to drama as someone who is happy "when there is motion going on, preferable chaotic motion," and in the absence of that motion, he says, they will create it. He compared this to being an adrenaline junkie. He also said that being overscheduled can be "another way to complain about their lives."

THE STIGMA

If you ask someone about a person addicted to drama, you may get reactions ranging from wincing to outright disgust. These reactions are usually lightning fast and quite visceral. People may not know exactly what it is, or what makes someone addicted to drama, but they know how they feel about it, and in general it's not positive.

All of this suggests a clear stigma about a rather fuzzy phenomenon. And stigmas create barriers: few people seek to be informed about the phenomenon, and fewer still are willing to identify with it or get support.

These barriers create a challenge to understanding the elusive, deeply layered, and widespread phenomenon of being addicted to drama. The stigma also prevents us from recognizing how the adaptive survival strategy of drama can interfere with healthy living.

My work has been focused on removing the stigma through defining, de-mystifying, and shining a light on our personal addiction with drama, and its global scale.

– – – – –

THE OTHER SIDE OF THE COIN: WHAT IT'S LIKE TO BE ADDICTED TO DRAMA

Although we've heard from those who interact regularly with people addicted to drama, nothing else conveys the emotional, mental, and physical reality of *being* addicted to drama as somebody living through it. As we will see, this behavior often took root as a survival strategy (in Part 2 of this book, we'll spend more time understanding the root causes of addiction to drama). Let's take a look at what it's like for the person who has this predilection toward drama: the view from the inside out.

Melissa: Unable to Stop Reliving a Traumatic Past

Melissa is a fifty-seven-year-old woman with a history of family trauma. She had grown up in an abusive and unstable home and experienced a significant amount of trauma, including parental abuse, fibromyalgia, sexual abuse, a sibling dying of brain cancer, an injury that left her unable to walk, illness that resulted in going on disability, temporary homelessness, the death of a cousin, and the loss of close friends. It's an overpowering list.

For Melissa, these details are on a constant loop in her head, and so she relives these traumas over and over. She attributes needing an outlet for this excess emotional energy as the reason she became a professional singer and actress. The high intensity that comes with being onstage is a way to channel her dramatic tendencies. Without that outlet, she worries about what further damage the constant revisiting of her trauma would do.

Many of those with a propensity for drama are survivors of extreme and dramatic events, including illness, abuse, accidents, and injuries to themselves or members of their immediate family. But for some people, like Melissa, the incident doesn't happen only once—because the memories don't let up, the incident occurs over and over again, a constant noise that needs to be drowned out in an effort to control the internal world. So, they cannot move on to healing from these events.

Just as not feeling at home in one's body reinforces the feeling of not being at home in the world, not feeling in control of one's own thoughts, emotions, and actions feeds into the sense of the world being out of control. Simultaneously, it is nearly impossible to experience a sense of internal control when the world around seems well beyond individual control.

Helen: Taking Control of Space as a Way to Cope

Those addicted to drama can also exert control, as an attempt to counterbalance their lack of it, by taking over space by being what interviewees described as bold, intense, or larger than life.

Helen describes herself as "an outgoing and sensitive person" and says she makes people's lives interesting. "I can make a lot of jokes," she says, "and it's sort of in a dramatic way and I can overreact in a lot of situations." Helen also notices her tendency toward drama, and the tendency to take over a space.

"When I'm telling a story I really exaggerate it with my language, and my body too. My body is more dramatic without me telling it to be: my body posture and facial expressions. When I'm in the drama, I can feel it in my body, like in my stomach. . . . I can feel it in my heart, and my body takes over. It's like my body takes over my emotions and reactions and it can feel more alive."

Helen says she hates drama but wonders if she is subconsciously looking for it. She considers herself entertaining but adds that she doesn't create drama for entertainment. Upon further reflection about the effect she may have on others, Helen says, "I'm not an evil person. I do it without knowing most of the time." Helen sees her tendency for drama as a way to avoid conflict. "I don't communicate what I'm feeling in the moment," she says. Over a long period of time, the feelings accumulate to an uncomfortable degree. "Things add up that are bothering me and I explode, and it turns into a bigger situation than it really should be." Drama, for Helen, is how she copes with things—but she realizes that "when I'm in it, I'm not really able to cope with what's happening or with the agitation." As a result, the situation gets worse instead of better. Helen acknowledges that her propensity for drama doesn't make sense. "I complain about being stressed all the time, and then I create more stressful situations, and there is a part of me that likes it." The internal world, for the person addicted to drama, can be full of such painful paradoxes.

Rafe: When Intensity Morphs into Anger

Rafe describes his anger when he is not seen or understood as so palpable that it manifests physically. "It is rage or complete hysteria. In the extreme version of it, I'll slam a door or break a glass." He admits that he needs to go to an extreme of being worked up to be able to let go.

Rafe says he grew up in a household that was filled with turmoil and a constant sense of unease. "There was a lot of anger and manic energy," he says. To Rafe, this is what passed as normal. "People would talk over each other. We had to say outrageous things, and do outrageous things, just to be heard and recognized. I didn't realize that it had become so familiar that I was looking for it in every facet of my life—my career choices, my romantic relationships, friendships, in what's happening in the world (news), and in the places I lived, like New York City. This omnipresent tension in the city is like the current I feel in my life."

Rafe was surprised to discover that lovers and friends described him as intense. "It took a lot of work to be able to step outside from my normal" and to observe it, he says, then another step "to know that anything different was possible."

Bringing yoga, meditation, and therapy into his life allows Rafe to contain the chaos in ways he couldn't previously, and he's been working on gaining insight into both others' and his own need for drama. "I've been gaining the capacity to see what's really happening underneath the false exteriors that people put on to convince themselves they have control over things in their life they have no control over," he says. "I've been trying to peel back the layers and understand where the need for drama is coming from and how it has been imprinted in myself. It was a process of finding or being able to receive comfort in states that are lower than the threshold of drama."

Although Rafe can see his propensity for drama more clearly and can choose when he goes into it and how far, he always can feel the draw of intensity and extremes. "Particular people or experiences bring the pull closer to the surface." At such moments, he says, intensity is "nostalgic and sentimental in its familiarity." Expressing his dramatic side is a little bit of a release—a rush. Rafe concludes, "It's okay sometimes to engage and eat the junk food of drama and have the things that aren't so good for me. I've learned to accept the intensity; I wouldn't want to be beige, anyways."

Rafe's comment about "being beige" aligns with the self-perception of others who are addicted to drama. They often see themselves as interesting people who make life more interesting for their friends and family. Rafe, for instance, describes himself as "a provocateur" who "stirs the pot" and enjoys seeing someone being uncomfortable or reactive to something he says or does. He thinks of this behavior as being "really honest with people, like a 'truth sayer,'" admitting, "I'll say things others won't say or things people don't always want to hear."

People addicted to drama and those living with or around them both recognize that the life of a person addicted to drama is intense, given to extremes, and preoccupied with stressors. While "outsiders" observed the need for attention and control, the "insiders" described continuous experiences of feeling unseen and out of control. Outsiders recognize that there is always something wrong, whether distorted or manufactured, in these people's lives; the insiders experience a constant sense of unease, as though misfortune is a constant companion—bad things follow them and happen. Those on the outside feel fatigued from being pulled into the crisis of these individuals; those from the inside feel alone, abandoned, and isolated.

KEY TAKEAWAYS

- If you know someone who is addicted to drama, you likely have observed some or all of these traits: there's always a sense of urgency, exaggerated language and expressions; the need to be the center of attention; reenacting and retelling stories with unnecessary intensity; they can take anything neutral and give it a charge; they are inflexible with any truth but their own; and something is always wrong—as they primarily focus on the negative, shocking, or exhilarating elements of their or other peoples' life.

♦ Those who are witnesses often feel controlled, exhausted, and sucked in to the drama.

♦ If you have or suspect you have an addiction to drama, you may recognize some or all of these traits: the pains of the past have an impact on how you perceive the world now; most things in life feel like a fight or a struggle; not feeling at home (comfortable and confident) in your body; experiencing a lack of control (e.g., of the bigness of your emotions or the crisis you find yourself in), a sensitivity to not being seen and understood; and the drama also gives you a sense of relevance.

♦ The intensities of that past that have been internalized can be brought back to life in the present, by seeking and matching with the places you live, the jobs you do, and the people you associate with.

CHAPTER 3

Common Symptoms and Impacts
of Addiction to Drama

H AVING SPENT YEARS HOPPING THE FENCE BETWEEN BEING IN THE DRAMA and observing it as a therapist and researcher, seven core themes (symptoms) emerged for those addicted to drama. Had I known how common these symptoms are while I was navigating my own addiction, perhaps I would have felt less alone and more hopeful.

"I have cravings for drama sometimes," Helen says. "Recently I felt like I hadn't done anything reckless or spontaneous in a while, and so I got a tattoo. The craving is like a need to spice things up in my life. I can also invent my own narratives—not really based in reality—that end up making me get mad with people, like my boyfriend. When my boyfriend and I fight, I feel like it's the only time he shares his feelings, and so I create these situations as a way to know he cares about me. The fight creates that spice and I get more attention from him. Same with my mom and the tattoo. I think the drama might come out of my insecurities and jealousy, a need for attention. When I'm anxious, I get into these more dramatic situations. It shifts my anxiety somewhere else."

Helen's story is just one example of how someone with an addiction to drama functions in their everyday. Every person with an addiction to drama has similar manifestations; these internal symptoms go with these individuals wherever they go, and whatever situation they're in. It's like walking around with a heavy raincoat through every season and every climate. Instead of a raincoat, people with an addiction are carrying around the pervasive experience of life as a lack of control, full of intensities and extremes, feeling alone, uneasy, and numb, as I briefly mentioned in Chapter 1.

As you might imagine—or as you know, if this is you—living this way isn't easy. Let's take a closer look at these common ways that addiction to drama can manifest, and to understand the toll that it can take on a person's relationships and their mental and physical well-being.

"I DON'T FEEL LIKE I CAN DIRECT MY OWN REALITY": LACK OF CONTROL

Many people who are addicted to drama have a tendency to feel—or be—out of control. They can feel out of control about things around them and out of control of themselves and their mental and emotional response to events. It feels like life has no options for them, everything in the world is coming at them, and they are buried under ten feet of sand. And their response to these feelings is so "automatic" that it seems predetermined by an outside force.

Of course, none of us can control many of the events or situations in our lives, but people addicted to drama may feel considerably less in control. Imagine those inflatable tube sky dancers you see waving about in front of car dealerships or other businesses. Their limbs bend and flex erratically because they're completely at the mercy of air compressors that inflate them and the wind that tosses them around.

This is how a person addicted to drama feels; their internal world is frequently painful and overwhelming. "I don't feel like I can direct my own reality," one client explained. Another person says, "Choice is what those with better luck are given, and hard stuff is always happening."

The inability to control (or predict) the external world leads to feelings of being overwhelmed, helpless, and victimized—something all of us may feel at times, but it's acute for those with a propensity for drama. Taking the wrong exit from a traffic circle may seem like a minor mistake or inconvenience for one person, but for another it feels like it happened "to" them and is an unfair catastrophe and failure.

From the outside, it seems that everything is being manipulated, measured, and controlled. From the inside, however, they are grappling with the many overwhelming forces simultaneously bombarding their life. They are attempting to make music out of a cacophony.

"LIKE A TEAKETTLE ABOUT TO GO OFF": ALWAYS INTENSE

Life is intense for people addicted to drama. The intensity fluctuates, but never goes away entirely. "It is a current that underlies everything," says Lisa, but "it's just that sometimes it's closer to the surface than other times. I'm always aware of where it's wanting to break through or erupt." Another client uses the metaphor of boiling water to describe the intensity of her anger during fights with a lover or her parents, particularly when she feels "wronged in some way." In such moments, she says, "The anger was so palpable that I would just feel like a teakettle about to go off." For her, the water was always simmering.

Intensity for people addicted to drama often translates to an unrelenting sense of urgency—without it, something feels wrong. To reinforce the urgency, they create a life that is overfull with commitments, projects, and deadlines, all competing with one another. Even the mundane is filled with this intensity, and thus the simplest tasks seem heavy and burdensome.

From the outside, it feels like they are bulldozing, overpowering everyone and everything by their speed and frenetic energy. Internally, the intensity feels like a driving force that pushes through everything, a high-throttle chaotic energy that is transferred onto every word and action. It can feel that if they slow down, if they take their foot off the gas pedal, they will die.

"NEVER, THE BEST, THE WORST, PERFECT": BEING PRONE TO OVERREACTION

For those addicted to drama, everything is perceived under a magnifying lens. Extreme thinking, creation of big stories, and the meaning and emotion associated with them lead to overreactions.

Those with an addiction to drama generally feel flooded with something, beyond the extent of what they can handle. Daily incidents feel like a big deal and their language reflects these extremes, with such words as *always, never, failure, absolute, the best, the worst, perfect, disaster, ruined, impossible, everything,* and so on. Finding and creating extreme situations can justify the bigness of feelings—like finding a big enough container to hold it and validate it.

To outsiders, the bigness of the response may appear purposefully manufactured—an expression of personality, a performance that seems to gravitate toward extremes. However, from the inside, it is not. The volume and magnitude at which things are expressed and actions are taken are on par with the volume they are experiencing them.

"NO ONE HAS MY BACK": FEELING ALONE, ISOLATED, AND ABANDONED

Many people addicted to drama feel that they are walking through the world alone. Helen says her "dramatic side" is "very vulnerable and soft and it's longing for being understood and to be heard."

Inherent in the sense of feeling abandoned and alone is a mistrust that anyone would or could support or be present for them. This feeling of aloneness is easily triggered by other people's actions, which is often interpreted as abandonment. Much of the need for drama for Karine, she says, is from "not having anyone at my back. I am completely alone, on my own, having to figure everything out myself." This common experience leads to continued hurt, which is called isolation pain.

From the outside, it appears that those with an addiction to drama are constantly seeking attention and won't take the advice or connection offered. From the inside, everyone else feels so far away and deep connection feels terrifying and overexposing to their vulnerabilities.

"THERE MUST BE SOMETHING BAD ON THE HORIZON": A CONSTANT SENSE OF UNEASINESS

One of the hallmarks of living with an addiction to drama is a constant discomfort or uneasiness, as though something is always about to go wrong. "I feel a presentient sense of malaise in my life," says Martin. "There's always something wrong or something to be fixed." And yet comfort and ease trigger a sense of danger.

Frank, a thirty-two-year-old event producer, says, "It's like constantly feeling in imminent peril—even when there's nothing there. When things feel good, my first thought is *then there must be something bad on the horizon.*" This creates a need for ongoing vigilance; those who are addicted to drama are constantly on the lookout, scanning for the unidentified forces of anxiety.

Many people addicted to drama sense discomfort that lingers and looms like a hungry vulture circling overhead. No matter where they go or what they do, that sense of uneasiness or angst follows. One client says, "Life always somehow feels like I have to be pushing a boulder up a hill, regardless of if the road ahead is flat and easy."

From the outside, this unease is palpable; it takes up all the space, vacuuming all the air out of the room. From the inside, the person addicted to drama is assigning meaning and trying to make sense of the constant sensation of dis-ease. They are battling to find a place between the looming discomfort and the perceived dangers of ease. For giving in to the comfort is conflated with being left defenseless, which can mean they are unprepared for the next bad thing.

"FEELING NOTHING AND TOO MUCH": NUMBNESS AND SENSORY OVERLOAD

Perhaps one of the most overwhelming and ultimately paralyzing issues of an addiction to drama is a feeling of numbness and sensory overload. The numbness or disconnect is most apparent when there is space between the intensity of responses to the world, business of life, or a preoccupation on what other people are doing. We all know what it's like when our foot has "fallen asleep"—for those with an addiction to drama, this is a full-body experience.

They have a continuous sense of too much and not enough of anything, but especially feeling. On one hand, they are highly sensitive people, or as many have stated, "extreme empaths." It's like being stuffed with cotton balls and soaking everything in, says Trina but on the other hand, "the cotton balls also feel like a buffer to the world, a familiar layer of numbness." That numbness and disconnection is often referred to as "boredom" for those who are addicted to drama. (I recognize this in myself: as a child, the closer I got to some version of calm, the more bored I became.) Boredom and being overwhelmed dance hand in hand, oscillating between which one takes the lead.

Felice, a client in her late twenties, describes this experience as follows: "Life is like having all the tabs open on the browser of your computer, and you can't address any of them, so you minimize the window and stare at the blank screen." This results in feeling helpless and a victim to the conditions of the world—intensifying the lack of control I described earlier in this chapter. Another client, Michael, said, "I don't know what to do with all of these sensations and feelings, so I just freeze, and then there is just nothing." As a child, he says, "I really had to be a statue and just kind of swallow all the pain."

From the outside, those with an addiction to drama seem nonempathetic and highly, performatively emotional, invested only in their own drama and narrative. On the inside, they feel way too much, and to survive, may feel nothing at all.

"IT'S LIKE THE AIR IS MOVING THROUGH ME": EXPERIENCING DISSOCIATION AND BEING ANCHORLESS

Accompanying a persistent sense of numbness and unease, many people addicted to drama experience variations of disassociation, or a sense of being anchorless, detached from themselves, and lacking solid ground and a sense of stability. As one client says, "It's like the air is moving through me." They feel like a candle without a wick, or a boat without an anchor or dock. Without this solidity, those with an addiction to drama feel utterly powerless, at the mercy of everything around them.

Being anchorless carries with it the heavy price of feeling lost. There is only confusion where a sense of purpose and meaning is supposed to be. Those with an addiction to drama may appear as though they are all over the place and yet simultaneously nowhere. They will often follow one direction before abandoning it and spinning off into the next direction. Even when there are major accomplishments, it can seems as though no one is home to take it in.

Because self-esteem and self-worth emerge from being able to feel safe and present in your body, those with an addiction to drama feel like there's something always lacking and wrong with them.

Without being situated in one's body, it is difficult to be present in what is actually happening and to judge what amount or type of response is warranted in any given situation. Their perception of a situation is distorted because of viewing it through their own internal storm. One longtime friend said, "When my therapist guided me back into my body, I realized that everything was like Alice in Wonderland, totally disproportionate to how it felt in those moments (of drama)."

To the outsider, those with an addiction to drama seem flaky, inconsistent, unable to sustain attention, and always late. On the inside, however, they are searching for a core sense of self and often mistaking it for the crisis around them.

THE PHYSICAL AND MENTAL COSTS OF DRAMA ADDICTION

No matter what side of the coin you are on, addiction to drama has many costs as the research tells us: it can affect relationships, jobs, and just about every part of a person's life. It also can lead to an assortment of emotional and physical problems. These possible results can include chronic fatigue, autoimmune disorders, fibromyalgia, immune suppression, joint and muscle pain, inability to focus, as well as interpersonal isolation and mood disorders. It can also affect the health of a person's skin, pancreas, stomach, heart, intestines, and reproductive functioning.[1]

As researchers such as Bessel van der Kolk have shown, the physical and the emotional symptoms often emerge hand in hand.[2] Basic quality of life issues are at stake here as well. If you are drawn to the stimulus of drama, it can lessen your capacity to attend to meaningful moments of life. You can easily miss the subtle intimacies and flavors of the day-to-day when riding on the roller coaster of extremes; your tolerance to normal stimulus can also be lowered. Ultimately, this can adversely affect your agency and resilience as well as your ability to stay present, foresee choices, and feel empowered to make informed choices. All of this impedes the ability to engage with meaningful challenges, the kind of adaptive responses that can stimulate personal growth.

Additionally, similar to other addictive behaviors, habitual drama—in essence, an addiction to intensity and chaos—may cause withdrawal-type symptoms when whatever triggers the drama is not present. And like someone addicted to drugs needs more or stronger doses to continue to get high, so can a person addicted to drama. People addicted to drama become accustomed to the volume or intensity of the dramatic situation and the internal chaos, and need more and more of it.

When a 10 out of 10 stressor becomes the new normal, we may start to seek the 11s and 12s to fill the hole of that hunger. In this way, drama changes from being a choice, one possible response to a situation, to being a characteristic of who we are.

Addiction to drama also deeply affects those around the person addicted to drama, creating stress, chaos, or turmoil. Multiple studies show that people exposed to the drama will experience similar psycho-physiological effects that the person addicted to drama does.[3] Just being in the vicinity of the inflated, dramatic situation creates a secondary stress response, a transmission from the person addicted to drama. Unlike nearly all other addictions, this one directly affects those nearby and can even be contagious—you can think of it as something like the dangers of secondhand cigarette smoke. To use another analogy, if you think of listening to an evocative story, the narrator's tone, rhythm, language, and emotionality can pull you into the story as though you were suddenly part of it. Drama can seem like this. Just as one driver slows down to view a wreck and then other drivers follow suit, people around drama can be drawn into it without making a conscious decision to do so—often resulting in a pileup.

Beyond these mind-body effects, addiction to drama creates major tension in relationships—so much that those impacts are addressed in a separate chapter. Let's take a look.

KEY TAKEAWAYS

- There are six key features of experience for those with an addiction to drama:
  - » A lack of control
  - » An intensity in both the force and magnitude of how they act and also as the underlying current and urgency with which they feel
  - » A familiar feeling and sensitivity of being alone, abandoned, and isolated
  - » A consistent sense of unease and discomfort, a pervasive sense that something is or will be wrong
  - » Feeling oversensitive and numb—creating an experience of life that there's either too much or not enough
  - » A common theme of disconnection with themselves; dissociation
- Slowing down or relaxing triggers an underlying anxiety.
- The cost of an addiction to drama is psychological, emotional, and physical.
- Like most addictions, a tolerance is built—requiring more drama to keep the cycle going and to avoid the withdrawal symptoms that occur.
- Also, like most addictions, it has an impact on those around them, ultimately creating similar physical and physiological challenges in others as those who are addicted.

CHAPTER 4

The Cycle of Creation and Destruction: Drama and Relationships

ERE'S HOW ALICIA, WHO IDENTIFIES HERSELF AS ADDICTED TO DRAMA, describes her relationship with her boyfriend: "When it's good, it's beyond great! And then, it can also be so painful and I just want to burn it all down. I can get really frustrated. Sometimes, my emotions are so big or strong that I lose sight of what I was originally frustrated with. I often feel wronged and unmet—but truth be told—it's hard being in touch with what I want or what I need in the first place." Alicia says she thinks if her boyfriend could just meet her needs, all would be well, but she's not always sure what those needs are. One of the hallmarks—and consequences—of an addiction to drama is the way relationships are in a constant process of creation and destruction.

Humans are a social species, wired for connection and building social bonds. Relationships can help regulate our mood, help us adapt, boost our immune system, and even reduce pain. But for those with an addiction to drama, relationships become more complex. Intimacy can feel dangerous, and relationships can become a place to project unexpressed and unprocessed feelings. The highs and lows of relationships become the hit that satisfies the unrelenting craving for drama. Drama can play out as jealousy, blaming, withholding, spying, cheating, intense fights, emotional affairs, passionate makeups, and a lack of boundaries—essentially, the real-life version of a sensational talk show and reality television.

The word *relationship* does not always mean our bond with a lover, friend, relative, or colleague, but it can just be the capacity to connect; the disruption of connection can extend to jobs, places, projects, or even things. However, for this chapter, we will focus on how connection and disconnection show up in relationships with other people.

RELATIONSHIPS THROUGH THE LOOKING GLASS

Relationships on all levels, even with yourself, serve an evolutionary objective: survival. It's the tension between simultaneously *wanting and rejecting social bonds (connection)* that creates many of the behaviors in a person addicted to drama.

Not all relationships built on chaos are considered negative—at least, not at first. People with a propensity for drama can seem quite alluring and exciting. There's something magnetic about their personality, and like a skillful actor or storyteller, they can draw you into their world, living a more enlivened existence vicariously.

Daniel says: "At first it's exciting, you feel drawn in, like you're special, like you're part of something more interesting than the mundane of the everyday. It feels similar to the way you're drawn into a good movie or performance, and your heart's racing—it feels exciting, fresh, new, somehow life confirming. The stories they share feel alive, you feel swept in and enlisted."

This level of validation in a relationship may not be sustainable, but it can be difficult to withdraw, as Daniel explains. "If I'm to be completely honest, it's like once you get a hit of the excitement, it's hard not to keep going in for more. So, the only thing to do is totally disengage . . . but then there's the fear and backlash of becoming the subject or target of their drama."

– – – – –

THE CYCLE OF CREATION AND DESTRUCTION

Addiction to drama is a constant cycle of creation and destruction of relationships and the tension that builds up in between. If you have interacted with those with an addiction to drama, you know this tension; it feels like a whiplash from a car wreck you can't get out of. If you aren't familiar with this experience, try this: With one of your hands, imagine pulling something or someone in—and, with the other hand, imagine simultaneously pushing them back. Let one hand take the lead (with the push or pull) before the other one comes in and takes the lead. This is the relational dance of those addicted to drama.

For the person on the receiving end of this tension, it feels as if you are being tossed around without any ground to land on, utterly disoriented. This push-pull dynamic courses through every relationship for those who are addicted to drama.

Elsewhere in this book we will talk about attachment theory: how early experiences of safety, connection, or disconnections form behavioral patterns that we may act out within our relationships, also called reenactments (Chapter 7). Before we go more deeply into *why* drama shows up in relationships (Part 2), we will first explore *how* drama manifests through the cycle of creation and destruction.

THE WATER IS ALWAYS SIMMERING: ENTERING INTO A RELATIONSHIP

Those with an addiction to drama don't begin to interact with others from a place of neutrality. I often say their starting point is more like a simmer. To understand what I mean, imagine if every time you turned on your faucet, the water immediately came out boiling hot instead of cool or tepid. Thinking about how to use—engage with—the water, whether for drinking, for showering, or whatever you might need, you'd assume using that water was going to be difficult or even dangerous and navigate from there. For those with an addiction to drama, it's like the water is always simmering, so that is where they begin.

Imagine a young girl who grew up in a house where family members were unpredictable. She wasn't sure when they were going to yell, ignore, or shame her, or when there would be another big storm. Her intuitive response to the fear and terror was to get small, as small as she could, and hide. If that underlying terror had a voice, it would say, *"Find a hiding spot within yourself and don't let anyone in."* That is exactly what she did.

Over time, the little girl developed a countermeasure to having to be small and hide, and like Alice in Wonderland, she created a version of herself that was so big that it was able to defend herself and not be ignored—a size that would be impossible not to see.

From the outside, these two versions of herself show up as big reactions that feel unwarranted, a reaction to being triggered that can morph into a blaming tantrum, a perpetual recycling of the same issues, or an inability to let go of the triggering element, followed by a collapse into what feels like the energy of a wounded child.

Both these survival strategies, simultaneously hiding and becoming exaggerated in size, kept her from getting what she ultimately wanted: to be seen and heard, to authentically express herself in her true size, and ultimately to be surrounded by safe connection.

The common symptoms described in the previous chapters form the starting point for those who are addicted to drama and influence how they engage in relationships. In the same way that relaxation can trigger a feeling of alarm for those addicted to drama, so can intimacy, sharing one's true self through closeness and connection. As I've mentioned, an addiction to drama involves layers of numbness and desensitization. To be intimate would mean to let go of the protective numbness—but the fear of letting go of numbness is that the "thawing out" of that deep freeze would be more painful than what caused it.

INTIMACY IS A TWO-LANE HIGHWAY

Intimacy, as felt through connection and relationship, is a two-lane highway. Meaning, we receive others as we are simultaneously received. For those with an addiction to drama, this bidirectional highway of connection is closed down as a means to filter out chaotic, unpredictable environments or to mitigate pain. Once this blocked highway becomes the new normal, it's not easy to open it back up.

When sharing something intimate with someone who is addicted to drama, it often feels like they are preoccupied and not really able to take in what you've been saying. With clients who exhibit this block in the highway of connection, it often takes a lot of work and patience for them to reestablish vulnerable connections. For example, my client Martina will look glassy eyed and blank when being told how well she is doing, how much she means to another person, or just any direct intimate connection. Martina shared with me a letter she received from her eldest daughter documenting how wonderful a mom she is. She immediately made a dismissive comment about how her daughter must have felt pressured to do so for Mother's Day. The moment I invited her to pause and take in the meaningful words of her daughter's letter, she began to fidget and change the subject.

To describe this inability to receive, I often use the metaphor of bringing a cup of tea to your lips but never actually taking it in or tasting its flavors. Being unable to feel, receive, absorb, or taste the flavors highlights a sense of perpetual absence in these people's life.

A simple practice to highlight bidirectionally of a relationship is to sit on a chair. Hold your body very rigid and tight, almost as though you are pulling yourself up and away from the support of the chair. Now, release the "holding" and focus on where your body is making contact with the supporting surface. Let your breath travel to those points of contact. Perhaps see if you can notice where the chair is coming up to receive the weight of your body. Notice where you can give yourself permission to be received by the chair.

This simultaneous flow of letting yourself receive and be received is that highway of bidirectional connection. Pulling away, becoming rigid and incapable of receiving the support or contact of the chair, is what it's like to walk around with an addiction to drama. (If this exercise was helpful for you—and I hope it was!—don't miss the Appendix at the end of this book, which offers many more useful practices and meditations.)

Someone who is addicted to drama is not truly making contact with the world around them. To those on the outside, it can often feel like the "[insert their name] Show"; it feels like it's all about them, that they relate to everything by telling stories about themselves and hijacking the conversation. But what may seem to be narcissism can be caused by the lack of this bidirectional connection. When cut off from taking in the outside world, people are unable to truly feel belonging or connected. They are trapped within themselves, where they are their entire world.

- - - - -

CREATION: FORGING A CONNECTION THROUGH A WHIRLWIND

If you happened to have missed the birth of the universe, well then, let me fill you in—it was chaotic. As the universe was essentially creating itself, simultaneously expanding and contracting, small changes were having disproportionally large-scale effects, like a butterfly flapping its wings in Mexico creating a tornado in Canada. For those addicted to drama, the processes of creating relationships are like the mayhem of the big bang; connections are often fast, exciting, high energy, creative, and intense. In this stage, those with an affinity for drama tend to become their own center of gravity, pulling everything and everyone into their orbit of chaos.

The challenge for people with an addiction to drama is how they seek connection and how they allow for it. We express love, and receive love, through our love language, a concept that Gary Chapman, PhD, developed in his book *The 5 Love Languages*. Chapman explains that for some people, acts of service, gifts, physical touch, quality time, or words of affirmation are their primary love language. Drawing on my work with clients and my interviewees, I would add that for others, their love language is chaos and crisis.

If someone grew up with caregivers who primarily showed attention when things were heightened, bad, or intense, that person likely began to adopt that as their love language. Intensity became their currency of exchange for love and became synonymous with what love means for them. This could include starting fights for no apparent reason, gossiping, being involved in other people's conflict, feeling closeness only when people are pulling away. The intensity of these relationships can often get confused with depth, but in reality, the connections are rather shallow or superficial. Being in relationship or simply in proximity to the drama can feel like being pulled into a perfect storm—the "whirlwind." For the person addicted to drama, pulling others into a dramatic whirlwind is the familiar and seemingly only "safe" way to get close to people. When bystanders get pulled in or become involved in the drama, they are matching the chaos frequency of the person stirring the crisis to form a whirlwind. And from the perspective of the person who started the whirlwind, it feels like someone has finally tuned into their radio station and they feel heard and seen—with a moment of connection. A person with an addiction may stir up the whirlwind to foster connection in the following ways:

Escalating Situations to a "Comfortable" Chaos Level

When your early relationships are built on presenting yourself at a higher volume to be seen and heard or believing that a stable connection is a chaotic one, it's going to be mirrored in any interpersonal relationship later on. Stirring things up re-creates the familiar connections, and as a result can create a sense of accessibility to connection. My client Elizabeth shared that she knew her son was wanting attention, but it just felt like he was "on Mute" until his chaos or the crisis around him reached a certain level. Suddenly, when his screams and actions reached a heightened decibel of intensity, she could hear him, spring into action, and attend to his needs. Before that, he would feel ignored, which would generally escalate him to the level of activation where Elizabeth needed to engage. This negative feedback loop is exactly what was required to connect. Elizabeth would say, "It's not that I want to fight with him; it just feels more familiar and easier when he's on my level."

Bonding Through Trauma

Getting bystanders riled up and activated enough to be pulled into their crisis is a learned skill for those addicted to drama. However, they soon discover it is much easier to pull in someone who is already primed for it. Someone addicted to drama might seek connection through affinity bonding—bonding through shared trauma—with people who get easily activated around similar things. Candace, whose sister is addicted to drama, shared, "It's like my sister can intuit when I'm upset with someone. Just the other day I was frustrated with our brother-in-law, and without missing a beat, she started sharing stories and gossiping about him until I was pretty riled up and furious with him. At first, it felt validating, and then I just felt like I lost my footing and felt totally immersed in something bigger than me."

When there isn't an affinity bond, those who are creating the whirlwind have to work harder to pull people in. However, the perceived reward for doing so extends beyond a momentary sense of belonging and connection.

Pulling people into the drama also makes it easier to confirm and justify the "rightness" of the cycle of drama. When you see other people convinced of your stories, it's that much easier to also convince yourself. Pulling others in allows the creator of that whirlwind to feed on the other person's activation—it's like acquiring an extra battery pack to maintain the cycle of drama.

Weaponizing Empathy

Another hallmark of those with an addiction to drama is connecting to others through weaponized empathy. Weaponized empathy is often accompanied with such language as "I just want them/you to feel what I am feeling . . . the stress, the pain, the hurt." Not being able to have a bidirectional relationship means not truly being able to receive empathy, validation, or even apologies—thus weaponized empathy emerges.

Weaponized empathy is creating or forcing the conditions in which you believe someone will have the same feelings or experience as you did. It can look like punishing someone: continuously bringing up the past "wrongs" of that person over and over again, using harsh language, shaming, intense and extreme stories or interruptions of what they said or did (or didn't say and do), and enlisting others to turn against someone.

While this seems like it would be an instrument to push people away, for those with an addiction to drama the intensified conflict is a way of connecting. The internalized belief is that "If others know my pain, I'm no longer alone in it." Or "My suffering has to be at a high enough volume for others to truly hear it." However, the inability to be validated, to receive someone else, makes it impossible to feel truly connected and empathized with. Those addicted to drama are trapped in a loop of being wronged or victimized, with constant relationship ruptures. This also manifests as perpetually demonizing, targeting, villainizing, and othering people.

For those who are addicted to drama, pulling people into their whirlwind creates a "safe" relationship, one where they finally feel in sync with those around them. However, whether from the person's intolerance for intimacy or that the others involved begin to return to their own baseline, that brief moment of connection and belonging becomes unsustainable.

AMPING IT UP: AFFINITY BONDING

Recently a friend's teenage niece, Lucy, came home from school and told me she had a difficult day with one of her teachers. I invited her to walk me through what happened and listened and validated her experience—a typical adult friend-as-a-psychologist situation. After talking with me, she seemed fairly calm, but then Lucy went right to a Zoom call with her friends. Within what seemed like seconds after sharing about her day, they were all throwing logs on the proverbial fire—voices shouting, revenge plots imagined, and so on. Because they all knew that particular teacher and were in the same "middle school nightmare," it took little effort for this primed group to take a spark and make a massive bonfire of drama.

After engaging with her friends, Lucy was more agitated and upset throughout her whole body than when she had come home from school right after the incident. On a scale of 1 to 10 of agitation, she was at a 5 when she came home. But after "affinity bonding" with her classmates, she was at a full 10. After the call, she was inconsolable and none of my psychologist skills could help her settle and reconnect to herself.

My mother, who was also there, leaned over to me and said, "Don't try to calm her; you'll only make it worse. She will eventually burn her way through it, but first she'll have to talk to her friends a few more times, let everyone know how much her life sucks and how she is a victim, and then likely do something irrational." When I asked her how she could so easily predict that process, she said, "Teenagers invented an addiction to drama . . . why don't you make that a chapter in your book?" We had a good laugh and watched, as over the next few hours, my mom's prediction played out exactly as she had said.

- - - - -

DESTRUCTION: RUPTURING RELATIONSHIPS

Every living creature has a fundamental impulse for connection and closeness. However, for those addicted to drama, once a connection has been made by pulling people into the whirlwind, there is only so much time before that person begins to feel overwhelmed with connection and needs to withdraw from the vulnerability that is emerging with sustained contact. It's a vicious cycle: People with an addiction to drama use coping responses that at one time protected them (from hurt or overwhelm), but that now prevent intimacy or create ruptures in relationships. In other words, these historic strategies of safety become default mechanisms for interrupting and disrupting connection.

Let's look closely at the four most common coping strategies: deflection, retroflection, projection, and confluence. These coping strategies are what lead the person addicted to drama to use lying, blaming, manipulating, creation of stories, and other actions of destruction that sever temporary connection.

- **Deflection** is passing focus/attention onto someone else. Deflection creates a barrier—nothing from the outside world gets in—and as such, creates an inability to absorb, take in, or be affected by other people's experience. It is typically associated with strategies of denial and gaslighting. Utilizing the strategy of deflection, the person addicted to drama might say things like "That's not what happened," "You're exaggerating my response," "You're making that up," or "This is actually about you." On a less extreme level, an example might be when you ask a friend how they are and they respond with a question about you, putting the focus on you. Using deflection is a defense against receiving any new information that may challenge their beliefs or their reality.

- **Retroflection** is turning something in on oneself, when people are unable to express their feelings with someone. Retroflection often emerges when the person has a history of not being heard, received, or allowed to express thoughts and feelings. When applying the strategy of retroflection, the person often becomes cold, rigid, and distant. Their jaw tightens and muscles in their chest, diaphragm, and arms clamp down, physically cutting themselves off from other people or the world around them. They are essentially shutting down all their feelings as energy is being diverted to armoring themselves. This in turn creates a sense of being trapped within themselves, unable to express what they truly need, and unable to effectively get other people or the environment to meet their needs. The self-generated pain reinforces the value—and necessity—of interrupting connection with other people. Utilizing this strategy might sound like "No one can ever meet my needs or understand me, so I'll just do it myself." For example, Alex is angry with his partner for something he said. But instead of being able to express his anger to his partner, Alex says cruel and punishing things about himself to himself. He becomes cold and distant, and then resentful of his partner for not making amends, even though his partner attempted to do so.

♦ **Projection** is moving all perceptions, feelings, and thoughts from oneself to another person or the environment. A hallmark of projection as a strategy is not "seeing" or "feeling" the people they are with or events that are happening, but only seeing them as the unresolved trauma, stories, history, and issues that are being projected out onto them. As a result, blame and paranoia tend to emerge, and the person addicted to drama will push their feelings onto another person, saying things like "You've disappointed me / let me down / got in my way" or feeling anger internally and saying to others, "You're so angry." An example here would be Maria's friend, who accuses people of persecuting her and believes they always mistreat her. "She was always the one facing injustice and unfair treatment but was the one creating fights—trying to pit some friends against others to create conflicts and dramas with them," says Maria. "She was your best friend one minute, but if you were two minutes late or didn't respond to her text quickly enough, she obliterated the connection between you, and then blamed you." Projection is often the stories that get put on other people or situations that create the conditions and/or justify the extreme feelings and behaviors that are part of the cycle of drama.

♦ **Confluence** is the opposite of deflection. The person, in essence, *merges* with what's happening around them, as though the crises of the world are personal. When this strategy is employed, the individual often is perceived, or views themself, as being very sensitive or a martyr. Speaking from this strategy might sound like "your pain is my pain," wherein there are no boundaries or filter between the world and that person. They may watch the news about a crisis happening overseas and feel like they are part of it, or feel the pain of a celebrity getting divorced. Or they can only be happy when in the presence of someone else's happiness. These responses go beyond normal empathy. Instead, it is as though someone else's pain or the pain of the world becomes fuel for their own fire. It can feel like the air is being taken out of the room when someone is utilizing confluence. Marcus shares, "I was married to a drama addict. I remember telling her my mother was diagnosed with cancer, and she became hysterical, sharing how scary that was for her and how she knew people who had died of cancer. She then began to cry for all of them . . . There was no room for me to have my own experience. It was like she vacuumed it out from me."

Addiction to drama is unique because there isn't one stable strategy for interrupting connection—but rather a continual oscillation between the strategies . . . which can often feel like being tossed around to the person on the receiving end. Each of these coping responses helps create and validate the rupture of any connection or the continual distance needed to feel safe. In essence, these coping responses are tools of disturbing connection and contact with other people, themselves, and the world around them.

THE DRAMA TRIANGLE

The "triangle" of drama was developed in 1961 by Stephen Karpman, MD, and is used in psychology to describe three rotating roles or personas that someone will take on in relation to conflict with other people or events. Dr. Karpman's work provides an easy handrail for looking at some basic characteristics of people with an addiction to drama. They will rapidly switch back and forth between the roles, leaving a wake of confusion and instability for those around them. Karpman describes the personas as follows:

- The "Persecutor" finds fault and accuses others, creates superiority, blames, threatens, or charges at others from a framework of injustice.
- The "Rescuer" is always trying to be "helpful," meddling, feeling guilty if not doing, perpetually sharing about all that they do, and enabling (a very classical representation of codependency and an avoidance of connection to self).

- The "Victim" will feel oppressed and victimized—and when there is an absence of conditions that justify the feeling, they will seek or create the conditions. As a result of rapidly shifting between these coping strategies, it feels like whiplash and a destruction of any connection that had been formed.

These are roles that people who are addicted to drama cycle through subconsciously—or project on other people.

- - - - -

RELATIONSHIP RECAP

In this relationship cycle, connection is often as intense and extreme as the destruction. Those with an addiction to drama pull people into their chaotic vortex (whirlwind), which allows them to feel in sync with the chaos of others, a variation of connection. When someone with an addiction to drama begins to experience vulnerability from intimacy, the person may begin to search for or create friction to interrupt that connection, which can turn into larger ruptures. The ruptures seem to start from something seemingly innocuous and be confusing to those involved. The person addicted to drama will create and share stories to justify their actions, claim victimization, and the wrongdoing of others. This moves them further and further away from the intimacy that provoked the rupture.

It's the push-pull relationship I described earlier. The dramatic patterns of relating can be a way of protecting oneself from further harm or abandonment *by keeping people at a distance*, using drama to feel power and control in the relationship. Dysfunction and mayhem create a predictability that is soothing to the underlying anxiety. To end a relationship or keep others at a distance through the creation of drama could seem less painful than if the other person were to leave on their own. One client, Susan, admits that it's much harder to have someone leave her than the other way around. She adds, "Drama comes out of needing to be heard and needing to be acknowledged, you act out to make sure they do, and then sometimes from that you end up losing that person."

In relationships, inner and outer scripts get acted out:

- **How could they?!**
- **I should have never trusted them!**
- **Why am I always the one to be wronged, why me?**

These internal stories are used to justify the feeling of profound alone-ness and as more fuel for the whirlwinds, which bring those with an addiction to drama back into closeness. And the cycle of creation and destruction continues over and over again.

By now, you have a clear perception of what addiction to drama looks like and the effects that it has on individuals and those around them. Now, it's time to deepen our understanding by looking at the roots of this addiction. As I've briefly mentioned, these behaviors often begin as a survival tactic. Recognizing where those behaviors come from, and why they can stick, is the next step on our path to interrupting the cycle of drama and moving toward healing.

KEY TAKEAWAYS

- We are evolutionarily designed for relationships and connection. For those with an addiction to drama, connection, intimacy, and relation-ships are both desired and triggering.
- Intimacy is a flowing connection within oneself or between two or more people. For those with an addiction to drama, this bidirectional-ity connection is shut down as a means of survival.
- Those with an addiction to drama develop unique compensation pat-terns to feel less alone. The primary method is by creating a whirl-wind of chaos and pulling others into it.
- Connection on any level over time will begin to trigger historic pains. This, in turn, triggers survival patterns of relational destruction, ultimately causing a cycle of creation and destruction.

PART TWO

UNDERSTANDING
THE CAUSES OF AN
ADDICTION TO DRAMA

CHAPTER 5

Building the Perfect Storm:
The Baseline of an Addiction to Drama

M ARIA THE FIGHTING FISH GREW UP PUSHING AGAINST THE RELENTLESS currents of the frigid Arctic Ocean. Her scales hardened to maintain her body temperature and give her additional protection against constant threat from predators. The toughness of her scales could move her through the unpredictable changes in turbulent currents and battering storms. Maria's vigilance and ability to quickly jump into action kept her alive in an extreme environment.

When Maria was caught, she was brought to land and placed in a tranquil pond with no predators or dangerous storms. You might think, "Oh, the pond is a safe place, with more predictability and a peaceful environment, so of course the arctic fighting fish would find happiness." But the warm, placid pond was so dissonant with Maria's habituated rhythms that she felt out of sync. Although there were none of the dangers of the Arctic, Maria could not adapt to the absence of stimuli that she had become accustomed to.

Maria soon began to take on the role of protecting the other fish, which then transitioned into starting fights with the other passive fish. Maria would often go to the center of the pond and swim in circles so fast that she created stormy whirlwinds. By creating havoc, Maria upset the balance of the ecosystem; the entire pond became dysregulated. The resulting anxiety and the cacophony of the pond felt familiar to her: she finally felt at home, from her tough scales down to her bones. Maria could spring into action once again, giving her back her sense of purpose. It's what she needed.

Upon first glance, most people assume Maria—or someone who is addicted to drama—is attention seeking or inherently disruptive. However, attention seeking and disruption are means to an end. In Part 1, I mentioned that addiction to drama often arises as a coping mechanism; now, we'll begin to unpack what that means.

No matter where you place Maria the fighting fish, in the dangerous Arctic or a placid pond, she has a baseline, a status quo, a way of being and existing in the world that has become foundational to who she is. A baseline is the starting point from which you interact with and operate from, in the world. Our accumulated experiences inform our baseline way of being.

Matryoshka Russian nesting dolls are a series of wooden dolls, each one incrementally smaller than and placed one inside the other. When you open up the largest one, there is another, smaller one inside, and so on, until you reach the smallest figure. If you were to halve a matryoshka doll you would see layers, like the rings in a tree trunk or the layers of an onion.

In the same way, the baseline of an addiction to drama is built upon layers of coping responses that are encasing deeper layers of numbness and pain:

First, innermost layer: the unmet primal need of being seen and heard
Second layer: isolation pain that leads to an undeveloped sense of self—a
    lack of personal identity, or sense of who you are
Third layer: numbness, which keeps pain from being felt
Fourth layer: sensation seeking, the response to being numb

When these layers intersect under pervasive stress, the experience becomes normalized to a state of perpetual inner chaos. *Emotional, mental, and even physical turmoil become the norm.*

To understand how this happens, let's take a look at each layer from the inside out.

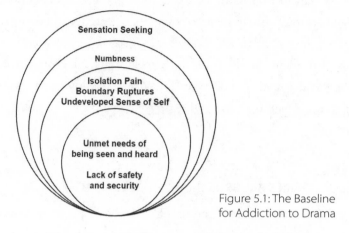

Figure 5.1: The Baseline
for Addiction to Drama

LAYER 1: NOT BEING SEEN AND HEARD

An unmet need to be seen and heard—the innermost circle in Figure 5.1—is the origin of an addiction to drama.

Nearly everyone I interviewed for this book described a lack of presence, connection, and support in their lives. Individuals with an addiction to drama often speak about the challenges and crises that were acted out within their family and the roles they found themselves assigned to. Some became the center of a crisis; others became the family's mediator. Some tell of parents who used their pain to draw attention to themselves rather than giving their attention to their children. And still others say the only way to possibly be seen or heard was when something was wrong or large enough to be attended to. As a friend once told me, "I used to think my mom only loved me when I was sick or in trouble . . . otherwise I didn't get much attention."

Being seen, heard, connected to, and allowed to authentically express oneself are primal needs. When those needs are met, we feel safe and loved; when they're not, we feel unsafe and isolated. This primary need of feeling connected can be affected by the presence or absence of trust, accountability, safety, respect, expression, honesty, consistency, patience, security, and cooperation.

Because the emotional and expressive processes of the person addicted to drama, as well as their fundamental presence, went unrecognized or unsupported, they feel a profound sense of loss. The feeling of being unheard and unseen become a core experience that sits within the foundation of who they are. It is the soil from which all things grow. In particular, a sense of isolation and disconnection—from both their inner emotional world and their outer world—tends to take root. This disconnection becomes an invisible and pervasive pain that drives this person's life, as do their strategies of coping with it.

LAYER 2: BOUNDARIES ARE BROKEN AND THE SELF IS LOST

The second layer that creates the baseline involves personal boundaries, core self-development, and the pain of isolation.

Boundaries are essentially our personal guidelines and limits, giving us a clear sense of where we begin and end. They can be physical borders or symbolic limits. They give us space and allow us to make choices between stimulus and response—what's coming in and how we express ourselves as a result. The functionality of our boundary sets the precedence for what we are able to say yes and no to. Types of boundaries include the following:

- **Physical/spatial boundaries**, which involve our personal space, our physical needs, and our comfort with touch; they allow us to express our need for closeness or distance between things (events, stressors, or people). For instance, giving and receiving consent to being touched is an important physical boundary.
- **Emotional/energetic boundaries**, which are arguably our most primal way of discerning between "I," "you," and "we." They are all about respecting feelings. This might mean connecting with others, internalizing others' emotions (or not!), and knowing when to share and when to hold back. Having emotional boundaries includes an awareness of how we express ourselves and how much bonding or connecting we need in any given moment.
- **Resources boundaries**, which involve an awareness of how much of your resources—whether time, energy, focus, financial, or material—are available in any given circumstance. This includes getting to

choose how those resources are distributed, used, and shared, and making sure you have the space to replenish them if they get depleted.

♦ **Mental boundaries**, which are the clarity, choice, and expression of thoughts, beliefs, values, and opinions. These include the ability to say yes and no to where your attention is directed. They also involve respect for other people's thoughts and ideas.

During our lifetimes, and especially in childhood, our boundaries have a profound effect on the development of self and our ability to identify and regulate our feelings, needs, and values. We can express our boundaries either consciously or unconsciously—their functionality and health can be revealed through our words, actions, thoughts, behaviors, energetically, and even the posture of our body—essentially how we move through the world.

Healthy boundaries represent an ability to feel stable, clear within oneself, and able to articulate feelings as an expression of one's needs—without trying to control someone else. Healthy boundaries are not absolutes; a healthy boundary is about adaptability with integrity. A healthy boundary is knowing how much "yes" and how much "no" is needed in any given moment. Thus, the adaptability and health of our boundaries reflects being able to be present in the moment, in the here and now. For a simple visual of a healthy boundary, imagine a water balloon. The balloon creates a boundary that holds the water and allows it to stay intact, but still lets it change its shape somewhat. The water, in this analogy, represents the core sense of self that our boundaries contain and protect. Our core self is a developed sense of who we are that influences how we think, feel, and act. Someone with a vibrant sense of self is motivated, balanced, and self-aware, readily able to "read" situations with acuity and to choose a healthy response to them.[1] Our sense of self grows and evolves through our interaction with other people and the environments around us—and this interaction is modulated by our boundaries. It is through our boundaries that we affirm our sense of safety, which allows for intimacy in relation to ourselves and other people.

Boundary challenges and violations are a much more common day-to-day experience. For example, a parent calls too often and asks too many questions, your roommate borrows a shirt without asking, or your boss texts you on the weekend. Think of the water balloon being pierced by a needle. The boundary remains intact; however, the healthy functionality of the boundary may be momentarily suspended.

Boundary ruptures, on the other hand, are the unhealed tears in the fabric of trust, security, and safety. Think of what happens to a water balloon that gets a large rip or tear. Boundary ruptures and their aftermath have a foundational presence in an addiction to drama. Boundaries can be ruptured in two basic ways: overstimulation (such as violations of personal space, overwhelming and unpredictable environments, or even feeding off the chaos) and understimulation. Understimulation occurs when a person feels unseen, unheard, unattended to, and perceives little or no opportunity to authentically express their innermost emotions and thoughts—in short, layer 1 of our baseline.

When the boundaries of the self are ruptured, our personal vitality and integrity are endangered. As an example, take my client Melissa, a self-proclaimed "second-generation drama addict," who spent her entire childhood navigating parents who would rope her into their drama. As a child of a person addicted to drama, you have two options—you survive by feeding off the fight as well or you completely mute yourself, essentially becoming numb to yourself and the world. Melissa would often jokingly say in our sessions, "Boundaries, what are boundaries?!" She struggled to identify her own needs and feelings, and the idea of not putting others first was excruciating. Both as a child and adult, her own space and sense of safety were never hers; she was constantly being pulled in whatever direction her parents, or the other people around her, were orchestrating.

To adapt after a rupture, people modify their remaining boundaries; they may try to change or control the environment, change or control themselves, or freeze. Essentially, we lose our ability to be flexible and adaptive in the present moment.

Some people compensate by forming rigid and inflexible boundaries, while others collapse into nearly nonexistent boundaries. When our boundaries are too rigid, we may miss important social and emotional cues. People with excessively rigid boundaries form rigid relationships; when closeness or intimacy starts to develop, they pick fights, project stories that create distance, or spiral in a way that pushes the other person away.

Those with an addiction to drama tend to simultaneously have rigid and leaky boundaries. Their day-to-day boundary challenges feel as though they are monumental ruptures. Eugene, a client who after some time identified with an addiction to drama, would often speak about his sense of boundaries being like Swiss cheese: full of holes. He describes himself as very sensitive, feeling and being overwhelmed by others' pain. For as long as he could recall, he would have no boundaries in the beginning of a relationship and then overnight became stiff and rigid in his relationships. Eugene described it like the aperture of a camera: it was either too open, overwhelming his senses, or sealed shut, leaving him alone. Ironically, Eugene could simultaneously feel overwhelmed by the world and yet alone in the dark, a familiar experience for those with an addiction to drama.

A person who has had ruptured boundaries will attempt to compensate to the best of their ability, but will often become hyperreactive or nonreactive, withdrawn, disassociated, and groundless with a stunted sense of self.

A well-developed core self gives a feeling of a solid, grounded identity that can mostly tolerate the ups and downs of ordinary life without feeling overwhelmed or victimized. For example, when facing challenges or stressors, you are able to stay present and stable within yourself—knowing and maintaining your desires, values, strengths, sense of purpose—and navigate that situation. A clear sense of a core self allows us to be present with another person or environment while still being clear on what is happening within us.

Not having a strong core is like being a leaf blown in the wind. One young entrepreneur describes the absence of this anchor as "feeling like I can't direct my reality or being in touch with what I want or what I need." For these people with an addiction to drama, there is a frequent feeling of isolation. Isolation can be the absence of others around us, the absence of being able to receive connection, and can also be the absence of a sense of self, which includes an ability to perceive one's own subtle sensations, emotions, needs, desires, and intuition. The result of these compounding sources of isolation is pain. (Many people experienced social isolation in the COVID-19 pandemic and can attest to the ache of this level of aloneness.)

Mind-body research suggests that the experience of physical and psychological pain are nearly indistinguishable.[2] Strong social bonds are at the core of our survival as humans, so we are designed to experience pain as a response to social rejection and isolation. Studies have shown that the disruption of social bonding in childhood—the inability to form warm, secure relationships with important others—is associated with widespread chronic pain.[3]

These social bonds are also interrupted when adult relationships end. People suggest that romantic breakups are the hardest, partly because of the unexpected physical and mental reaction. I grew up with Disney movies as my model of love, so for me, it was radically surprising to feel love for the first time, and the complex feelings that come with it—from joy to nausea, nervousness, and clumsiness—quite different than the imagined magic carpet ride I had learned to expect. The same can be said for the breakups—the feelings can come as a shock. With my first heartbreak, the level of ache in my body was on par with the time I broke my leg playing soccer . . . except it lasted longer and I felt it everywhere, in my chest, belly, and even my arms. How could this be? Why would a separation from another human being become a physical pain?

The purpose of pain is to keep us from doing anything else that could cause more pain—this is a form of protection. This can be physical or emotional pain. Whatever the source, it's natural that we brace, hold, and freeze until it's safe enough and the wound has been healed.

As noted in Part 1, often those with an addiction to drama describe a constant sense of unease and discomfort—an elusive and unidentifiable ache. Prolonged pain that becomes part of the baseline turns into a pervasive sense of an "underlying current" of discomfort and unease.

One client, Ismar, said, "The ache has been there for as long as I can remember. It's like how people describe feeling an old injury when it gets cold. Maybe it's a pain or maybe it's a longing, maybe that's the same thing. Often, I feel like that pain wants to grow, like it wants to be fed. And I go have more shitty relationships or find myself in situations that are hurtful. And bam, that inner ache has been fed, and it gets bigger! I think it wants to be fed so it can make itself big enough to be found or can't be ignored anymore."

Whatever the source of isolation pain, whether it's from being unseen and unheard in early childhood or a later boundary rupture, the coping mechanism is the same: forming a layer of numbness to keep emotional, physical, and social pain from coming to the surface. This brings us to layer 3 of our baseline.

SHAME

Shame is a by-product of a boundary violation or rupture. We've all likely felt some version of shame. We might have said or done something that we later regretted or felt humiliated by. Someone else may have said or done something to you that shrank you down.

Healthy shame is meant to be temporary. Like pain, shame on a physiological level is intended to immobilize our biological processes, even for just a moment, to give us time to pause, reflect, and evaluate the potential harm we are enacting on others or ourselves so we can then repair. In healthy shame the focus is on the behavior and not the person; ultimately there is a way back to connection and belonging. Here's an example of healthy shame. A playful child runs into the street to chase a runaway ball. The parent sees the child doing the very act they were just warned against. The parent runs over and pulls the child back to the yard. They begin to scold the child saying how wrong the action had been, how dangerous it was—and for what, a ball?! The child and parent have a temporary rupture of the relationship. This allows for a pause to evaluate and learn from what is happening, then there is an opportunity for the parent to mend the rupture and say, "I love you so much, and it scares me when you are in danger. When I raise my voice, it's because I really need you to hear how important it is that you stay safe. I love you very much." A hug ensues and the cycle of healthy shame (rupture and repair) has completed itself.

Humans are not designed for prolonged shame, which is toxic shame. Toxic shame is pervasive; the act of the rupture continues beyond a singular moment. In toxic shame the person considers themself to be the problem (such as bad, risky, problematic, intense, etc.) and they internalize it as the label of who they are (consciously or subconsciously). In toxic shame, the individual stays in the rupture. The same playful child from the previous example is scolded and told how stupid she is for risking her life for a ball, that she doesn't think before she acts. She is then sent to her room on a time-out to think about her mistake. When the child emerges from her room to apologize, her parents respond by reminding her that she has to start to think before she acts—or there will continue to be serious consequences. There was no repair to the rupture, and the shame begins to make itself home in the young girl's body and mind.

Angela's mother used to shame her for loving her father more than she did her. No matter what Angela accomplished musically or academically it was viewed as trying to impress her father. Over time, Angela believed she was someone who overshadowed other women and made them feel small. She spent a lot of energy trying to make herself small around other women and refused to accept compliments from them. Having absorbed and identified with the pain of unhealthy shame for so long, Angela became hyperfocused on the aches and pains, often using those as an excuse not to focus on her feelings. No matter what type of physical therapy she attempted, it wasn't until she started addressing the internalized shame that she began to get physical relief.

As children, our parents or caregivers, even with the best intentions, can leave us with a confusing sense of rejection and shame. Studies show that the children of parents who are depressed and have flat affect internalize the lack of parental feedback as rejection—which results in toxic shame.[4] Shame leads to a fear of rejection and an isolation to avoid further rejection. Ultimately this becomes a part of their baseline.

Toxic shame leads to a feeling of being unworthy of connection, bonding, and belonging. It creates a deeply rooted sense of being flawed and worthless. These beliefs get integrated into beliefs around the self, sealing in the original moment of shame—the original rupture. Because the original rupture or trauma is held in the body as implicit memory, it is experienced as though it's continuing to happen in the present moment, and the person is stuck in the shame spiral.

Long-term shame leads to long-term numbness—it becomes more difficult to handle challenges and sensory input from relationships, and our fundamental stress response becomes impaired.

- - - - -

LAYER 3: BYE-BYE FEELINGS, BYE-BYE SENSATION. . . . HELLO NUMBNESS

After many months of working toward tolerating the feeling of a nonexaggerated emotion, a client, Ian, turned to me and said, "Wow, we can be aware of ourselves and still not be in touch with ourselves." Ian was referring to the level of numbness that had become his baseline—the distance in the way he experienced himself and the world. For those with an addiction to drama, numbness follows pain.

Numbness has many forms, but fundamentally it is a coping mechanism for surviving when sensation and feeling exceed a tolerable threshold. The proverbial cup that could hold the experience is either overflowing or broken, subsequently sending the person into energy conservation mode—a freeze response. Morgan, a young client, affirms this, saying, "I have felt frozen in life, like a lack of movement, and often because of that, I feel like I'm at the mercy of the world."

Numbness is associated with psychological dissociation in which someone is essentially taking a vacation from their body. When numbness becomes a habit, a part of baseline functioning, it creates challenges. This is often why those who are addicted to drama seem like they are "performing"—there's a palpable distance between the bigness of their feelings and behaviors and what's happening within themselves. People addicted to drama have some version of dissociation in which a part of them is continually cut off from the rest. One person described it as "like having one foot in the door of myself and one foot out—all the time."

In chaotic environments, people learn to filter out stimuli. Medical professionals often experience "alarm fatigue or alert fatigue" in response to being exposed to frequent alerts. They then become desensitized to the alarms and may miss them completely. Similarly, ER doctors, nurses, and paramedics become more and more desensitized to the intensity and severity of what occurs in emergency rooms.

Desensitization is imperative in some situations, but it impacts the ability to emotionally connect with oneself or others. When the adaptive and necessary strategy of desensitization gets generalized and used in other settings, it creates a challenge to being adaptive or responsive to what's happening in the current moment. The same is true for emotions that may have been suppressed due to a lack of safe space, permission, or support. People cannot avoid a single sensation or emotion without affecting all sensations and emotions. They are part of a global system, and thus strategies of suppression and numbing have a global effect.

During our first session, Melinda told me that she came in for treatment because her friends all said she was a drama queen. I asked Melinda what emotions she was allowed or had permission to have.

She immediately responded, "All of them."

When I asked, "What of all of those emotions do you feel?" she looked at me as if I were speaking a foreign language. She took a few moments before saying, "When I have these big feelings, it's like I'm drowning in them, and I guess I am not feeling what I'm drowning in."

I then asked her to pick up the apple she brought and hold it. "What is your response to the apple?"

Melinda responded, "Neutral."

I invited her to take a bite and notice her response.

Melinda again responded, "Neutral."

I invited her to describe the qualities and characteristics of the apple . . . the taste, the weight, and so on.

As she was describing it, she said, "It's strange, I suddenly feel more connected to it . . . like before I was distant to it and now I'm closer."

I had her call up a memory of something we were talking about earlier in the session and we took some time for her to feel into the emotions like she did with the apple. She was able to do it for a moment before she felt something shut down inside: "I could start feeling the texture of the emotion like I did the apple," she said, "and then all of a sudden it was like I hit a wall and got kicked out of my own body, whoa!" In that moment, Melinda was able to recognize how distant and numb she had been . . . how walled off her inner sensations and feelings had been, despite the big emotional explosions that would make her friends call her a drama queen.

While a hallmark of an addiction to drama is extreme feelings, reactions, and behaviors, the intensity is not actually part of someone's baseline—it is in *response* to it.

The confusion between how an individual could be both numb and disconnected from their sensations and feelings, and yet be seen with large and unregulated emotions, can be answered quite simply. These individuals are essentially responding emotionally to the memories of the past and the stories of the future they are creating, as opposed to being in touch with what is happening in the here and now. The past and future serve as an escape from the underlying feelings and sensations of the present. Thus, they can be quite responsive with large feelings, but feel out of touch to the given circumstances of that moment. In turn, living outside of the present moment becomes part of the baseline.

BIG FEELINGS, BIG DISTRACTION

I once witnessed a woman at a dinner table clink her fork on her plate, smile at the sound of it, and say, "I guess I was starving."

I replied by asking, "Didn't you know you were hungry before, seeing how fast the food left your plate?"

She responded, "I guess not!"

We often look for large external or peripheral cues to indicate how and what is happening in our body and mind. The truth is that the further we get from the subtle cues of sensation and emotions, the more external cues we rely on, and the more distanced we become from ourselves.

Here is another example: Often when we are taking a yoga class, we assume we aren't doing the work unless we feel some extreme stretch sensation in the body. In reality, the profound effects of yoga arise from a state in which awareness and feeling merge and we experience the subtler sensations of the body—emotions, gut feelings (intuitions), and safety—as our inner guidance. We are able to acquire that information from a quieter, more introspective state. However, sensations such as stretching, burning, and pain reach the brain faster, thus they take up our brain space and attention—overriding by sheer speed and volume our body's subtler sensations and cues.

For those with an addiction to drama, the bigger and more intense reactions and experiences, not to mention the heightened focus on activating and painful things, distract from underlying more subtle sensations and feelings. For example, my clients often say "I feel a lot . . . I feel angry or abandoned all the time."

However, they have difficulty locating and feeling these responses in their bodies or other emotions such as sadness or disappointment. The big global intense state takes the driver's seat, while the smaller, isolated emotions become quiet passengers. When clients who are addicted to drama came into contact with true sadness, especially, they often immediately begin sensation seeking (as a means to avoid that feeling). So, the extreme emotional states often associated with addiction to drama are in fact a loud distraction from being able to contact the subtler underlying emotions.

People addicted to drama tend to use particular feelings, such as anger and frustration, as an expression of all other emotions. The scenario might go like this:

> If I can't feel sadness or joy, I will pour that into the only container I have for expression, which might be anger, and the only way I can get that feeling is to create a scenario in which I've been wronged or abandoned. The sensation of anger also confirms my sense of aliveness. I feel alive and real when I'm angry.

A client, Veronica, recalls her first dissociative experience when she was a child, saying, "Like I'm half in my body and half running away from it. Like I can see myself from the outside." The emotion of anger helped anchor her: "My anger helps me stay in my body. I can feel it. It helps me feel my core."

Those with an addiction to drama have revealed that explosive anger was often used as a grounding cord to come back from feeling dissociation as well. In this way the big and more extreme feelings are both grounding and distracting.

– – – – –

LAYER 4: FEELING ALIVE (SENSATION SEEKING)

One of the ways we confirm our aliveness is through what we feel: I feel, therefore I am. I have meaning. Thus, out of numbness and the desire to be part of something or someone, we begin to deliberately seek big sensations.

Sensation seeking is a willingness to take any social and physical risks in an attempt to find or create an experience that produces a response that rises above the threshold of numbness, and confirms a sense of being alive— no matter the cost.

Research has shown that those who score high on addiction scales also generally score high on sensation-seeking scales and are more easily bored.[5] In fact, sensation seeking and the propensity to take risks predispose people for substance abuse and other addictions.[6]

Have you ever experienced your foot falling asleep, and to try to wake it up, you tap it or hit it against the floor? And then increased the amount of tapping and hitting as you go along? Now imagine, instead of your foot, that disturbing sense of being asleep extends through your whole body, and the only feeling you have is unease or discomfort. In response to the numbness, people seek sensation to feel more alive by engaging in drama, which can momentarily rectify some of the numbness. In this way, sensation seeking is finding the right volume of stimulus, something high enough to confirm one's aliveness.

When my dog, Charlie, began to lose his hearing, he would start howling for no apparent reason. He presented numerous signs of anxiety—as though the world as he knew it was disappearing, leaving him in an empty vacuum. To soothe him, I would place a radio near his bed. As the months went on and Charlie's hearing got worse, he began howling again. That was the sign to turn up the volume on his radio, increasing the decibel level to essentially keep him company and mitigate Charlie's feeling of being alone.

For the person addicted to drama, craving sensation becomes part of their baseline. **Drama is not about making sense, it's about making sensation.** The blaze of drama offers a false sense of release and completion, while simultaneously providing distraction and even satisfaction. It is an adaptive response to trauma and emotional loss. The challenge is that when we are sensation seeking, we can simultaneously be inundated from it and build up an immunity to it. In the end, like the tolerance phase of any addiction, we require more and more stimuli, relying on stress to feel something—anything at all. That's what leads to the dependence on drama, as we will see in the next chapter.

THE FIGHT TO FEEL ALIVE

The sensations of the dramatic situation help those with an addiction to drama feel that they exist, that they are alive. Or, as one person put it, "Who am I without my problems?" The physical, mental, and emotional sensations derived from extreme situations helped them to feel "something," and in feeling that something they can feel more alive.

Here is how some people try to feel more alive:

- "I have to really rise above the threshold of numbness to feel connected and alive," says Karine. But her intensity ends up pushing people away, she says, then she just feels abandoned.
- For Miki, certain emotions help them feel alive or, rather, don't cause them to freeze, go numb, or shut down: "I can feel anger and shame without shutting down, so I evoke those feelings. To feel something, anything, is to know I'm alive."
- Kyle says: "There is numbness, but there's also another part where I'm doing all this stuff to really try and feel something. So, if it's burning myself or taking a drug that's going to really, like, change my experience in a remarkable way . . . [then] it's to feel something. Maybe the numbness is there first, but then it's just this explosion of a kind of self-destruction and acting out in violence."

Ordinary life with its routine aspects can seem potentially threatening for the person addicted to drama. Ordinariness is uncomfortable rather than calm or peaceful. To the person addicted to drama, it can feel like nothing, or nonexistence.

– – – – –

KEY TAKEAWAYS

- ◆ A baseline is the starting point of how someone with an addiction to drama interacts with the world. This baseline comprises four primary layers of experience:
  - » The unmet need to be seen and heard
  - » Ruptured boundaries. Those with an addiction to drama form extreme boundaries that oscillate between rigid and leaky, ultimately

resulting in unmodulated emotions, inaccurate assessment of the present moment, and a loss of connection, which forms a pervasive isolation pain.

» Numbness, which takes several forms including dissociation and an absence of being able to connect and express the feelings and needs of the present moment

» Sensation seeking, which entails creating, or finding, the conditions for them that will produce sensations big enough to supersede the widespread numbness

CHAPTER 6

Wired for Drama: The Role of Stress

Y OU ARE GOING TO DIE.

We all are, of course, and on some level, you know it. But that knowledge didn't stop your eyes from widening, your heart rate to increase or skip a beat, your breathing to instantly become shallow, or your mind to race when you read those words.

In one sentence, I have created a stimulus and response cycle, an electric stirring of excitement—a moment of chaos. We humans don't enjoy being reminded of our inevitable deaths (the stimulus), but when we are, we experience a spike of physiological arousal that sharpens our attention and creates a thrilling surge of energy coursing through us (the response).[1] It's just the way we're wired; this surge is an integral part of adaptation that has helped *Homo sapiens* survive and evolve for millions of years. Our brains receive this burst of sensation as a reward—and so, paradoxically, the reminder of death is also a tactile confirmation and affirmation of being alive.

That's just a little taste of what the person addicted to drama feels. If you are addicted to drama yourself, hopefully this helps you to continue to recognize and contextualize what's happening. In the previous chapter, I mentioned that when the layers that form the baseline intersect under pervasive stress, a constant sense of chaos becomes normal. But what does stress have to do with addiction to drama? Well, it has to do with the psychology and physiology of stress and our capacity to adapt to it—and in this chapter, we'll break all of this down.

Let's begin unpacking the addiction to drama by considering the two main ingredients, *chaos* and *crisis*.

- *Chaos*, which originates from the Greek word for an abyss or void, is a state of confusion, unpredictability, and dis-order. In this book, we will use it to define the internal experience of drama.
- *Crisis* is an event or condition of instability and danger affecting an individual. In this book, it will be used to define external experiences, those arising from the surrounding conditions, relationships, or environment.

In the same way that addiction to drama can be unpacked into the elements of crisis and chaos, stress can be unpacked into its two elements: stressor and stress response. A stressor, simply put, is a stimulus; a stress response is the internal change in relation to the stressor. As we saw in the previous chapter, someone who is addicted to drama has a dependency on both crisis and chaos; they are reliant on stressors and their stress response.

But what *is* stress? Do you understand what stress is and how it affects your body? Most of us weren't taught the full, complex picture. A high school science teacher of mine once said, "If you didn't have stress, you would die." On one level, this makes sense; to a certain extent, we all need stress for stimulation (and some stress is necessary and healthy). On another level, it doesn't really make much sense at all: Why would something destructive be necessary for survival?

WHAT IS AND ISN'T STRESS

Write down your nonacademic definition of stress, the one you might tell a nine-year-old.

Next, write a sentence or two about your relationship to stress.

Now, read your definition out loud a few times and notice what happens in your body as you read.

Did you perhaps notice some activity in your body? A little heat or tension? Perhaps a shortening of your breath or narrowing of your vision? Well, that response is all part of your body's natural reaction to a stressor—in this case, the stressor was stress itself! (That reaction also holds a big key to understanding an addiction to drama, as we'll see later in this chapter. But let's stick with stress itself for now.)

This is the moment in the conversation when people typically say or think, "Stress is awful; it gets me sick and makes me unable to deal with things well." The statement "stress makes me sick" has merit—but it's not entirely true. Understanding the processes of stress can illuminate its more nuanced complexity.

Contrary to what you might think, stress is not an evil villain lurking around the corner placing cinder blocks on your chest. Rather, it's a biological process of adaptation and survival.

Although the relationship between stress and diseases is well known now, it wasn't always so. Hungarian-Canadian endocrinologist Hans Selye (1907–1982) introduced the term *stress* in the early 1930s, defining it as "the non-specific response of the body to any demand for change."[2] And stress, as it relates to the body, is essentially our biological means of adaptation. Rather than viewing stress as a villain, Dr. Selye explained it in his 1956 book *The Stress of Life* as the way we adjust to what's going on around us: "Life is largely a process of adaptation to circumstances in which we exist."

We all have some inner capacity to adapt to the stressors of life. However, not every person has the same adaptive capacities. The important point is that stress is not inherently good or bad. It is the body-mind's response to an event, situation, or person. It's about getting the body-mind ready to take action—and inevitably to adapt.

LET'S ADAPT: THE STRESS RESPONSE CYCLE

If someone throws a baseball and it's coming straight at your head and you just stand there, it's a fair assessment to say you are not adapting to life's

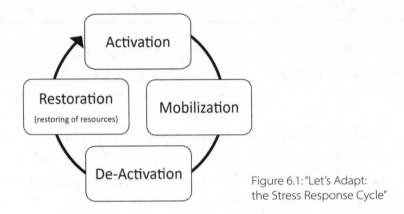

Figure 6.1: "Let's Adapt:
the Stress Response Cycle"

circumstances. And if you're responding to a baseball that isn't even near you or are unconsciously running directly into the pathway of an oncoming ball, you may not be adapting optimally to life's circumstances either. The stress response cycle is your biological process of interacting with the stressors (stimuli) of the world and adapting to them.

In interacting with a stressor, a series of effects prepares us to engage and then helps us recover. Whether the stressor or stimulus is real or imagined—you're running late for an important meeting or seeing a stick on the ground and thinking it's a snake—the body response will be the same.

As the illustration shows, there is a four-stage cycle. Your nervous system plays a large role in how you react to stressors.

Activation or arousal, the first stage of the stress response, is the state of preparing ourselves to engage with the stressor and adapt. Our nervous system and endocrine system respond by releasing stress hormones that make our pupils dilate, cause our blood vessels to contract, and put nonessential functions (e.g., digestion) on hold. Our field of vision narrows, so the stressor comes sharply into focus, and everything else is blurry and ignored. The world in this state is experienced differently, like shifting from a panoramic view to a portrait view. This is often referred to as the "fight-or-flight" response, and it's the stage most of us are most familiar with: we feel the tightening of our muscles, our heart pounding, and energy building inside of us as our body gets ready for action.

Mobilization is when the surge of energy is used. That could include running, jumping, moving toward or away, ripping, pushing, and so on. Mobilizations are by no means violent in nature; they are simply the action of response and adaptation. The part of our nervous system that controls our skeletal muscles kicks into action, allowing the physical response.

Deactivation is like a coming-down process. A relaxation reflex occurs, which includes a shift of blood pressure, heart rate, digestive function, hormonal levels, and attention as a counterresponse to activation. You've reached the meeting room; you've realized the snake was a stick all along. Your muscles lessen their engagement, tunnel focus begins to expand out to include the periphery, and you are more tuned in to underlying feelings and sensations. This is the "rest-and-digest" stage, when you process or "digest" the feelings of activation and mobilization.

Restoration is the final stage. In this stage, you are recovering and rebuilding resources that will be used to fuel the next stress response cycle. If you've ever worked out, you might know that you should have a rest period between sets so that you can restore and lift the next round more effectively. Similarly, restoration is the means that allows us to continually adapt and navigate the dance of life.

At least, that's what is supposed to happen. However, it's possible to get stuck in the activation or mobilization stages (common for those with an addiction to drama). And that is where the problems that we commonly associate with stress arise.

A THWARTED STRESS RESPONSE: GETTING STUCK IN STAGE 1 OR 2

It is possible to have a strong activation/arousal response (preparation for action) without the mobilization (completing the action); then we say it is thwarted. To help explain thwarted action/adaptation, imagine you turn on a faucet to fill a cup with water. When the cup is full, you turn off the faucet, drink the water, and are satisfied. However, if you never turn the faucet off, and don't drink the full cup of water, the cup will overflow, while you remain thirsty. A person who is not able to complete the stress response cycle, and therefore adapt—whether because they don't have time, space, or permission—is essentially flooded with arousal response with nowhere to go.

Dr. Selye was the first person to prove the existence of *generalized biological stress* (ongoing stress) as distinct from *acute stress* (the response to an occasional stressor, after which we can recover). He noticed common complaints among patients who were diagnosed with distinct diseases, and these included fatigue, loss of appetite, weight loss, and loss of interest in work and social life. Inadvertently, his research proved a cause and effect relationship between external environments and internal physiological and psychological processes.[3]

Remember, in his book, Dr. Selye described life as "a process of adaptation to circumstances in which we exist." He continued: "A perennial give-and-take has been going on between living matter and its inanimate surroundings, between one living being and another, ever since the dawn of life in the prehistoric oceans. The secret of health and happiness lies in successful adjustment to the ever-changing conditions on this globe; *the penalties for failure in this great process of adaptation are disease and unhappiness*" (emphasis mine).[4] Essentially, as Dr. Selye noted, the conditions that we associate with stress are *by-products* of our biological adaptation system (our stress response) being challenged or thwarted. This bears repeating: when our stress response system gets messed up and the cycle is left uncompleted, that manifests as disease in the body. (Thus, he challenged the notion that the mind is separate from the body, a philosophical view that has prevailed for 1,500 years.)

Our understanding of stress's role in disease has only grown since Dr. Selye's time. We now know that a disrupted stress response can lead to building neurons in the brain that create higher levels of anxiety and wear and tear on the hypothalamus (the part of our brain that maintains biological cycles, temperature, appetite, and physiological and emotional responses to stimuli). This results in decreased ability to regulate hormones; reduced digestive and sexual function; immune system challenges, such as Graves' disease, fibromyalgia, chronic fatigue, and numerous other symptoms. However, we might reimagine that these diseases are signals from the body saying that something is challenging our biological processes of adaptation.

We know that an unregulated or chaotic stress response can wreak havoc on your internal physiology. Yet, rather than attempting to reduce stress, some people also respond in ways that *increase* their stress or their response to it. Talk to people like this and they will say they don't want this stress . . . drama and stress just find them. An observer might notice, however, one of two things happening: The person projects crisis into their environment, seeing (and experiencing) crises that others do not. Or they help build crisis, worsening a mild, relatively undramatic situation into something more severe. Crisis is their "normal" comfort zone—their baseline, as we saw in the previous chapter.

As one example, look at my client Francesca, who came to my office with massive anxiety that was presenting itself as headaches, fainting, chronic fatigue, and a general full-body ache when she would get up in the morning. She also had a chronic sore throat that she would describe as the world trying to choke her. Francesca recognized she had an "intimate relationship" with drama but said it was not her fault. If a doctor told her that her lab results were slightly off, she would be incapacitated for days, which of course just made her symptoms worse. Francesca found it easy to express her woes about her health but very difficult to share or trust her feelings. Francesca grew up being told that her feelings weren't valid, that she was too much, and always overreacting. As we worked together, she began to trust her own sensations and feelings. After we talked through what stress really was, she became open to the idea that the reactiveness in her body (activation) was actually the way her body was preparing to respond to a lot of the hardship (stressors). She came to recognize that her physical symptoms and anxiety were unresolved activation stuck in her body. As she allowed for the unprocessed activation to mobilize she began to feel significant improvements. For example, learning to express the word and gesture *no* released a lot of the tension in her body, and her physical symptoms started to disappear.

This can be a bit of a radical shift in the understanding of stress. Language and outdated notions can have a lot of power over how we perceive and experience something like stress.

THE LANGUAGE-PERCEPTION-REALITY LOOP

It is important to recognize that we can also create our own stressor or crisis without it having to be real, especially if some part of us is craving the stress response and inner chaos.

Often we talk about stress with a vague idea of what it is, after reading some two-dimensional textbook or online article trying to capture our attention with heightened language. We talk about being "so stressed out." Not surprisingly, stress has become the big bad monster that everyone's talking about but few have been given the opportunity to fully understand or even appreciate.

Earlier in this chapter, I asked you to write down your personal definition of stress and your relationship with it. I hope this exercise highlighted the lens through which you see stress—the same way a pair of glasses affects your vision. Your perception of stress in turn affects how you receive and understand it.

Going one step further, your perceptions, the way you interpret something, creates your experience and constructed reality of it. Your experience, filtered through your perception, is what we call your individual reality. This is an important concept in understanding the world of someone who is addicted to drama, as their constructed reality might be quite different from someone who is not addicted to drama.

Here is a tangible and playful example of the loop between language, perception, and reality. When he was very young, my nephew came to visit and I steamed some broccoli as part of his meal. I noticed that he wasn't eating the broccoli and asked him why. He said, "I don't want to eat them because they are baby trees that never got a chance to grow up." Now, besides being very endearing, this was a perfect example of this language-perceptual-reality loop. His definition of broccoli—baby trees robbed of their opportunity to have a full life—affected what he saw when he looked down at his plate. But it didn't stop there.

Because he perceived lifeless baby trees, my nephew also had a flood of feelings (sensations) and emotions. He reported feeling sad and confused and described a weight in his chest and stomach, which is a somatic re-

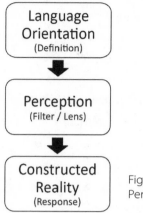

Figure 6.2: Language Perception Chart

sponse. He had a visceral response that reinforced his perception and definition, and it became his lived reality. Now anytime my nephew hears the word *broccoli*, he has that visceral response, typically below his conscious awareness.

In the same way, every time you hear or read the word *stress, drama,* or *addiction*, it is being filtered through your definition of it, your feelings about it, your perception of it, and any familiar experiences (memories) of it. You also have some level of physiological response creating and reinforcing your reality of it. Right now, as you read these words, whether or not it's obvious, you are bringing your own definition and bias to these terms.

So, while there are some universal physiological processes that happen in the body—the stress response being one of them—"stress" is really as unique as the individual who is experiencing it. There is a subjective component, because the cocktail of a stress response includes that individual's unique *relationship* to stress, as well as the stressor they are responding to, and their body's reaction to it.

If we begin to recognize that every stimulus (stressor) is not actually a threat and our stress response is not a "threat response," but rather our innate ability to adapt and thrive, then we can begin to ask ourselves different questions:

What happens when someone does perceive that all stressors are an impending crisis?

What happens when the flooding of that internal cup is what someone is used to and becomes their status quo?

What happens when the arousal response becomes something a person seeks and creates? How does it benefit them?

When working with clients with an addiction to drama, I will often ask, "Is your activation response in your body more than is useful for this situation?" I also ask, "Is how you're mobilizing that energy adaptive for you at this moment?" This is a tricky question, as we are evolutionarily designed to be overresponsive—it's better to mistake a stick for a snake, than a snake for a stick. However, those who are addicted to drama take that evolutionary propensity to an extreme level. Some of it has to do with their personal perception of stress and some is because of their personal capacity to adapt.

WE EACH HAVE A DIFFERENT CAPACITY TO ADAPT TO STRESS

All ecosystems, whether in humans or in nature, are in constant interaction with stressors. Some ecosystems engage with these stressors and flourish. Some ecosystems are challenged and depleted by the stressors and still return to balance. And some ecosystems interface with stressors and fail to thrive.

What makes some ecosystems flourish and others not? What allows some systems to have the capacity to navigate the ups and downs of life, and others not? Essentially, these are questions of resilience and adaptability.

To illustrate, imagine you are running late to work. For whatever reason, you slept past your alarm and woke up to a text message from your boss asking you to email the presentation before the meeting starts in an hour. Your internal activation spikes so that you can take action and adapt to the circumstance. What do you think you'd do? Here's how different people might react.

- Allison bolts out of bed and gets dressed, chugs some coffee, and rushes out the door.

- Lexi is overwhelmed by an incredibly tight feeling in her chest, paces around her bedroom, splashes water on her face, contemplates calling in sick, then calls a friend for a suggestion of what to do. She eventually arrives to work disheveled just a few minutes before the big meeting.

- Erik is completely frozen, unable to think or move, and starts to envision how he will be fired and kicked out of his house and forced to live in a shelter where he will likely die an early lonely life.

Same situation, very different responses. Some people are more resilient to stressors, while some have less capacity to adapt—and they look outside themselves for ways to keep going in the face of stress.

Resilience is often thought of as the ability to bounce back from adverse situations. Imagine a blow-up punching bag, like a clown that you can bop around. From the outside, every time you hit it, it bounces back to its original stance . . . therefore it must be resilient, right? The harder you hit it, the faster it bounces back.

What we don't see if we're simply watching it bounce back is the significant impact of each hit on the inside of that punching bag. If you were to imagine that punching bag as a person, you might now have a visceral response when they get hit, even if they stand back up. That visceral response lets us know something isn't okay. Just because someone or something stands back up does not mean that there isn't an unseen lasting imprint of that hit. You can override pain and stand back up . . . but still have internal bleeding. Many psychological and emotional wounds, of course, are not visible to the naked eye, and the person may not even be aware of them. Not all hits are "bad" or "negative"—sometimes even positive experiences or "good" emotions can knock someone down. Resilience is not the ability to bounce back from adversity, but the capacity to be present, to inhabit the moment, with an awareness and felt connection to what is happening in one's self and in the environment. Resilience allows us to be responsive and flexible, to be able to change, move, and adapt to whatever the situation demands, and to glean meaning and purpose.

Returning to the image of a blow-up punching bag: with each impact there's air escaping, sometimes a minimal amount and sometimes a significant amount. We can think of the air that has filled the blow-up punching bag as symbolic of it feeling alive, aware, and able to take action. As humans when we experience the impact of stressors it takes some resources and energy, and then we recuperate or fill back up. So, as the air slowly drains from the bag, it begins to have a global effect on the whole bag, which begins to droop, sagging as it loses structural integrity. To stay upright, the bag must be propped against something or someone. (If what it is propped up against is well hidden, we might believe the bag is standing up on its own.)

In people, that propping up is what we call a dependency, typically on people or substances. It's easy to be distracted by what a person is using to prop themselves up and lose focus on the real underlying problem—the fact that they're being hit and deflating.

While we are hardwired for resilience, there are events, circumstances, and even genetic dispositions for an inability to optimally thrive. Your capacity to adapt and your level of and resiliency to stressors will be different from someone else's, based on genes, where and how you were raised, and environmental conditions.[5]

STRESS RESPONSE SCALE

The stress people feel falls along a scale of reactions, from "good stress" (called eustress), which motivates you; to distress, which is when you're overwhelmed and can't adapt; with "tolerable" in the middle. Think of Allison, Lexi, and Erik.

Allison's response is an example of *eustress*. A person can feel rejuvenated from engaging in this. *Tolerable* describes Lexi's response to her late morning—she has enough resources to meet the challenge and weather the storm. And Erik's reaction to waking up late on the big presentation day—being unable to cope at all—is an example of *distress*.

It's worth noting that the key determining factor is the person, not the event—the exact thing that causes eustress for one person could cause distress for another. It's very individual; for one person a promotion at work could produce a eustress response, while for another person the promotion might be more accurately placed in the *tolerable* category.

Some people are more sensitive to stressors; some people are flooded with stressors; some grow up without the vital resources of support, and some bond with the stress response.

People at high risk for chronic stress and stress-related illness may have

- Less flexibility in adapting to stressors—this can manifest in being hyperready to respond, or being underprepared.
- Catastrophizing, or more colloquially, making a mountain out of a molehill, and taking a negative viewpoint.
- Hypersensitivity that is easily activated or reactive. Similar to catastrophizing, this is the tendency to go from "0 to 100" with no gradation of response.
- Compound stress—psychosocial life stressors in the form of major life changes and daily hassles, often happening in a condensed period of time.
- Lack of or insufficient social support system and coping skills.

- - - - -

THE FACTORS THAT SHAPE OUR INDIVIDUAL STRESS RESPONSE

Allison, Lexi, and Erik demonstrated that the same stressor could have widely varying responses, and their very different responses indicated the impact the stressor had on their lives. Their responses to stress had been wired in their nervous system.

There are several main contributors, typically early in life, that shape our nervous system, direct our thoughts and behavior, and can disrupt capacity and resilience. Some of the main factors that determine how we respond to stress include the following:

- Early adversities in life
- Transgenerational experiences and hereditary predispositions
- Interactions with the environment
- Attachment styles

Once we understand the origins, we can explore the ways people cope and adapt to these conditions, including (surprise) an addiction to drama.

Early-Life Adversities

Early challenges and trauma can leave a lasting imprint well into adulthood. As an example, consider the exploratory study evaluating the adverse childhood experiences (ACE) of a group of Chilean girls placed in foster care. The study found that girls who were exposed to experiences such as emotional and physical neglect, sexual and/or physical abuse, household dysfunction—which could include household members who are substance abusers, imprisoned, mentally ill, or suicidal—were highly vulnerable to developing behavioral and psychological issues.[6] The cumulative exposure to such adverse experiences—trauma—also resulted in poor quality of life, poor physical well-being, poor psychological well-being, challenges with autonomy and parent relationships, and poor life outcomes.[7]

In another study, researchers discovered that people who had at least one ACE were two to five times more likely to attempt suicide. Additionally, the study found a significant relationship between ACEs and alcoholism, depressed states, and illicit drug use.[8] If someone had four or more ACEs, they were twelve times more likely to develop risky behaviors and diseases in adulthood. In some cases, the person with a history of ACEs chooses the risky behavior consciously, although many of the impulses leading to the behaviors are unconscious.

Many of these early life experiences create a deep pain, which many people wish to escape, sometimes by finding sanctuary in whatever helps them avoid it. After experiencing trauma in early childhood, people often develop adaptive behaviors, such as addiction, numbness, and dissociation (and as we'll see shortly, these behaviors can also be the result of transgenerational trauma).[9]

Very early childhood stressors, both before birth and after, profoundly affect adult stress responses and have long-lasting effects on the central nervous and endocrine system.[10] In thirty-three research studies that evaluated how adversity in children in utero to age five influenced their response to a controlled stressor, the results showed abnormal responses to the stress hormone cortisol. Even children who are too young to have language to describe what was happening registered stressors in the early environment and responded to them. Other stressors, such as poor nutrition, economic uncertainty, and fear—and the resultant stress responses—elicited reactions that fell outside of the normal cortisol levels.

People with severe adversities before or after birth may have a baseline that is not (nor ever has been) stable and resilient. For them, adult decision-making serves to maintain the dysregulated baseline because dysregulation is familiar and normal. As one client, Justin, reported, "I like being in high-pressure situations. I like leaving things [until] the last minute. I don't know why. It's like I put myself in a pressure cooker. I like having that stress."

Transgenerational Trauma and Inherited Vulnerability

Epigenetics is the study of how your environment and behaviors can change how your genes work. It's why scientists are now able to say, "Your genes are not your destiny." Epigenetic variations do not change your DNA sequencing, but they do affect how your body reads a DNA sequence, determining what genes are *expressed* (or turned on and off) and how the cells are registering that expression.

As noted earlier, epigenetics research has discovered a similar correlation of early childhood stress and disrupted stress response *between* generations. As one example, the offspring of survivors of both the Holocaust and 9/11 with PTSD showed lower baseline levels of cortisol, rendering them less adaptive, which resulted in higher levels of anxiety. Other studies that focused on survivors of war trauma, refugees, and torture victims all depict similar transgenerational effects on the stress response system because children can inherit a genetic "response to environmental challenges even when the young do not experience the challenges themselves."[11] The child of a parent with a history of trauma or distress does not have to have an adverse experience to show a disrupted stress response.[12] It is as though the adversities of the parents or grandparents leaves a biological memory of the unprocessed trauma.[13] We might call this a trauma imprint.

A mother's level of stress during pregnancy and the presence of anxiety or depression during her lifetime or during the pregnancy and afterward could create higher cortisol levels in infants and children. Other stressors that raise a child's cortisol levels include prenatal tobacco exposure, prenatal alcohol exposure, negative interactions between parents or caregivers and children, maternal/paternal anxiety and depression, and exposure to violence and aggression.[14]

Martina, a self-identified drama addict I interviewed, said that people would be more sympathetic to her behaviors if they could have met her mother and grandmother. "It's like the trauma of the Great Depression, and the wars, and whatever else they all went through is coursing through my blood," she said.

How does transgenerational trauma manifest? Research suggests that it is highly likely that people inherit a vulnerability to stress. This can produce a person who is continually vigilant, on high alert for stressors in their environment, like prey species constantly scanning the horizon for the predator. A person who is searching for crisis as a means of matching their inner chaos is a person who is addicted to drama.

WHEN TRAUMA HAPPENS

Trauma can occur when

- There is too much too soon.
- There is too much for too long.
- There is not enough for too long.
- Power and agency have been taken away from the person or collective.
- The stressors outweigh the resources available to navigate them.
- Our primal protective instincts, intuitions, and responses are thwarted.
- There is not enough time, space, or permission to heal.

Trauma can lead to feelings of powerlessness, helplessness, and groundlessness. It interferes with our ability to feel real in body and mind; it disrupts our very sense of existence and takes us away from the present moment.

- - - - -

The Impact of the Environment

Think back to your childhood, and the mood of your environment. How would you describe the surroundings: calm, frantic, playful, dangerous, etc.?

Foundational relationships between you, others in your life, and your environment shape your experience of who you are and how you experience the world around you throughout your entire life.[15]

Jack, a friend who self-identifies with an addiction to drama, grew up in a small town in Alaska. The weather was always extreme: −60°F in the winter with no sunlight, 90°F in the summer with two straight months of only sunlight. "You always had to stay vigilant to what's coming in on the storm front," Jack explained. "This became my baseline, the main place I learned extremes as the normal. As a kid and young adult, I was always trying to find the extremes, pushing the edges, climbing dangerous mountains." For Jack, his home environment was also intense, with the house filled with the voices of his parents fighting. To get their attention, he said, he had to turn his volume up to the extreme.

Still others inherited the propensity for drama from parents who developed a habituated response to crisis around them, even when children did not experience the challenges themselves. For example, Lincoln, a young man I interviewed for the book, said that his mother is addicted to drama; the extremes and intensities he learned are from her modeling it and his interpreting it as the normal way of being in the world. He could recognize that, while for him, those behaviors feel like something he learned, his mom was dependent on them to get through her week.

Studies show that children who grow up in more chaotic physical and social environments—with noise; lack of order, structure, and routine; crowding; unpredictable stimuli and emotions—have a lower capacity for self-regulation, diminished language abilities (including the ability to identify and describe feelings), reduced learning and motor function, higher incidence of behavioral challenges, and learned helplessness.[16]

All of us develop core beliefs, thoughts, physiological function and rhythm, and even our physical capacities and posture in response to our environment. We are sponges; we soak up and filter in our surroundings, and we shape ourselves to it and are simultaneously shaped by it. According to Bernard J. Baars's *In the Theater of Consciousness: The Workspace of the Mind*, most of us are conscious of about 6 to 8 percent of all the stimuli we are absorbing.[17] Yet there is much more than what we are aware of that we are simultaneously absorbing and responding to—all of which have a lasting effect.

Attachment Styles

Our sense of self is also influenced by other people in our environment; they help shape our unique developmental trajectory.[18] A simple example of this is, if people laugh at your jokes, you get confirmation that you're funny—and thus you start to believe that you are a funny person. The same can be said if you are cared for and loved. The ways in which these relationships are formed (or not formed) help create the lens that guides someone's perceptions and actions throughout life. The quality of these relationships—as well as the coping mechanism the person uses in the absence of them—influences the connection to family members, first, and later to adults in the greater environment.[19] Such early-life connections are referred to as the relational and social-developmental *attachment style.*

When caregivers are available, patient, consistent, and responsive, they create a positive childhood environment characterized by a harmonious relationship. This is known as *secure attachment,* which is highly correlated with self-esteem, social competence, self-control, empathy, ego resilience, and positive affect. Such adults tend to be attentive, social, cooperative, and able to give and accept care.[20] Self-regulation and resiliency comes from co-regulation with a caregiver, which happens through the secure bond (attachment) with a caregiver. When there is a secure bond, and resilience and self-regulation, distressing feelings are manageable and the child or adult can make their way through it.

Some childhood experiences include emotional neglect—lacking warmth, attention, and consistency, including early separation from a caregiver. This results in *insecure attachment*—which in turn shapes the nervous system and stress response. Those who grew up without secure bonds often didn't get the opportunity to process through stressors or trauma and are likely to suffer anxiety, depression, addiction, and physical pain as adults, as well as an inability to cope with stressors.[21] Insecure attachment in turn begets one of three general coping styles to reduce or avoid the pain of this rupture in the fabric of social bonding.[22]

Here are the three insecure attachment styles:

1. **Insecure-anxious.** These people often have a hyperactive nervous system. They tend to act out in response to stressors, get upset, and lose their emotional balance easily. They are more primed to think negatively and will catastrophize what is happening. They want connection with other people but struggle with communicating their needs and taking that connection in. They often create stories that they are unloved and seek approval and reassurance that they are loved.

2. **Insecure-avoidant.** People with an insecure-avoidant attachment style have an underresponsive nervous system, and shut down, run away, and minimize their needs. They suppress emotions to protect from vulnerability. They downplay the importance of relationships, avoid connection, and appear extremely self-reliant. They view others as not providing safety or comfort.

3. **Insecure-fearful.** Those who have an insecure-fearful style strongly fear rejection and become dependent in relationships. They are in a tug-of-war between wanting intimacy and fearing it. They often experienced mixed messages from caregivers, such as "Come closer" and "Go away!" They often view both themselves and others in a negative perspective.

Recently, Danny, a client who displays many elements of an addiction to drama, reminded me that a damaged bond between siblings can manifest similarly to a wound with a caregiver. Danny was the youngest of three children, with his older two siblings much older. "I wanted nothing more than to be close with them," he said. "While my mom was way too attentive and my dad was dismissive, it was my siblings' love that I craved—and usually tried to get it through acts of service. There's this feeling that's attached to me that I've never been able to shake. It's a pain in my stomach and then this sense that I'm being engulfed in a cloak of darkness, and I'm the only one there. Every once in a while, someone's voice or action pierces that darkness—but I can't get out of it."

EARLY ADVERSITIES IN life, transgenerational trauma, and challenging interactions with the environment influences that person's resilience and capacity to navigate stressors. As a result of these wounds and continual challenges, each person creates coping responses that affect how they make decisions, perceive their reality, and behave in the world. And this is where our survival strategies can become an addiction.

KEY TAKEAWAYS

- Drama can be deconstructed into chaos (internal experience of drama) and crisis (external conditions), in the same way that stress can be deconstructed into a stressor (stimulus) and a stress response (internal response to stimulus).

- Stress is our process of adaptation, and our stress response cycle is the steps toward adaptation and well-being. The cycle includes four primary stages: activation, mobilization, deactivation, and restoration.

- Stress responses are unique to each person. The same stressor can have different responses and capacity toward adaptation—this is also reflected in how resilient that person is.

- Factors that can affect each person's adaptability include early trauma, genetic factors, adverse environments, and attachment styles (reflection of early relationships of safety and security with caregivers).

CHAPTER 7

Caught in the Grip: When a Survival Strategy Becomes an Addiction

N O MATTER WHAT, WE, AS HUMANS, ALWAYS SEEK TO MAINTAIN OR RETURN to equilibrium. To keep this internal state of steadiness, we use cognitive, emotional, behavioral, and physiological processes to adapt to the stressors that challenge it. Like a thermostat making adjustments to maintain the ideal temperature, or finding a sweater when you're cold, we are fundamentally driven to find balance as a means of survival.

Humans are so wonderfully complex that we use both conscious and unconscious strategies to address the conditions of our environment and internal experiences to maintain this equilibrium. These are called *coping mechanisms* or *adaptive (survival) strategies*.

According to a 2001 article, "Coping with Stress During Childhood and Adolescence," there are three kinds of coping mechanisms:

- **Primary control**, which is "intended to influence *objective* events or conditions
- **Secondary control**, which refers to coping aimed at addressing current *inner* conditions
- **Relinquished control**, which is "the absence of any coping attempt."[1]

We either try to change the conditions or environment, change ourselves, or don't do anything in response. As you might recall, those with an addiction to drama have often experienced early pains or chaotic environments that they, like all of us, have had to adapt to and cope with, including adopting this chaos as their state of steadiness.

It is important to realize that coping mechanisms, in general, are neutral. They are merely a way that people direct their efforts at "maintaining, augmenting, or altering control over the environment and the self," according to the authors of the article.[2] They are inherently the way each person is trying to do their best in the dance of life, to navigate, adjust, survive, and prevail. If the coping response seems helpful to the short-term objective, then it is rewarded and repeated.

However, while all coping and adaptive strategies have a positive intention, in the long term they can have a negative impact on someone's well-being. They include using a substance or behavior that, over time, becomes a pattern—a predetermined way of thinking, responding, and being. Those with an addiction to drama seek sensation as a coping mechanism, a means of maintaining their normal. (Think of Maria the fish from Chapter 5.) Subsequently they may have found themselves in situations—whether relationships, jobs, and/or physical locations—that mirrored earlier intense, unstable, and unpredictable experiences. In short, they were seeking conditions they had adapted to as a way of maintaining an internal balance, becoming dependent on drama to maintain their status quo. This is how the very coping mechanisms that we use to maintain and restore balance become the objects of our dependency, the grip of our addictions.

VIEWS OF ADDICTION

Addiction is essentially a dependency on something, regardless of the consequences. Among various theories of addiction, two main perspectives include the following:

- **A medical model**, which considers addiction an illness, as if a treatable brain disease, caused by a combination of genetics and environmental factors[3]
- **A biopsychosocial model**, which recognizes environmental, developmental, and genetic factors, and that takes into account many underlying conditions and is more likely to acknowledge non–substance abuse addictions

The biopsychosocial model offers a more nuanced understanding of addiction to drama. It is a self-soothing coping response characterized by a need to perpetually create or seek high-intensity environments to match a similarly intense internal state. Mark D. Griffiths, PhD, a professor of behavioral addiction, believes there are six main components that qualify a substance or behavior as an addiction:[4]

- **Consuming:** when the substance or behavior is the most important thing in a person's life or occupies a significant amount of their time
- **Mood modification:** an altered mood state, such as getting "high" or "a buzz," that emerges from engaging in the activity or substance that serves as a coping or escape mechanism
- **Tolerance:** an increasing amount over time of the substance or activity is needed to maintain a mood-modifying effect
- **Withdrawal:** an unpleasant physical and emotional response, such as moodiness or irritability, that comes from terminating or doing less of the substance or activity
- **Conflict:** a disregarding of consequences that results in conflict—with others as well as within the self that may lead to a loss of control
- **Relapse:** a regression back to the activity or substance after a time period of improvement

All six components are present for those who are hooked on drama, as we will see in more depth in Chapter 8.

Addiction is highly correlated with low self-esteem. Low self-esteem and sensation seeking share a lack of feedback to the self and an absence of the self at a fundamental level—as if from the inside a person is not fully real or present. Think back to Chapter 5, when we discussed the factors that form the baseline for a person with an addiction to drama, and that boundary ruptures can lead to a lack of sense of self. This lack of an internal sense of identity creates a craving for feedback to validate one's realness—the sense of being alive.[5] It's like trying to fill an unfillable void.

A FRESH VIEW OF ADDICTION

Johann Hari, author of 2015's *Chasing the Scream: The First and Last Days of the War on Drugs*, made an important point: "The opposite of addiction is not sobriety. It's human connection."[6] Hari's view reflects the new lens on addiction that has been emerging from such researchers and journalists as Gabor Maté, MD; Peter Cohen, PhD; and Bruce K. Alexander, PhD, among many others. Hari notes that early models of addiction—the medical models—thought of it as something an individual is hooked on, a chemical response produced by a substance, with the drug the issue and focus of addiction. This theory was perpetuated by experiments with rats. They were isolated and given two bottles, one filled with water and another laced with a drug, such as cocaine or heroin. As one might expect, the rats kept coming back for hit after hit of the drug-infused water until they died. The researchers, however, failed to take into consideration the rats' environment, including their habitat and resources.

In the 1970s, Bruce K. Alexander designed a different experiment. He wondered what would happen if the rats were exposed to drug-infused water in a supportive environment, and so Dr. Alexander built Rat Park, a place in which there was ample food, toys, mates, and friends. Lo and behold, the rats in Rat Park, who were living a more optimal life, were not interested in the drug-laced water even after tasting it. The small fraction of rats that did drink the drugged water did not consume it to the point of mortality. And when rats that were already addicted to opiates were introduced to the colony, they chose to drink the pure water rather than the drugged water— essentially choosing to withdraw from the opiates.[7]

Additional research has demonstrated that supportive environments and substantial social connections counteract high use of drugs.[8] Social bonding helps with overall emotional regulation, allowing people to more effectively address a stressor before it becomes distressing. This new view of addiction recognizes that we are social beings and, when we are not able to bond with one another, we bond to something else that substitutes for social closeness.

In the *Journal of Restorative Medicine*, Dr. Maté describes addiction as consisting of the following:

♦ Something creating relief or pleasure
♦ Conscious or subconscious cravings when it isn't present
♦ Negative consequences due to that need
♦ Difficulty giving up despite the challenges that emerge from those consequences.[9]

In his book *In the Realm of Hungry Ghosts: Close Encounters with Addiction*, Dr. Maté asserts that within all addiction is some form of trauma or pain deriving from loss in childhood. That loss can be something tangible—an adverse experience or the absence of something good, such as bonding or the supportive presence of a caregiver or the environment. The loss affects the neurodevelopmental processes of reward and, in addition, the individual will seek that reward somewhere else. Thus, according to Dr. Maté, the addictive behavior either soothes pain or is an escape from pain.[10] I would add one observation, based in my own research: the intention of the addictive behavior is to mitigate the level of numbness that emerges from trying to soothe or escape pain.

When speaking about managing pain, it is important to realize this includes physical pain as well as emotional pain: they share many of the same neurological pathways.[11] Emotional responses can elicit physical sensations, and physical sensations can trigger emotional responses.[12]

Some individuals in emotional and physical pain use high-risk situations and catastrophizing to distract themselves.[13] Dramatic thinking and behavior can stimulate the nervous system to release endorphins, which inhibit pain signals and also causes euphoric feelings—in short, alleviating both emotional and physical pain.[14] In this way, drama can potentially and momentarily alleviate both emotional and physical pain. So, if drama can make someone feel less pain and euphoric, they get attached to drama—it is their way of finding relief.[15]

These coping mechanisms that create relief from the unmet needs that emerge from trying to maintain equilibrium become habits; and these habits that are left unsupported become addictions. When a coping mechanism becomes the reflexive status quo, we lose our agency over being responsive to the present moment and become predictably reactive. The ways we make decisions, perceive the environment, move through the world, engage in relationships—indeed, even our identities—become entangled with the maintenance of this adaptive survival strategy.

DECISION-MAKING, COPING, AND ADDICTION

The decision to engage in crisis and stoke the inner levels of chaos doesn't make sense to an observer, nor does it make sense from within the lived experience of drama. Decision-making doesn't always mean there's a conscious choice, especially when it's driven by a coping mechanism.

When we're in a stable and balanced state, we're aware of and responsive to thoughts, emotions, psychological processes, goals, and conditions in our environment. This state optimizes ideal decision-making, as our best decisions come out of an ability to assess our own current state and the perceived future, and evaluate the outcomes from previous decisions. The decisions you make can change your state of well-being.[16] In the moment, making decisions is like finding your balance while stepping from boulder to boulder while crossing a creek. Deciding which stone to step on and how to approach it requires being able to assess the current moment. People who are more prone to addiction tend to have less awareness of the present moment, including their current state of being;[17] in turn, a lot of the decisions are being made as though they are operating from the past or a fantasized future.

Some decisions are clearly nonoptimal for long-term well-being. Making less optimal choices is often caused by a misguided attempt to achieve stability and balance, like having a hard day at work and consuming a massive amount of alcohol to level it out. When someone perceives a situation and acts in an exaggerated or intensified way, they may be attempting to return to what they consider normal. My client Martina told me that even when a problem has been resolved, she always decides to go back in to make sure everyone really understands "the truth" of what they did wrong. She recognizes that it often disturbs the peace, angers people, pushes them away, and leaves her feeling alone—but she is steadfast in her belief that the truth sets people free. While Martina believes that the drive for these decisions is about setting people free, in actuality the decisions to stir things back up is about returning her to a normalized state of chaos.

Research has shown that patterns of dysregulated decision-making and sensitivity to stressors exist before the development of an addiction, which suggests that addictions are formed out of dysregulated nervous systems and inabilities to adapt to stressors.[18]

THE COPING RESPONSE (AND ADDICTION) BECOMES EMBEDDED IN THE BODY

In Chapter 6, we talked about how the body is activated during the stress response cycle; the neuromuscular and hormonal changes that happen during activation (increased heart rate, muscle tension, and so on) are also known as a *stress response*. Stress responses can far outlast the presence of the stressor, so the body is still ready to fight or flee even when the stimulus is minimal or long gone. As we will see, for those with an addiction to drama it's like always being in a state of readiness to respond—regardless of the presence or absence of the stressors. When the size of the stressor finally matches the state of readiness for it, the person with an addiction to drama feels satisfaction. When their stress readiness is at an 8 out of 10, when there is a stressor that is also an 8 out of 10, life suddenly feels affirmed, and they feel validated.

When we are in conditions, situations, and environments that feel unsafe, our sensory systems (sight, hearing, smell, and even taste) adapt, altering our perception; in a person with an addiction to drama, this altered perception can become the norm. The following are how all our sensory systems adapt to stressors, and where it can get stuck:

- In the stress response, our field of vision narrows, so the stressor or thing we are adapting to comes sharply into focus and everything else is blurry and ignored.[19] The world in this state is experienced differently, like shifting from a panoramic view to a portrait view. Prolonged stress exposure maintains tunnel vision, keeping us locked into stressors, while simultaneously limiting the peripheral vision of our surroundings, making it hard to see anything but stressors. Someone who grew up in a chaotic or unpredictable environment zooms in on those elements—and doesn't necessarily know how to zoom back out to the panoramic view.
- In heightened distress or threat, the muscles of our eardrums adjust to focus on nonneutral (lower and higher) frequencies to keep us tense and ready for danger. Lower frequencies are more associated with noxious and threatening stimuli, such as the buzzing of a light bulb or a predator approaching. The nervous system transports this sense of danger taken in by the auditory system and moves it to the gut—where we have a gut instinct that something is or will be wrong.[20] In these moments it's more difficult to hear and receive neutral frequencies, such as the soothing voice of another human being. (This can explain why, when someone is in distress or traumatized, it can be difficult to receive words of empathy or a soothing human connection.[21]) For those with an addiction to drama, becoming more attuned to low and high frequencies of sound can become the new normal.
- Neutral smells become more unpleasant, which is intimately connected to the emotional systems of the brain.[22] In other words, unpleasant smells can affect someone's mood, and even alter the emotional quality of how something is remembered.
- Prolonged stress and the feeling of being unsafe even alters our taste perception where we become more sensitive to bitterness.[23]

People who are addicted to drama may also experience time differently. In a state of activation, the world around us feels slower than the timing and rhythm on the inside.[24] Consider this scenario: you are running late for a meeting and waiting in traffic behind someone who appears to be driving very slowly. But it only *feels* that they are moving in slow motion, when they are actually moving at a normal pace or the same speed as you are. Often for those with an addiction to drama, there is a perpetual sense of urgency— and the slowness of the world or those around them is anxiety producing.

This is how the person addicted to drama walks through the world, and everything they are attuned to reaffirms that the world is full of potential or actual danger. The stress response of these individuals is oriented and activated in these ways regardless of the presence of stressors. Like a television getting stuck on one channel, those who are addicted to drama's sensory systems are primarily attuned toward chaos.

Having your senses stuck on the channel of danger in this way alters your sense of reality. The result of this altered reality is living out of sync with everyone and everything around you. There is nothing more physically and psychologically disturbing than to feel out of sync with the environment, other people, or the world. If even for a brief time, your external relationships and environment are in opposition to your internal state, a sense emerges that you are out of sync and that something is inherently wrong. You can't put your finger on it, but you feel a sense of dissonance and doom. So, there is value in finding or creating the environments that coincide with your innate rhythm. As a way to decrease this cognitive dissonance, the person addicted to drama will seek relationships and places that affirm this sense of normality. My client Alistair says, "There was always a lot of anger in my household. It was somewhat of a manic environment. That's probably a part of the reason why I actually chose to live in a city like New York is because there is a constant underlying tension throughout every day. On the subway, the grocery store, the laundromat, there's always this underlying current. And I think that's part of the reason why I feel so at home in a city like this." These unconscious changes to a person's perception filter all incoming information about the world, and become the background operating systems of that scanning, searching, finding, and creating things to be activated by. The constant threat of the world feels compounding, like life is an inescapable attack, and you are the victim of it. Hypervigilance is not an attitude, it's a survival mechanism, a way in which our senses have locked us into the perception of a terrifying, lonely, and unsafe world. A person becomes primed to be attentive to certain stimuli and filters out other information to fit what they are scanning for. What you are oriented and attuned to, you will always find, or it will find you.

Take Mark, for example. Mark had grown up playing baseball, so it was no surprise that as an adult he did it recreationally on the weekends. Mark played shortstop, and that position between second and third base required a heightened readiness to respond to the multitude of directions the ball might come from, what each opponent was doing and could do, and a readiness to pounce into action at the slightest movement. Mark's eyes would dart between the player with the bat at home base, the player on second base, and the player on third base. He would watch all these players simultaneously and then scan the opponent's coach, trying to predict and capture whatever information was being relayed.

He had a laserlike focus capturing the minute details of everything around him: wind velocity, readiness of his teammates, and an eye on the clock. His weight was always on his toes so he could spring into action at a moment's notice. He could predict the sound and trajectory of the ball— sometimes even before it was hit. This level of prediction, vigilance, and attention would last throughout the game. But it didn't stop there.

After the game, Mark would travel back to his house to take a shower. The game had ended, but Mark's vigilance had not. In the shower, he was observing the showerhead with a hawklike attention, predicting the pressure of the water, listening for the phone to ring, looking at how much soap was being used, and anticipating how soon he should order the next bar of soap online. The same readiness of response that was required for the precision of playing shortstop had been transferred to every activity around him, which didn't require this level of attention. Mark couldn't shift the level of readiness for response and the sensitivity to stimulus. It was very useful in the game but did not allow him to rest or relax at home. Stress readiness was embedded in his body.

This would be like maintaining the hypervigilance you might have while walking through a haunted house, scanning for and ready to respond to the many ghouls that might jump out—when you are simply walking through a serene garden. The sense of being always "primed for action" can lead some individuals to fill that readiness with sensation. This pattern in the body creates an unconscious seeking of stressors, hyperresponsiveness to stressors, and a sense of justification when the body pattern gets to be fulfilled. Let's look at Zoe. If Zoe is reliant on external crisis and internal chaos, the many mechanisms that she uses to preserve and defend her sense of self make it difficult for her to recognize these patterns as coping mechanisms that are overreactions to stress. Thus, when Zoe—or any person who is addicted to drama—acts from this place, she will try to normalize it, justifying her behaviors.

Beyond changing our senses, stress readiness can also live in the posture and tension of our body. In a study, when people were placed in slumped-depressive physical positions, those participants became more helpless and less responsive on tasks they had performed earlier, and reported a greater sense of stress. Additionally, observers who witnessed participants in these body positions perceived the individuals as depressed.[25] This suggests that how observers perceive an individual will affect how they treat that person, and that person will in turn act in accordance with the observer's actions.[26] If an observer perceives someone's emotional state as "stressed out" or "dramatic" based on their body language, they will treat them as stressed or dramatic. In turn, the person observed in this way will go further into being "stressed" or "dramatic." Multiple studies suggest that habituated neuromuscular patterns in the body can induce emotional and cognitive states even *without* an external stimulus. For example, simply biting a pencil for twenty minutes can activate the same muscles involved in a smile, generating positive affect.[27] Such results suggest that not only is the pattern of addiction an adaptive strategy on a cognitive level, but also that the body stores the stress readiness as a muscle memory that is primed for activation.[28]

In short, it is as if those who are addicted to drama have preinstalled "software" that is running the show. And even though there are little notifications that are inviting them to download an updated version of the software, they stay steadfast to that operating system and deflect any updates. When we are stuck in old trauma, and the survival strategies become not only our operating system but also a sense of who we are—our fundamental identity—then there's no way we are going to hit the update button and lose our identity and the strategies that have kept us alive to this point. The updates or any challenges to this operating system are interpreted as a threat. In turn, we remain in our programing, staying immersed in our perception, internal scripts, and biases—which both create our world and reaffirm that our perception of it is valid.

REENACTMENTS: THE WAY TRAUMA AND ADDICTION PLAY OUT

Reenactments are a form of repeating and reenacting the unfinished emotional and psychological pain of the past. By subconsciously finding or re-creating familiar situations and scenarios, it's an attempt to work out unresolved trauma—replaying the past in hopes to heal it in the present. It will show up as the continuous dramas in relationships, work, or even as compulsive thoughts or reoccurring physical sensations. Nancy, a self-identified drama addict, would often say, "I don't understand how I keep dating men that treat me so bad!" Reenactments are essentially why drama seems to "find" people despite their "best" efforts to avoid it.

Reenactments rarely, if ever, lead to resolve. They do, however, reuse and reinforce the same coping mechanism that created the addiction in the first place.

As a bystander, it is not uncommon to be pulled into someone else's reenactment. Unbeknownst to you, your response to their whirlwind is part of the reenactment, and possibly some form of catharsis for them. In a sense this is *cocreating* their reenactment, without you being aware of it.

Suppose Marisa walks into a medical building and sees two front desk workers, one smiling and friendly and the other not. Marisa grew up with "conditional" love, meaning she had to work to appease her mother to get any connection. Seeing the front desk worker who seems cold and unavailable triggers her sense of familiarity. In some deep, unconscious desire to relive and potentially heal the past, she is drawn to approach the worker who appears emotionally unavailable. Unsurprisingly, the front desk worker plays her predictable part and no matter how hard Marisa works, she can't get her to connect. Marisa feels dismissed and deeply hurt and tries to turn to the other front desk worker for help, but that person is now preoccupied with someone else and unable to attend to her.

Before you know it, Marisa has a complete emotional meltdown in the waiting room, convinced that all the people who work there have "victimized" her. Some people in the waiting room come to Marisa's defense, the office workers come to each other's defense, and the doctor comes out and asks everyone to settle down. In that moment, the doctor plays out the exact role of her father, trying to make the peace and not coming to her defense. Marisa storms out of the office devastated that the staff "drove her away" from getting the medical attention she needed. The entire group within that office had been seized by the drama of Marisa's story—helping her reenact familiar scenarios from another time in her life and the adaptive strategies that came along with them.

These drama reenactments and the coinciding coping mechanisms require constant confirmation so as not to create further dissonance.

CONFIRMATION BIAS: VALIDATING THE COPING MECHANISMS

A confirmation bias is interpreting new information as a confirmation of your beliefs. It can be a way of creating stories and interpreting situations that justify behaviors. For example, someone may feel hurt by someone or troubled by something, and then seek out information that would validate the hurt or the sense of being troubled. They disregard any information that could counter their claim or story they have created. All their effort goes to justifying their feelings and validating the actions that followed. For people addicted to drama, sticking to their own story is a form of safety and preservation, and they will do whatever is needed to avoid the cognitive dissonance that might emerge between the conditions and their exaggerated or generated response to those conditions.

Chaz walked straight into my office, burst into tears, and said, "My boyfriend doesn't want me and thinks I'm ugly." When I asked him to walk me through what was happening, he let me know that he had barely heard from his boyfriend since they were intimate the night before. Chaz said, "He's totally disinterested in me now!"

I asked Chaz how he knew this was true. He shared a whole laundry list of things, like his boyfriend not asking how his day was and responding to a group email but not responding to Chaz's last message. Chaz spent so much time playing out his speculations in his mind that he became convinced that this must be what happened and thus had a hard time discerning between the factual truth and story/speculation. I had the benefit of perspective: this story was nearly identical to what Chaz said about his previous boyfriend, so it was evident that this was his software, his programing, playing itself out.

I recently worked on a project with someone who was furious about an email she thought didn't get sent to her. So, I forwarded her the email that originally went out weeks prior and pointed out she also responded to that email. Instead of saying, "Oh, goodness, I'm so sorry," she responded, "Well, you should have sent that email an hour earlier." It was clear she had been so worked up over this situation that she found it impossible to pull back the anger and intensity, get out of her original story, or turn in a different direction.

To be fair, we all tend to create and share stories whose facts we interpret to confirm our beliefs and perceptions. Confirmation bias is universal. For example, if you look at the Figure 7.1, what shape do you see?

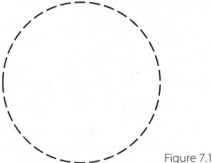

Figure 7.1

You may say you see a circle, but it's not actually a circle—it's a bunch of lines on a page. You mentally filled in the spaces and concluded that it is a circle. Yes, I admit that was a bit tricky, but this is what we do as human beings. We take in a small portion of information, quickly make the leap to fill in the gaps, and then make an assessment about it—just as you likely did with the lines that don't quite form a circle.

There are benefits to creating cognitive shortcuts—they can save time and energy. Say you're walking through the forest and hear a rustling in the bush and see something that resembles fur. You can quickly interpret it as a bear and respond accordingly, like running or playing dead. If you were to take your time to gather 100 percent of the data—such as, this creature is large and has sharp teeth and claws—you could have already been mauled by the bear. At the same time, we could jump to conclusions that aren't accurate, such as thinking there was a big bear, but it was really just a squirrel. People addicted to drama fill in those gaps using thoughts, stories, and habits based on a lifetime of crisis and chaos.

According to Bernard J. Baars's *In the Theater of Consciousness*, only about 20 percent of what we see and interpret in the present moment is happening in the present. The remaining 80 percent is being filled in by memories of the past and expectations of the future. And what we are creating from the past and future—and to some degree the present—directs our judgments. We make decisions, adapt attitudes, and take actions based on our subjective interpretation. Most of what is being infused into a given moment is coming from the memories, stories, associations, and patterns of the past and future. And for those addicted to drama, they are often filled in with high intensity and extremes of feeling alone and unheard. This filling in process is lightning fast, an automatic process that is a subconscious reflex, taking only about 200 to 300 milliseconds.

By contrast, a new thought develops in roughly 500 to 600 milliseconds. It takes a considerable amount of attention and resources because the new thought doesn't involve automatic filling and interpretation. Receiving the subtle sensations of the body, such as feelings and emotions, and becoming aware of them, takes roughly eight times longer than that superfast reflexive thought process, according to psychologist Alan Fogel, PhD, in his book *Body Sense: The Science and Practice of Embodied*

Self-Awareness. For people who have to keep moving and staying activated to feel okay, slowing down to get in touch with these subtle sensations and feelings is nearly impossible.

In this way, their big responses and behaviors are coming lightning fast, from thoughts, stories, and patterns that have been formed and used so often. This leaves no space to get in touch with the subtle sensations and feelings that are present in the body or to respond from those true needs that arise from those feelings. It's very hard to escape.

WHEN CONFIRMATION BIAS BECOMES A SELF-FULFILLING PROPHECY

Someone with an addiction to drama will likely see themselves as a victim. It won't take much then to confirm what they are seeing, regardless of the situation. And when they feel victimized, it triggers similar memories from the past, flooding them with familiar sensations and feelings that overpower their perception of what is actually happening in the present moment. They then respond and act in a habituated, extreme way from that flooding—and create details to justify their extreme response.

The world tends to respond in kind. Chaz, for example, confronted his boyfriend, saying, "I know you no longer want me and find me ugly." No matter what his boyfriend said, Chaz was convinced of his own story. Like all those with an addiction to drama, he saw the world through the lens of his programing and the stories of the past and projected future. He filled in those perceptions with the anticipation of crisis and chaos, sought and confirmed his stories as truth, and finally acted upon this perceived truth. His boyfriend in turn got very distant and stopped responding to Chaz's texts. Chaz created a self-fulling prophecy of being unseen, unheard, not enough, and too much; and his worldview was reaffirmed.

- - - - -

INSIDE THE GRIP

Nearly everyone I interviewed or have worked with who has a propensity for drama spoke about the experience of being pulled back over and over again into the grips of drama. A dear friend of mine from art school, Kristen, explained her experience this way: "It's just really fast. There's no space in it at all. So, usually that's an indication to me that it's some kind of addictive response that I'm having . . . it kind of gets back to that idea of normalizing in a way where it feels really like a fish [in] water."

Here are how some other people explained it:

+ Allissa, a former graduate school colleague, said, "It feels like a really quick pull toward something. It feels urgent and big . . . I can feel it's charged with this energy that doesn't feel like a grounded energy. I think that in some ways there's a quality to that experience where it feels nostalgic. It feels a little sentimental. It also feels like a little bit of a rush."

+ A client, Craig, says, "The need is like an emptiness that has to be filled—and I get pulled in every time. If I don't fill it—I feel like I've failed, it's like an addiction."

+ Marko, another client, described a felt sense of being drawn to a force that would either create or feel like a familiar situation or environment from their past.

+ Nikki, a friend I made along the way of researching this book, added another layer that has really impacted the way I view an active pattern of drama. She said, "When I follow the grip, when I get pulled into my own really strong brewing storm, it's like a voice that's calling me into it, a voice I can't resist. And strangely enough, it feels meaningful."

Several others echoed Nikki, that when going into the active drama cycle (which we'll explore in the next chapter), a momentary sense of importance emerges, creating a full sense of purpose and meaningfulness. From the lens of psychology, purpose and meaning give a sense of direction and reason for our own individual existence. They also give us a sense that we have value, and most important, that we are part of something greater than just ourselves . . . that we belong. An underlying lack of worth (which many who are addicted to drama have, as we saw in earlier chapters) can momentarily be subdued by the intoxicating and distracting hit of drama. It's no wonder why anyone affected by this addiction would cling to it.

KEY TAKEAWAYS

- Coping mechanisms are the way we try to maintain equilibrium in the face of stressors. We can become dependent on these coping mechanisms, as they shift from a temporary means of adaptation to something more habitual.

- Addiction is essentially a dependency on something regardless of the consequences. An addiction occupies a significant amount of a person's focus or time and modifies their mood state. A person who has an addiction will build a tolerance for the "high"—requiring more to feel more. They will then experience withdrawals when it's not present, and will often relapse into the substance or behavior that creates the high.

- A fresh view of addiction recognizes that the opposite of addiction is not sobriety, but rather human connection.

- For those with an addiction to drama, the drama is a coping mechanism to distract from dis-ease and even acts as a pain reliever. The coping mechanism to early pain and chaotic environments gets stuck in the body (the senses and posture)—altering the perception of the present.

- Those who have experienced trauma or pain, and especially those with an addiction to drama, will find themselves in reenactments. Reenactments are essentially seeking or creating the circumstances that evoke the core wounds—as an unconscious means to resolve them.

- Confirmation bias reinforces both the worldview and accompanying actions for those addicted to drama. It becomes the justification for what emerges when they are caught in the grip of the addiction to drama.

CHAPTER 8

The Drama Cycle: Chaos in the Blink of an Eye

I F YOU HAVE EXPERIENCED OR BEEN IN PROXIMITY TO SOMEONE IN THE GRIP of the drama cycle, chaos "in the blink of an eye" may not feel like such an overstatement. Often those in proximity will feel whiplashed and confused by the speed at which things escalate or drained by someone's constant attention to crisis. But even though it often feels like going from zero to one hundred in mere seconds, there are stages of escalation in drama, and they tend to play out in a recognizable active cycle:

- Phase 1, revving
- Phase 2, dysregulated activation and the merging of crisis and chaos
- Phase 3, uncontained catharsis
- Phase 4, hangover/boredom

Now that we understand the conditions that can lead to an addiction to drama—the early pain and trauma, numb baseline that leads to sensation seeking, the role of stress, and when a coping strategy becomes a dependence—it's time to understand what's going on in that "blink of an eye" when a dramatic episode ensues. This cycle overlaps with the body's natural stress response (activation, mobilization, deactivation, restoration), but—as we will see—that cycle is interrupted in addiction to drama.

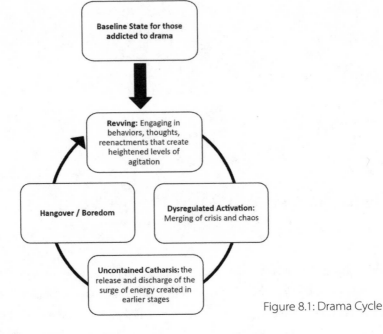

Figure 8.1: Drama Cycle

PHASE 1: REVVING

Revving is the tactic of fueling the proverbial whirlwind, the drama. It is about building an energizing charge. It is a process of stimulating yourself into a level of agitation through thoughts, behaviors, and focusing on what is inherently triggering. It's sourcing and creating the things that create the drama.

While people who are addicted to drama can use any number of ways to keep themselves "revved up," the following five are very common.

External Sourcing and Focusing

This involves a heightened focus on challenges, issues, and negativity in or with other people or the environment. It's not simply focusing and dwelling on these external events, but also communicating to others about them—venting—and getting into heated situations that help generate more intensity, in essence adding fuel to the fire. External sourcing might be a locked focus on what other people have or are doing, how they caused hurt or harm, or listening to or spreading gossip.

Internal Sourcing and Focusing

In contrast, some people with an addiction to drama demonstrate a fixed focus on what is "wrong" with them psychologically or physically. This internal focus, which can include negative self-talk or an internal war between parts of themselves, serves a similar revving function as the external focus, generating intensity to distract from one's inner wounds.

Oppositional Thoughts, Desires, or Actions

I also call these double binds. As an example, someone might say to themselves, "I wish my house was cleaner, but I'm too tired to clean it, but I can't hire a cleaning person because I should be able to do it myself." Or "All I want to do is help people, but everyone takes advantage of me, but if I don't help people I'm selfish, and if I do help them I'm a pushover." The tension between conflicting ideas traps someone in a charged thought loop that keeps them revved up for drama.

Reenactments

This is creating or seeking conditions in which highly intense experiences trigger a familiar activation. You may continuously and unconsciously choose partners that will disappoint you, for example, so you will be engrossed in the familiar experience and the reaction to it—creating the conditions and circumstances where you can justifiably complain and cause drama. A reenactment is also retelling stories over and over again that create a spark that puts you back on the emotional roller coaster.

Creating and Living in Stories

Those with an addiction to drama will often view the world as though they are a character in their own movie: watching themselves living out the scenes of their real and imagined life. A person will create stories and repeat the story (reenactment) to themselves or to other people. These could be projected stories, such as seeing someone else's fabulous life on social media and creating a story of comparison or being left out. A revisionism loop is when someone gets stuck going back and replaying over and over again how things could have been.

No matter how it happens, revving serves its purpose—creating rising levels of intensity in oneself or in the environment to move that person to the next stage of escalation, dysregulated activation and the merging of crisis and chaos.

REVVING TO GET UNSTUCK

In the frozen tundra of Dakota land (also known as Minnesota), where I grew up, getting your car stuck in a snowbank was nearly a daily experience in the wintertime. And because it's the kind of cold that freezes a sneeze in midair, you do whatever you can to never leave the comfort of your heated car. Instead of digging yourself out, you might rev the gas over and over again to spin the tires and melt the snow around them, allowing you to become free of the snow's grip and be on your merry way. This is exactly what those with an addiction are subconsciously trying to do through the continual revving and catharsis, and is the underlying intention for reenactments.

To understand how this process happens, let's take a ride into the wonderful world of neurophysiology with neurobiologist Stephen Porges, PhD. His 2011 book *The Polyvagal Theory* explores the relationship between the autonomic nervous system (which drives the bodily functions beyond our control) and social behavior, as well as its connection to physical and mental health. Our well-being emerges from our social nature and bonding to others, and any interruptions to that capacity for social connection have profound implications on our health and function.

In a conversation with Dr. Porges, we spoke about chaos, crisis, and drama as a tool to avoid intimacy and social connection. Dr. Porges defines intimacy as feeling safe in the arms of another person—or safe enough not to evoke a defense response in the presence of another. He says that individuals with an addiction to drama will go into a defense response (such as fight or flight) in the presence of others because they are not comfortable being vulnerable.

Often when we witness someone who is addicted to drama, we can get distracted by our interpretation of their overt behavior. Instead, Dr. Porges recommends that we need to understand their underlying physiological state and how cues of safety and rest operate as a threat for those with an addiction to drama.

When a child's safety is challenged (whether by something as fundamental as not feeling seen or heard, or having to manage an unpredictable and erratic environment), they may not be able to address it through social engagement or fight/flight. So, they default to freeze (immobilize) as a survival response. Because the child does not feel safe in their own body, a numbness sets in as a means of protection. This numbness includes a lack of sensations, feelings, and connections with oneself and others. It's a defense strategy or adaptive response. The immobilization can show up as constant uneasiness, fear and anxiety, and an intense inner critic, underscored by deep pain.

Imagine an ocean wave that freezes in midmotion before it can complete its return into the sea: all that kinetic energy never had a chance to be used. The same is true when a person freezes or experiences numbness. The underlying feelings and activation never get an opportunity to be completed—they are unfinished business. Interrupting the completion of the stress response registers as another threat, which in turn creates a secondary response from the brain saying, *keep moving or you will perish.*

That intolerance for slowing down should seem familiar for those who are addicted to drama and to those around them. If you can keep moving, you don't have to touch the vulnerability of what's beneath the immobilization and you don't have to experience stillness, which is perceived as a death.

So, in this case, there's both a freeze in the nervous system and a simultaneous adaptive strategy to rev out of that freeze into mobility. It's two things in direct competition, being in a dead stop but being compelled to try to keep moving at the same time—like keeping the car in neutral and revving the engine in hopes that it will somehow drive.

In an active drama state, a whirlwind is created when someone slams on the brakes and the gas at the same time, hoping that if they keep pressing on that gas, it will somehow get their foot off the brakes. This is how people try to mobilize themselves out of a freeze response, and how revving is born.

During the accelerator process, or revving, they focus on whatever outward crisis has caught their attention and become frantic, angry, or excited. If the brakes win out, they fall back into the state of freeze and numbness. However, when the revving wins out, there's a catharsis. It feels as if you are flipped out of yourself (and the numbness) into the crisis at hand—giving you a sense of relief or even power and control. I used to think of these moments as taking my life back.

- - - - -

PHASE 2: DYSREGULATED ACTIVATION AND
THE MERGING OF CRISIS AND CHAOS

If we think of revving like taking a "hit" (like using drugs or drinking alcohol), the dysregulated activation phase produces the first part of the "high" in an addiction to drama. Like all drugs, it has its limited time before it wears off—and thus revving is utilized as the hit to come back to this unexpectedly exhilarating merging of crisis and chaos. This phase of the drama cycle feels like the battery pack has been fully charged—there's way too much energy to know what to do with it—but it still feels exciting and powerful.

Recall that activation is a natural part of our body's response to a stressor, the physiological preparation to act. Dysregulated activation, however, is when the level of activation exceeds the amount that is functional or needed to adapt. Revving keeps us at our baseline level of stress and seeks or creates the external conditions to match that internal state. In the phase of dysregulated activation, there is a moment of synchronizing that internal state and external conditions where the world feels connected and there is a false sense of wholeness and relation. In Chapter 6, we defined *crisis* as *external* situations arising from the surrounding conditions, relationships, or environment and chaos as an *internal* state of confusion and disorganization that is created from past experiences. Chaos is also unprocessed stress and trauma that take up residence in the body. The merging of chaos and crisis is like the vinegar and baking soda volcano science experiment many of us did as kids. Before the volcano erupts, there's a moment in which the excitement and activation level has built up so high that it feels like absolute power. In the state of dysregulated activation, the merging of crisis and chaos feels like power, unlimited potential, excitability, and most important, aliveness. Once you've had a taste of that aliveness and power, you may feel that this is exactly what has been missing in your life . . . and, oh boy, do you want more of it.

When I was younger, I often felt lost and disconnected from what and who was around me. I used to imagine my superpower was to be able to siphon electricity and energy from lights and the moon—and, in response, I would feel these little moments of electricity surging in my body. For a brief moment, I would feel connected to who and what was around me. As years went on, I found that "surge" through other means. Sometimes, it was performing in front of hundreds or thousands of people. Other times, I would get into emotionally charged situations that could easily be made more intense. I would initiate calls with customer service departments whenever there was a discrepancy in the bill, for instance, or interruption to the service. It didn't even have to be my own issue—I would also call on behalf of other people. I was known as the teenager who could get apologies or charges reversed. Just the idea of it got that inner surge going. I was already revving up before anyone picked up the phone. As soon as the customer service representative was on the phone, I began scanning for where and what I could use to further rev myself up. I could feel an urge and this desire for things to be wrong, for them to have screwed up. Something in me was being fed by it—as if I were directly connected to a battery pack of energy. When the person on the end of the line picked up on my dissatisfaction and the tension (crisis) between us matched my inner agitation (chaos), that was the moment of dysregulated activation. And the stronger and bigger the activation, the stronger and bigger I felt. It was like a massive shot of coffee. It woke up every part of me from my malaise.

PHASE 3: UNCONTAINED CATHARSIS

Uncontained catharsis is the second part of the "high" of an addiction to drama. Catharsis is the release of emotions and the discharge of energy/tension—which ultimately activates the reward systems of the brain.[1] Catharsis is positively rewarded and reinforced by a prompt increase of social support.[2] However, for those with an addiction to drama, an uncontained catharsis pulls those social support resources in, bringing them closer through an intense whirlwind.

Back to the volcano science experiment: once the baking soda and vinegar mix and the carbon dioxide produced by the mixture has filled the entire opening of the volcano, it then seeks more space to fill and to let off the building pressure, which results in an erupting mess.

In the stress response cycle, the stage after activation is *mobilization*. In a healthy stress response, the rise of physiological energy (activation) is then used to address and adapt to the stressors (mobilization). In the drama cycle, however, the dysregulated activation energy builds up, and rather than being able to mobilize and adapt the person will either collapse or go into an uncontained catharsis—a haphazard attempt to discharge an enormous amount of energy built up in the previous phases.

Uncontained catharsis is like overfilling a balloon, regardless of its strength or capacity, until it pops. It is a disorganized release of energy that can look like strong anger, a panic attack, emotional dumping (venting), freaking out, or any frenetic or dissociated action (e.g., overeating, oversharing, overconsuming, etc.). It's as though the person's boundaries are completely dissolved and everything spills out onto the world around them. In a catharsis, the energy is often explosive, without anything being processed or understood. This makes it nearly impossible to connect with their inner needs or those of others.

After Robin reaches what she calls "the buildup" of overstimulation, she finds herself in a walking blackout where all she can do for relief is to obsessively clean her house or work out until exhaustion. This is the phase in which the person addicted to drama feels out of control and possessed, like they are rolling down a massive hill, collecting speed and intensity, and unable to stop.

The release of endorphins and discharge of pressure is euphoric and empowering—but ultimately short-lived.

PHASE 4: THE HANGOVER AND BOREDOM

After an uncontained catharsis, those with an addiction to drama collapse into a temporary and an artificial relief. When people addicted to drama start to relax, there is a subconscious voice that asks, "Is silence and space safe?" Since silence and space may have been unfamiliar, or they were associated with the calm before the storm, it can make someone feel very vulnerable (see "Revving to Get Unstuck" on page 114). Additionally, the space and stillness can be quite full of dis-ease, which are often the sensations and emotions that individuals with an addiction to drama are avoiding for self-preservation.

The momentary release from the catharsis is fleeting. Lillian, a former client, says, "I think at times it's enticing and it's seductive to have the re-lease—but it's also not sustainable; something always gets me going again."

A cathartic release in the drama cycle leaves people with an emotional and psychological hangover, as opposed to feeling restored. In the space that's created from the explosion, momentary relief gives way to a growing discomfort or boredom—a sense that this empty space needs to be filled. Feelings of fogginess, disorientation, being drained, moody, or disconnected can also occur as a response to withdrawals. Allison, a longtime client, says, "I know I'm going to have my hangover tomorrow, but I promise myself I'm just not going to come back here [to the drama] for a long time."

Sebastian, a self-proclaimed drama addict, described coming down from the dysregulated arousal state and catharsis as a wicked hangover, cou-pled with feelings of regret, loneliness, and sadness. "It feels almost like a breakup . . . it doesn't feel clean . . . the energy feels kind of dirty. And there's this certain level of fatigue, I guess, and a feeling of regressing . . . like I just fed something that I didn't want to feed."

A German Chilean neuroscientist named Susana Bloch Arendt coined the term *emotional hangover* in the early 1990s, describing performers who were unable to leave behind the emotional connection they created with a character on the stage. She described two typical time lengths: *phasic*, if short-lived; or *tonic*, if maintained over time. The longer tonic state can have serious consequences for the actor's mental and emotional health. In 2016, researchers at New York University discovered more evidence for emotional hangovers, characterized by a physiological residue and an emotional brain state that lasts longer than the event itself, and has an altering effect on how the event is remembered.[3]

Another theory is that during the stage of activation, there is a surge of endorphins, the body's natural pain relievers. After the dysregulated and un-contained catharsis is complete, and there is a short break from activation, endorphin levels return to normal, and the underlying discomfort and pain returns.[4] Essentially, this theory also suggests that the hangover is a withdrawal from the high that emerged after the dysregulated activation and catharsis, mixed with a combination of how someone feels about themselves and how they perceive others feel about them.

As boredom or withdrawal sets in, it means the anesthetic response of the drama is wearing off and they are coming closer to the underlying truth of their baseline discomfort and disconnection, that feeling of being out of sync with those around them and the world. The urge for the next hit of drama starts to stir. I have seen and heard many clients rev themselves up as soon as they start to relax, saying things like, "The settling is terrifying" or "What if I need to run into the street to save my child? How could I even do that if I'm relaxed?" For those with an addiction to drama, an arousal reflex emerges to protect the individual from falling into the abyss of relaxation and jump-starts their engines back into revving. Out of the relief of the cathartic release comes the withdrawal, the boredom and anxiety, and they need to throw logs on the fire again to build up to the next fix of drama.

As in any addiction: you bite the dog that bit you and reenter the cycle, through the compulsive worry, repetitive thoughts, stories, reenactments of the past or projected future, and all the things that keep you revving toward the high and catharsis, to feel some sense of power, importance, and meaning.

When there's no integrated way of coming down from activation, there's no stage of recuperation. In turn, the individual never gets to metabolize the emotions associated with the event or regenerate the energetic reserves that were used for adapting or responding to stressors—and so is left in a chronic state of depletion. It's no wonder that people who are chronically depleted will keep defaulting back to crisis and chaos as a way to lift themselves back into life—returning to the revving stage so the drama cycle can begin again.

Now, if all of us were always revved in activation without the ability to rest, we might see an epidemic of chronic fatigue or addiction to drama on a wider scale. Actually, in many ways, that *is* what is happening . . . as we will see in the next chapter.

A SNAPSHOT OF THE CYCLE

Malerie has an internal seedling of a feeling of sadness. Sadness isn't a tolerable feeling for her, so it defaults to something more familiar or acceptable: loneliness. That escalates into a projection—*Where is everyone?!*—which forms into an internalized story about why she is alone, such as, *I do so much for others and they never show up for me!* It continues, *Why is everyone against me? No one has my back!*

Because Malerie isn't able to express this core feeling of sadness, she now has multiple streams of revving from stories and internal scripts, as well as a full-body tension. All of these streams of revving are building a significant load of dysregulated activation. There is also a rise of discomfort and unease. And this makes Malerie rev more to try to find a way to dispel it.

Malerie goes out walking with all of this happening in her. At the grocery store, she believes she has been cut off in line. She is furious and demands to speak to the manager. When the manager is befuddled by what is happening, Malerie launches a victim campaign: "Why won't you defend me . . . this store doesn't respect its customers!" She begins to explode onto the manager, depositing all of what happened before into this moment. Malerie is building a whirlwind—she pulls people into the bigness of her experience. "Isn't this store the most awful store?!" she declares, and some people might even get pulled in and agree with her. Then, Malerie is justified and validated. Because the intensity is so big, she's also not able to register when that dysregulated activation has been used and moved through . . . and so she just keeps revving until she explodes in an uncontained catharsis. She blasts it on all her social media and replays the story to herself and others, repeatedly.

To point out the obvious, no one, including Malerie, is anywhere near addressing her original underlying sadness. And because she is not mobilizing her core feeling, but rather a secondary one that is masking the first one, she is not able to heal the original pain or emotional wounding. While some individuals may have been sucked into the whirlwind and cheered on or validated Malerie, ultimately she did not get the connection of being seen and heard that she truly desired. This is even more apparent as she wakes the next day with a hangover and the ache of aloneness still present.

From the perspective of those witnessing the escalation, Malerie's extreme response can seem like a peaceful mountain becoming an erupting volcano in the blink of an eye. However, when slowed down it is clear that Malerie went through stages of experiencing intolerable unprocessed feelings, avoidances, activation, perpetually scanning for more logs to add to the fire, a self-perpetuating reaction to the last log she put on the fire—and is also pulling other people's responses into the situation, like adding oxygen to the fire. This shows up as the phases of the drama cycle: revving, dysregulated activation, uncontained catharsis, and a hangover. Underneath this enormous blaze is a human being yearning to heal and experience the safety of social bonds—and yet is so far from what they yearn for.

- - - - -

KEY TAKEAWAYS

- The active drama cycle consists of four different phases:
  - » Revving: creating conditions or focusing on specific things that create a charge of activation. This can be done through catastrophizing, unconsciously reenacting old wounds, getting stuck in emotional binds, and creating and living in stories.
  - » Dysregulated activation: the payoff of all the revving in which there is a satisfying and powerful experience of synchronizing of the internal state of chaos and the external crisis.
  - » Uncontained catharsis: the haphazard and uncontrolled way to rapidly discharge the built-up tension. It also serves as a medium for connecting, and stimulates the reward systems in the brain.
  - » The hangover: a collapse and short-lived (false) state of release. This is then followed by withdrawal that triggers the cycle to begin again.

CHAPTER 9

Overstimulated and Underconnected: The Global Drug of Drama

TAKE A DEEP BREATH, BECAUSE ON SOME LEVEL WE ARE ALL ADDICTED TO drama.

Did that truth hook you in with one of your most precious resources—your attention? There's only so much attention to go around, and the competition for your focus is extremely high. In fact, your attention is one of the most valuable, sought-after resources and commodities on the market. If you're reading this book right now, it means you aren't attending to what's happening all around you, and I have succeeded in capturing your focus. You aren't checking your texts, updating your Instagram, or watching CNN. Your focus is on this book and my bid for your valuable attention has won. This is no small feat!

We in Western culture are living in an attention economy that is created and perpetuated by a variety of media, including television, radio, social media, newspapers, magazines, and more. While each of these uses predictive marketing models to capture and maintain your attention, social media has a more powerful means of watching, tracking, monitoring, and recording your actions. While you have not given explicit consent, the collection of this data is used to predict your actions and redirect your focus to maintain your attention. In the same way textile experts create color trends years before those fabrics saturate the market, a small handful of engineers are creating the trends to get your attention—along with billions of others. The manipulation of your attention is, of course, a means to grow brand devotion and maximize profits from advertisements.

In this open market of attention, we might not even realize that our own agency—in this case, of controlling our attention—is being usurped. As neuroscientist Richard J. Davidson, PhD, put it, "Our attention is being captured by devices rather than being voluntarily regulated. We are like a sailor without a rudder on the ocean—pushed and pulled by the digital stimuli to which we are exposed rather than by the intentional direction of our own mind."[1] The more our focus is pulled into these external sources and technologies that are bidding for our attention, the more reliant we become on them, and the harder it becomes to bring our attention back to ourselves. Similar to how those who are addicted to drama get pulled into whatever they are revving about, or how those in proximity to a whirlwind get pulled into someone else's drama—we are being baited away from attending to our underlying needs. Perhaps it's the fear of missing out, or of being left behind (and out of sync with) the fast-moving currents of the world—but it's becoming increasingly harder to slow down, evaluate, and process what we're consuming. As our ability to attend to ourselves lessens and the amount of stimulus increases, significant consequences emerge, and we start to lose our ability to regulate our own focus, emotions, actions, and energy.

When our attention wavers, we miss essential cues taking place in relationship between ourselves and the environment, including a connection between ourselves and others. We move further away from experiencing the world from *within* our core self. Our decreasing agency over our attention can cause us to neglect our own important biological cycles, such as resting. Our fundamental needs get bypassed or ignored. It's like shoveling in food without recognizing if we are hungry or full, let alone if it tastes good. *We can't process what we don't feel, and we can't feel what we can't attend to.* If outside sources are owning our attention, they begin to have ownership of how, when, and what we feel.

As we have seen, a painful childhood or chaotic environment can create the conditions for an addiction to drama. When the conditions are right, every human has the capacity to use drama as a means of adapting and coping. Social media, and today's attentional economy, produce the same dynamics that create and perpetuate an addiction to drama, globally. The drive toward capturing our attention is in a sense an "incubator" nurturing our exposure and reliance on drama. This mirrors the conditions that create a dependency on crisis and chaos, and drama becomes our new normal.

The conditions that emerge out of this include loneliness that perpetuates a sense of being unseen and unheard, a relentless stream of stimulus that both numbs and overwhelms, a constant flow of activation that revs us to feel more alive and attentive—and the social media platforms that are a stage and a place to deposit the unregulated catharsis that burst from the forced revving.

THE LINK BETWEEN ATTENTION AND ACTIVATION

The truth is we don't live in an attention economy, we live in an *activation economy*.

To gain your attention, something must stimulate the arousal in the nervous system. The same part of your brain involved in the arousal response and pain modulation is integral to attention and focus—attention is simply a by-product of activation.

The activation that makes us focus on whatever is demanding our attention is the same activation that occurs in a stress response, and more important, the same activation that is the fuel for those with an addiction to drama.

When every app, show, newspaper, and person is bidding for your attention, what will win out? Whatever is more emotional and sensational for you. While every person will have a different response to something based on their level of connection to it, relatability, timing, and desire for it, that which is more sensational is almost always more captivating and memorable. It's no wonder that the content of our screens and information sources are filled with ever more taboo, evocative, and sensational material. It is what creates activation and wins our attention. Even as magazine sales overall started declining in 2012, over one million gossip magazines were sold each week. And now, in the age of accessible gossip, we receive unlimited amounts, directly, from the celebrities and influencers themselves in real time. In the 2000s, 70 to 80 percent of the television audience was devoted to reality television, and in 2017, one-fifth of all American prime-time TV shows were reality shows.[2] These posts and shows are highly staged to evoke the most stimulating responses. We get absorbed in other people's drama—the more sensational, the better.

Sexual explicitness in advertisement has continued to increase since the 1980s, while occurrences of violence in television, news, and video games also continues to rise.[3] Multiple studies have demonstrated that violence and crimes are exaggerated in the telling of the news, creating an increase of fear, despite declining crime rates in many categories.[4] These sexual and violent stimuli that capture the audience's attention elicit a physiological arousal as well as aggressive thoughts and feelings, which keeps them locked into whatever they are watching or listening to.

Not all emotions or stimuli are created equal. Or better said, not all stimuli and emotions are used equally in the bid for our attention. We've evolved to learn from (and attend to) negative information far more than positive information.[5] Now, negative doesn't necessarily mean "bad." Positive stimuli are associated more with security, while unpleasant or arousing information is associated more often with fear, which stimulates our survival responses. *Negative*, in this context, means more arousing, intense, disruptive—and typically is deemed less desirable. In this sense, negative emotions let us know that something needs to be changed or adapted.

Emotions are intended to be our compass guiding us on a primal level to action. For those with an addiction to drama, however, the question is: How much emotion is required to guide or gain attention through activation?

This bias toward negative stimuli and emotions is found neurologically—in spikes in activity in the amygdala. The amygdala, the brain center for evaluating incoming information and generating an arousal response, responds to all stimuli, but the intensity of response to negative stimuli is greater than the response to the same amount of positive stimuli.

As a result, we are far more attentive to (and influenced by) negative than positive stimuli.[6] If you ask any author or performer, they will likely remember their negative reviews more clearly than they remember the details of all the positive ones, even if they have many more positive reviews than negative ones. Many of us have experienced this negative bias; a painful truth in today's "trolling" society, as more and more people leave negative and harmful comments or posts.

Similarly, after watching the news, observers are more likely to recite and share negative content rather than positive content. Sadly, we perceive negative news as more truthful and more valid.[7] So, the reward for exaggerating stories and spinning a more negative perspective is that you win the attention of the viewer, and sustain it.

When our survival response is activated, we are preconditioned to pay attention to fear over security, or negative stimulus over positive. As our attention becomes more fixated on arousing negative stimuli, that becomes what we tend to use in our decision-making. For example, if you walk into a room of people, and one of those people evokes a negative response but the rest of the people do not, the decision of what happens next will be based on the negative feeling. We are evolutionarily designed to use negative stimuli as activation—which would make sense if we were responding to a real threat. Many people not only dwell on the negative but use it as a fuel to take action. Some studies indicate that some people see a more neutral, ambiguous stimulus as more threatening, such as assuming danger from seeing a person who doesn't look like them, and they will devote an excessive amount of psychological energy to that stimulus.[8]

Words have a strong impact on where attention will go. Research on social media, journalism, and advertising all indicate that negative words get more attention and arouse more emotion.[9] The speed at which this happens also influences the receiver's behavior. The more intense the language, the longer it will stay in that person's memory. The intensity of the language will also predict the amount of attention captured and for how long. "That was a terrifying experience" will get more attention than "That was an unexpected experience."

Besides replacing neutral words with more intense ones, other tactics to get our attention include additional escalating words ("extremely bad" as opposed to "bad"), stylistic devices (e.g., metaphor, "It was like he saw right through me and I melted into the abyss of space" versus "He ignored what I had to say"), and typographical elements, such as exclamation marks! You could take note of how often those with an addiction to drama use these "devices," and how often these strategies are used in marketing, storytelling, social media posts, etc.

There are two stages to this process: getting your attention and keeping it. In a 2004 study, the time an office worker sustained attention before switching tasks was three minutes and five seconds. In 2016, the average time for sustainment on any screen, for the same population, was forty seconds.[10] In twelve years, our attention spans shrunk by nearly 79 percent. These studies are groundwork for the emerging field of interruption science. Interruption, the disruption of our focus, has been increasing through the use of a multitude of tactics. Think of all the banners and alerts that you have on your phone.

As I was writing this paragraph, a news notification on my phone popped up that read *"How America's deadliest serial killer hid in plain sight. Plus: the 100 smartest inventions of the year, and weekend reads."* Even though I mostly ignored the absurdly irrelevant and tantalizing clickbait, it did cost me energy and attention.

And that's not all it costs. Research shows that interruptions cost the US economy $588 billion a year.[11] In response to all interruptions in focus, people typically feel more frustrated and it takes more time and exertion to complete the same tasks. As they become more cognitively fatigued, they need a higher dose of activation to bring them back to focus. You might recall how those with addiction to drama used chaos and crisis like some people use coffee to keep them engaged. Being continuously sidetracked and distracted replicates an unpredictable chaotic environment, one in which it becomes increasingly more difficult to settle into, and hypervigilance is born. Thus begins a frenetic and frantic rhythm that has become known as "urgency culture," and we begin to associate and adopt this as normal.

And as people become acclimated to being constantly interrupted, they begin to *self-interrupt* in the absence of disruptive stimuli. This is similar to how those addicted to drama create stories and reinterpret reality as a means to rev up in the absence of real crisis. Self-interruption might look like checking your phone even when there have been no notifications, or being in midstream of a conversation and you start thinking about what you have to pick up from the grocery store, or soaking in the bathtub and starting to ruminate and replay a story from the day. This could be easily mistaken as adult ADHD.

GLOBAL ISOLATION PAIN

As attention becomes scarcer and distractibility grows, we must adapt to continue to feel seen and heard. The race for our attention via activation is not limited to social media—it's just that social media has become a more attainable means for us to enter into the race, and possibly prosper off its rapid reward cycles. We are all bidding for one another's focus.

When my best friend had a baby a few years ago, our daily phone calls became daily texts, and then weekly texts, then dropped down to monthly texts. Her attention was being consumed by the needs of her child. When I went to visit her last year, she asked me how I was doing, and before I could finish a story about my parents, she was scrolling on social media. I recognized in that moment that I was also competing with everyone she has access to online, on her phone, as well as whatever other notifications that could interrupt and steal her attention. So, I did what any "good friend" would do, I turned on some music and pretended to do a striptease (or, wait, is that just what *I* would do?). It wasn't until I started belting out the lyrics of the song that she turned to me and said, "Oh, sorry, I got a notification and fell down a social media hole."

If you're anything like my friend—exhausted and finding yourself reflexively scrolling out of fatigue or distracted by messages or news stories—chances are that preoccupation of your focus has led to a momentary absence of attention to yourself or someone else.

When we or others around us have less attention capacity and more distractions, we are drawn further and further away from attending to ourselves or being attended to—and subsequently are less likely to have our needs recognized and met.

The distractibility of those around us is connected with the growing prevalence of loneliness. And the degree of loneliness is directly connected to an absence of feeling seen and heard—part of the baseline of an addiction to drama, as we saw in Chapter 5.

The World Health Organization names anxiety and depression caused by loneliness and isolation as one of the most pressing health concerns of our time. Loneliness is a gap between the amount and quality of social connection we would need to have, and the amount we experience. It's an internal state that directs us toward a primal initiative—forming more secure bonds for survival. The absence of connection extends beyond just ourselves or other people.

I consider there to be six variations of loneliness or isolation:

Intrapersonal isolation can emerge as a result of separating from our feelings, sensations, wants, needs, intuition, purpose, or even a sense of separation from our own body (dissociation).

Interpersonal isolation can emerge from not having meaningful face-to-face contact that feels rewarding, supportive, and enlivening. It can also potentially emerge from a shortage of social resources and skills, attachment wounds, boundary ruptures, lack of feeling empathy/validation/understanding, self-protection strategies, or loss.

Collective isolation can emerge from not feeling part of a group or collective, and is often associated with an absence of community connection and a sense of belonging.

Social/cultural isolation can emerge as a perceived sense of "otherness" that we created or is created by both implicit and explicit bias, hate, oppression, power differentials, and transgenerational trauma.

Environmental isolation can emerge as variations of grief, despair, and pain from the loss or deprivation of our innate bond with nature.

Spiritual isolation can emerge from feeling that you are not part of something beyond your individual existence. Spiritual isolation can be associated with an absence of clarity, guidance, and a true source of belonging.

Accessibility, responsiveness, and engagement are the factors that define the quality of bonds to others, and when they are not present, we begin to experience isolation pain. This pain is a signal from our body that feels like an underlying issue, letting us know of the absence of these secure connections and that our fundamental needs are being missed. It creates a pervasive sense of dis-ease and forms the underlying anxious current of our lives. As isolation pain from loneliness increases globally, so do the coping responses to navigate it—including an addiction to drama.

The next layer that emerges is numbing and the need for more sensation to feel alive (and attentive). However, in this activation economy, the overwhelming stimuli that create the numbness and the subsequent revving is not coming just from us, but is something that is being done to us.

BEING OVERWHELMED AND REVVING ON A GLOBAL LEVEL

We know that more heightened language, images, and stories will be used to arouse an emotional response, typically geared toward negative feelings as they are more arousing, attention grabbing, and sustaining. Add to this the repeated exposure of those images, video clips, words, stories, etc., multiple times a day, from many different sources.

In the same way those with an addiction might cycle back over and over again to the same story, each time getting a hit off of its activating content, we are often exposed through many media sources to intense content repeatedly.

Here's an example from my life. On September 11, 2001, I was walking down Fifth Avenue in New York City toward Washington Square Park on my way to my first day of college. I vividly remember watching a plane go into the side of a building. My first thought was that it was an expensive movie set. Throughout the succeeding days, I moved from shock to fear and began to share and process what I witnessed with many other fellow New Yorkers.

I made a conscious choice not to watch the news after speaking to my parents who had been glued to the television in fear of their son's life. I remember my mom saying to me, "I can't look away; I must have seen the videos of the planes, from all sorts of angles, go into the World Trade Center at least sixty to one hundred times today." My dad kept telling me he was going to drive to New York City and pick me up. I kept explaining to them I felt safe and wasn't leaving my new home. I couldn't understand why they seemed more alarmed than I was when I was the one just a mile from the incident.

Then, it occurred to me: they were being constantly inundated and bombarded with activating video footage while sitting still in front of the television, without a break, and certainly without any way of processing that much information. Whereas I had walked through the city and had connected, wept, and bonded with complete strangers.

After that experience on September 11, I began to study and research the long-term effects of information overload, specifically information that was repeatedly activating. No matter what generation we are, we have seen significant events repeated throughout multiple media sources: the assassination of John F. Kennedy, the murder of George Floyd and others, and the stories of those dying from COVID-19.

A 2013 study on the Boston Marathon bombing explored the stress response of those who had direct exposure to the event versus those who experienced it through the media. Those who were exposed to many media sources several hours throughout the day had a *more acute stress response* than those who were directly exposed to the event.[12] The onslaught of images and retelling of the narrative kept the stressor more active and alive. The repeated exposure of these types of events sustains the audience's attention and is linked to increased and extended stress and trauma-related symptoms.

And addiction is a way of coping and relieving the pain from these stress and trauma-related symptoms.

Not only are we being exposed to a flood of activating images, words, and stories, but our exposure to other people's emotions can be contagious, adding to what we are already experiencing. Emotions and other physiological states are contagious, and the most contagious of all of these states is activation, or a stress response. A good actor on a stage doesn't just draw you in to what's happening but transmits their experience until you begin to feel what they are going through.

Several studies have clearly shown that viewing others who are experiencing or have recently experienced states of activation has a contagious physiological response in the observer, what some researchers identify as secondhand stress. In one study, participants were part of a Trier Social Stress Test (TSST), in which some of them had to give an impromptu speech to a panel of judges. Stress response markers were measured in both the speakers and observers. The observers' release of these stress markers was directly proportional to the speakers: the more stress from the speaker, the more stress the observers felt.[13]

Additional studies have shown that the contagious response also occurs in reaction to "passive" stressors, such as videos, images, and perceived tone of voice in writing. The ability to "catch" a person's stress response is an evolutionary development aimed at better navigating our environment and communicating nonverbally the complex dynamics of adapting.[14] If a friend of yours were to come running into your house after seeing a massive snake outside your front door, before they can speak, you're already registering their body language, breath, pacing, and other subtle cues—and beginning to mirror that level of activation so you can also adapt to the massive snake without ever having to see it. In short, every time you might see someone around you who is totally "stressed out," on some level, so are you.

The level of arousal response also activates the observer's implicit memory, in which that sensation "lights up" associated experiences from the past and floods the present moment. When your friend comes in from having seen the giant snake, not only are you catching her activation level, but this also triggers other times you have been activated—and suddenly you may also be responding to the past as though it was the present. The hurts and pains of the past flood the present and all projections of the future.

Every post you see, advertisement or new story you're exposed to, elicits from you an emotional and psychological response. Some of that arousal response is generated from you, and some of it comes from others. That's a lot of activation.

The commodification and manipulation of our activation has been hijacked by a global enterprise that doesn't care about the well-being of our nervous system or the long-term effects of overstimulation. These sources of activation cannot recognize each person's window of capacity for activation—and err on the side of flooding our attention and ability to digest. This information overload, without the time, space, and support to process it, leads to an inability to manage what happens internally. We either collapse under the pressure of it or in essence spew this overload all over the place.

If the physiological response of activation isn't allowed to progress to mobilization, as in the stress response cycle, there are severe consequences. Prolonged unresolved exposure to activation can impair the brain's executive functions—located in the prefrontal cortex—which allow us to observe thoughts, feelings, and emotions objectively. We can recognize that those with an addiction to drama have challenges in observing a moment objectively, as opposed to being flooded by stories of the past or ones being created about the future. The overload of stimulation coupled with today's more sedentary lifestyle creates an imbalance between sensory input and motor output—leading to unfulfilled stress-response cycles that have long-term significant consequences, such as type 2 diabetes, high blood pressure, gastrointestinal disorders, a suppressed immune system, reproductive issues, learning and memory complications, emotional dysregulation, and impaired judgment and decision-making. To put it simply, being overstimulated and sedentary is making us sick.

It doesn't stop at overstimulation. Over time, we become habituated to that level of stimuli coming at us. The same amount of suspense, violence, intense images, and language becomes less effective at capturing our attention. This is the stage called *tolerance*. Just like doctors who experience alarm fatigue and block out sounds indicating an emergency (as first mentioned in Chapter 5), we, too, start to level off on the amount of stimulation it takes to incite activation and capture our attention. It now *takes* more to *feel* more. Hence the game commences of one-upping, of increasing the stimulus to regain our attention.

If we are not revving ourselves up from this numbness, then certainly these media sources needing to capture our attention will do it for us.

If we were to imagine growing up in a chaotic and overstimulating family like this, we would clearly be able to see how this could form an addiction to drama. Instead of a family disrupting our environment, we have a whole culture creating these conditions.

IN A LONELY WORLD, DRAMA BRINGS US TOGETHER

Pain, despite its challenges, acts as a social glue that brings groups into a synchronization of experience, rhythm, cohesion, and cooperation. Those with an addiction to drama pull people into their whirlwind as a means of connecting, to feel less alone. This is mimicking the evolutionary truth that in the midst of feeling alone and isolated, humans bond over crisis.

After the events of 9/11, there was a sense of community among those of us in New York City. Typically, there was such a coldness and autonomy among people that no one ever smiled or said hello to each other on the street—and for a brief time, all of that changed. Suddenly, every person you walked by acknowledged you; it was as if we all knew one another through our shared experience. People waved and smiled at each other; I remember sitting on a bus and a woman turned to me and said, "How are you? Did you lose anyone?"

A study at a university in Australia observed two groups of participants: one group had to submerge their hands in painful cold water to complete a task, and the other group had to complete the same task in tepid water. When evaluated, the group that completed the painful task showed much higher social bonding with other members than the group whose task was painless. The painful task group also showed more collaboration in future tasks, as members of that group continued to risk their own outcome for the benefit of the group.[15]

Individuals in a shared group experience of crisis tend to report fewer feelings of isolation and loneliness than individuals who go through a crisis alone. In fact, the division between class and culture momentarily dissolves, allowing more trust and connection to form, ultimately creating bonding. In this way those who experience some variation of loneliness may feel the rewards of bonding through crisis. It is perhaps not dissimilar to those who are addicted to drama reporting that crisis was the currency of love within their families. And if there isn't a true crisis to go through together, a person *can create it* through the processes of telling stories and reenactments. In a culture where there is an epidemic of loneliness and access to billions of people at the swipe of a finger, there is no more powerful substitute for true connection than drama bonding.

ALL THE WORLD'S A STAGE

Damn, take a breath. It's one thing to recognize the powerlessness at which you have been inadvertently pulled into someone else's whirlwind of drama—and in doing so cocreating their trauma reenactment; it's another thing to recognize that the media conglomerates of our culture have replicated the very conditions for a perfect storm—an addiction to drama in all of us.

Like Alice falling down the rabbit hole, anyone can find themselves in the story of someone else's drama or a reality that is manipulated by others. We are evolutionarily designed to react to the stressors of life, and the contagious nature of these responses are being used to capture our attention vis-a-vis our activation. As our attention is pulled away, our primal feelings and needs are being abandoned. The constant interruption of attention and connection pulls us out of sync with ourselves and subsequently with the world around us.

A massive exposure to this level of activation builds a tolerance like a wall that must be continuously scaled and conquered by those who need to capture, contain, and maintain our focus. The more tolerance, the more desensitization (numbness) sets in—and the more sensation is needed for us to feel alive and vibrant. Isolation pain replaces authentic connection,[16] and we enter into the rat race for being seen and heard, competing with billion-dollar companies that have armies of engineers and marketing psychologists at their whim to capture and maintain our attention.

The higher the tolerance, the bigger the withdrawals. Our responses to what is happening around us becomes less regulated and in turn deactivation and restoration become foreign or intolerable. Decision-making gets made from this state of withdrawal—and we begin to seek or create the circumstances to bond. And as you might recall, there is no more powerful substitute for true connection than drama bonding.

What has been seen as a condition for seeking attention is truly a fight for connection. I often think of the saying "The child who is not embraced by the village will burn it down to feel its warmth." *The intention is not malicious even though the aftermath is devastating.* Whether you are the one setting fire to the village or witnessing the fire, there is one essential question: What would each of us do to once again feel the warmth of connection?

So, take another deep breath, because at some level we are all addicted to drama. But, more important, we can all take steps toward healing and getting free of the conditions that created this storm.

KEY TAKEAWAYS

- Our attentional economy predicts our focus and behavior and redirects it to optimize marketing. The attentional economy produces the same dynamics that create and perpetuate an addiction to drama.
- The more our attention is being pulled to technologies and media sources to direct us, the less we are able to bring our attention back to ourselves. This neglect to ourselves and others results in an absence of feeling seen and heard.
- Attention is achieved by creating an activation. Media sources have been capitalizing on this fact by creating more sensationalism and dramatic narratives. Over time, we become more tolerant toward the level of information overload and activation, and require more to feel more.
- This eventually becomes the new normal—and the coping responses begin to mirror that of those addicted to drama.
- As feelings of isolation and loneliness become more prevalent, pain and crisis continue to act as a social glue. Bonding through drama can momentarily replace a deprivation of connection.

PART THREE

THE JOURNEY OF HEALING AN ADDICTION TO DRAMA

CHAPTER 10

Breaking, Finding, Releasing, and Learning: Stories of Healing

I F YOU HAVE DRAMA IN YOUR LIFE—EITHER FROM BEING AROUND SOMEONE who appears to be addicted to drama or because you are the one who craves drama—there is hope. There is a path to a life filled with more ease and connection.

To inspire your journey or someone you know, here are stories of several people with an addiction to drama, and how they broke free of the dependency on crisis and chaos.

MARTY: BREAKING THE SCRIPT

A former client, Marty, used to tell everyone he knew he had the worst luck finding love.

"The dating scene is just full of people who don't know how to communicate or have fun—it's hopeless, absolutely hopeless," he declared.

It became more painful when Marty saw couples on social media who seemed to have found each other effortlessly and were (apparently) living their best lives together. He wondered, *Why can't that be me?!*

After some time working together, Marty realized he keeps picking similar people to date—ones who aren't actually available. He convinced himself that he did want a relationship but also created distance from people who could fulfill that. He described it as a simultaneous push and pull within him. *He created the external conditions to maintain distance,* so as not to see the underlying patterns. He used his job, his friends, his exhaustion, or even the state of politics to rationalize how he was energetically and emotionally unavailable for a relationship.

Upon further therapeutic work, Marty realized there was a harsh, repetitive inner script that was feeding the pattern: *that he was stupid and ugly, which is why no one would ever love him.* He believed that other people would find him unattractive and unintelligent—and so he would interact only with people who wouldn't get close enough to him to discover these flaws.

Over time, Marty was able to differentiate himself from the script. Yet, while he believed he reached the core issue, he was still far from it. Marty had articulated the script but did not yet understand where it came from or why he clung to it. Then, he recalled one of the first times he heard this script: after the breakup with his first partner. At this point, he realized he never got closure after the end of that relationship and couldn't understand why the person had left him—so he had invented that script (and kept repeating it) as a way of finding the understanding he needed. Marty had projected his feelings onto his partner—and then responded by feeling useless and pathetic about being ugly and stupid, as though it were the truth.

Marty and I were getting closer to the core but not quite there. One day, I asked him, "What is this script protecting you from?" The script was pulling his attention away from something else that was going on at a deeper level. After some time, Marty contacted what was beneath the script: his unresolved heartbreak, a physical sensation that felt like a dagger from the top left of his heart to the back right, where it seemed stuck into the lobe of the lung. Marty wailed when he contacted this underlying heartbreak that he had avoided acknowledging. There were no words or stories as he reached the core pain, just pure sensation and feeling.

He mourned for nearly six weeks, unpacking the layers of this heartbreak, sadness, despair. When it was done, the old script felt like an empty whisper of wind—it held no power. Shortly thereafter, Marty was able to feel excitement about prospective partners again and started having depth and joy in connecting with people.

I call the process I guided Marty through "clearing the layers of dust off the mirror and arriving at core experiences." Many of us form our sense of self around the layers of dust that we created or were created for us. We humans are incredibly complex in the way we create layers and compensations in response to some core feelings that are intolerable or when there isn't the safe space to be held and seen to move through those feelings. Those who are addicted to drama are operating from these outer layers of dust. Intensity and extremes help maintain distance from the original core feelings, yet are pitched at a decibel loud enough for someone to finally respond—or so they hope.

SUZANNE: LOOKING UNDERNEATH THE COPING RESPONSES

Suzanne came into my office fuming about how disappointed she was with her relationship. She was sure she was with the wrong person, even though often she would say it was the best relationship. This particular day, her partner hadn't seemed interested and engaged when they went to a history museum, leading Suzanne to believe that he was incapable of being intellectual. And if he couldn't be intellectual, then what were they going to talk about? Furthermore, if he wasn't smart, then her family might disapprove and make her choose between them and her partner. Suzanne didn't stop there.

She went on to conclude that if they couldn't have an intellectual discussion about history, then a year from now she would be bored by their conversations, which meant she just wasted another prime year of her life, and if they were to break up then, then she might be too old to find another partner and would feel stuck. But if they break up now, what if she finds out later that it was a mistake? Because she was in her midthirties, and who knew how long it would take to find another partner who she would want to have a child with, Suzanne had to stay in the relationship. *But,* her persistent inner voice asked, *if he can't stay interested at a museum then how is he going to stay interested in their child?* Or worse, would their children also be unable to engage in deeper thinking and contemplation, like their father, and so she would be all alone?

If you, the reader, are feeling whiplashed and confused but simultaneously feel drawn into Suzanne's processes, then you have entered into her drama whirlwind. Take a moment, a few exhales to notice where your body is being held by the chair or ground underneath you. Then, let's head back in . . .

Suzanne went on with this a little while longer, cycling and revving through many layers of her story. When there was a space, I asked, "How was the museum for you?"

She paused for a moment and then launched back into speaking about her partner.

I smiled and tried again: "I really want to hear how the experience with your partner was. . . . and I'm curious what was your experience of the exhibit."

After a few more times of going back and forth, Suzanne slowed down enough to say, "I thought it was a bit dull."

I replied, "Oh, it sounds like both of you might have found it dull. Do you know what, if anything, was dull about it for your partner?"

"I don't," she said—and then tried to jump back in talking about the future of having kids together.

I asked, "What would happen if you found the museum dull?"

Suzanne took a long pause before saying, "Then, I would be dull and unwanted."

What you're seeing in this session is a prime example of the dynamics of unproductive coping responses. You may have noticed that as Suzanne came closer to her own fundamental experience, there were fewer techniques of revving and the whirlwind lessened. That is because the coping responses to avoid contact with herself started to soften, allowing for more clarity about the difference between reality and the perceived reality she had constructed through various coping strategies. Suzanne now feels like she can step back and see the pattern as it is occurring and is able to find moments of deescalating her revving tendencies so that she can break free from the drama cycle.

LORI: FINDING SAFETY IN SILENCE

At our very first session working together I asked Lori, "What would you like to work on?"

"I feel stressed out all the time," she responded. I paused to wait and see if there was more she wanted to say. I could see her becoming visibly agitated, and finally she said, "I'm super uncomfortable with the silence—I need you to say something."

This began Lori's journey toward healing an addiction to drama, as we spent months exploring what happens in the silence or pauses of life, and all the ways she has filled it. She filled it with a stream of thoughts, fast talking, intense exercise classes, watching the news, and a jammed schedule. When there was less going on in her life, she still felt busy, as if there was somewhere she forgot she was supposed to be or something she was supposed to be doing. Our primary objective was to make silence more tolerable—and discover what all the busyness might be distracting her from.

We discovered that various resources, such as a weighted blanket and the image of running water, helped soothe her as she hung out in the deep discomfort of silence. She began to recognize a sense of being pulled into anything that would take her out of the silence. She said it felt like she was being sucked into all sorts of distracting thoughts.

Over time, we were able to slow down her process of getting pulled into thoughts and actions that were keeping her in a high state of constant activation. In one session, she described being able to zoom out and watch as the desire to be pulled into the busyness showed up, and for the first time, she was able to have enough space to say no to the relentless craving of getting another hit of activation.

As Lori created more space from responding to the craving, she began to become more aware of basic needs, such as when she was hungry and when she wanted to rest. Previously, she had just gone to sleep or eaten because she knew she needed to. As she allowed herself to feel more of her primary needs, other desires—for companionship, humor, and support—started to surface. As she became aware of more needs, the feelings that came with them also emerged. We explored the history of what needs were met and which were unmet, and which feelings had been expressed and possibly even heard or recognized by her parents.

She told me that her mom was always there, but it never felt like she was present. "It was like she could never look me in the eyes, only adjacent to them," she said. For weeks, she mourned the absence of a present parent—part of her had always known this, but she had never let herself feel it. Lori said, "I was always keeping so busy looking outward, as though to find 'her eyes,' and being pulled in and distracted by everything else that was outside of me."

Later, Lori would report that some days were hard, and that she felt the pull to be distracted from herself. Sometimes, she got sucked into other people's stressful situations before recognizing she was abandoning herself, just like she had felt as a child. Through practices of compassion and love and kindness, she learned to forgive herself for these "abandonments." We celebrated the times when she was able to stop that temptation to be distracted from herself by becoming aware and connecting with how she was feeling and what she needed in that moment.

I spoke to Lori recently after she returned from a silent meditation retreat. She laughed for much of the session at the irony of feeling empowered and at ease during an entire week of silence.

MEGAN: RELEASING STORIES AND EMBRACING AUTHENTICITY

Megan, a young college student, would come into sessions and immediately start to cry as she told stories of her week. Her stories were filled with hardship, in which she was often being abandoned, forgotten about, and victimized. Any compassionate statement that mirrored how she was feeling was seemingly ignored, as was any advice to help change the circumstances. The only response that she would take in was if I were to echo how villainizing the characters of her stories were. The only thing she could receive was commentary about all the other people and places in her life.

While some of what she shared happened in real life, quite a few things came from posts she read or exchanges over text—mediums that allowed for a fair amount of interpretation and creation of stories based on limited information. Someone would cancel hanging out with her and she would immediately decide that her friend was choosing to be with someone else, which would escalate to thinking that person didn't like how expressive she was. "I'm too much for them," she would think, assuming that they were never truly friends.

One day, after a few weeks of the same conversation, I asked her how many times she had shared this story today. She counted seven people she had shared the story with. "If we were to compare the story you told the first person to the story you are sharing now," I asked, "how has it changed?"

She was quite honest in her response and recognized that, with each retelling, she added quite a few more details. I then asked her what happens as she adds those new elements. She responded that it kept the experience fresh and also intense.

I asked her to slowly retell me her current version of the story and then share what she knew was absolute truth in that story. That was difficult for her, but she was able to distill what was absolutely true to about three sentences.

Over several weeks, we unpacked why keeping the stories fresh and intense was valuable to her. One day she said, "It's like something in me wants to feel bad and disempowered all the time—like somehow that feels empowering." She began to realize the retelling of the story was only creating more drama than the original event and actually making her feel worse.

A few months into working together, Megan realized it wasn't just negative stories that were exaggerated and intensified—all her posts and photos were. She had posted about finding some beautiful flowers on the road and how much they reminded her of her childhood (captioned "beauty on the dirt road"). She turned to me and said, "That's not actually that true, but I nearly convinced myself it was true when I reread my post and all the comments that were written about it."

We called this her social avatar, a constructed and curated version of herself that had been created to tell stories that would yield attention in the form of comments and likes. The further her social avatar got from reality, the further she pulled away from her core self and the needs and feelings buried there. So, we created a system that before she posted anything on social media, she would ask herself why, and what it was she needed from that post.

We would ask, "What are you really hungry for?" The answer could be connection, attention, or someone knowing that she was sad. She recognized that she had spent so much of her life abandoning her authentic self to be a peacekeeper to her parents, and then created an avatar of herself that kept her even further from her authentic truth.

Eventually, Megan began to let go of the stories she was creating, including the new variations and subplots that developed in her mind, and instead started to address the underlying and unprocessed experience of the event itself. She was able to separate her awareness from her interpretations of what other people were saying or posting and connect with herself. "It's like I can start to feel the difference between truth and story," she said, describing truth as a feeling of alignment that seemed to help her stand tall. Conversely, when she told stories that were untrue (or not entirely true), it had felt like a heavy weight and as if her whole body was buzzing like having had too much coffee.

Over time, we began to have a shorthand to identify what was an empty story and what was something that needed to be processed. I would say, "Is the sandwich bag (the story) empty or is there actually still some sandwich left to process?"

During one of our last sessions together, Megan reflected that her life had been ruled by the creation of stories, and that she was so much happier and fulfilled to stop being caught in those narratives. She felt empowered in her life, and not from being the victim of her own stories.

DEAN: FINDING A DIFFERENT USE FOR ENERGY

Dean, an accountant in his midforties, came to work with me at the recommendation of his friend, a yoga teacher who told him that it seemed like his breath never went any lower than the top of his chest.

At our first session, I asked how he would describe himself and how others would describe him. "I think they would see me as anxious and argumentative," he replied—but he thought of himself as an adrenaline junkie who doesn't do any extreme sports and someone who loves to debate. He made it quite clear as we began to work together that he doesn't like being empathized with or being validated for his past. "Just tell me what's wrong and how to fix it," he said.

Over many months, we began to identify what was underneath the sense of being an adrenaline junkie. He had grown up in a fast-paced environment, with his family moving from military base to military base. Nothing ever felt settled, and neither did he. If he made friends and found roots, he would have to give them up.

As an adult, he lived in a bustling city but didn't feel rooted despite living there for years. He moved houses and jobs as soon as they started to feel like he was settling in. He was still trying to find his purpose and none of the jobs made it clear. We took many weeks to explore that his sense of purpose and direction was connected with his self-worth. Self-worth comes as a response of being comfortable in one's own skin, and Dean admitted to being out of touch with himself, as his shallow breathing made evident.

Debate was his alternative to extreme sports. This was when he would feel more excited and connected with people, because they were passionately talking about something.

In response to his feeling constantly uprooted as a child, we explored grounding practices, imagining himself connecting and rooting into the ground. At first, he was uncomfortable and told me how stupid this was. As with any breath work we did, the moment he would start to breathe deeper, he would begin to feel anxious or experience pain.

As we continued, he identified that connecting to his body didn't feel safe, as if it could be taken away from him. We worked on finding things that could be considered consistent and not taken away from him. I had a very basic painting of an ocean in my office at the time, and one day, he said, "I feel like that painting is never going to move." This small recognition was a significant breakthrough. For perhaps the first time, he could connect with something that felt consistent, and he could even breathe a little more deeply. He was able to look at the painting and allow his feet to feel the connection to the ground.

Slowly but surely, he was building trust. He opened up and shared more of the hardships of moving, the pain of feeling pulled away from people. He felt that every place his family ever moved still had a piece of him, because he didn't have any choice about leaving. He recognized other places where that felt true, such as in his job. As he began to let go of some of the chronic tension evident by the shallowness of breath and the stiffness of his body, he realized that to survive he had armored himself. "I've been bracing since I was a kid, like I was frozen in ice," he said.

He did much meditation work on healing the boundaries that had been ruptured when he was moved without choice. That included identifying where he does have choice in his life and attuning to that feeling of empowerment. We also did practices for reclaiming the parts of him that were left behind—inviting them to come back to this time and place. The bracing and armoring lessened, his breath was filling into more of his body, and he could feel more present.

Dean spent several sessions crying for all the times he never let people in. He cried for all the times he wouldn't allow himself to feel relaxed or comforted. He mourned lost time in which he was frozen and unpresent. I shared how sad that was. He looked up. "Thank you, I really needed to hear that," he replied—and just as he said that, a deep breath filled all the way down to his lower belly. He smiled and said one of the sweetest things I have heard: "I think it's actually okay to be here," pointing to himself.

KAY: LEARNING TO TOLERATE JOY

When I began to work with Kay, her addiction to drama was very evident. She came to sessions with a long list of the things wrong in her life, herself, and the world. It would feel like she was unknowingly trying to pull me into what was happening with her via her stories and experiences. No matter what we did, it was as if she refused to let go of what was wrong. As soon as it seemed that we were nearing a resolution around one thing, she would spontaneously jump to talking about something or someone else. Sitting there listening, it would at times feel disorienting and like being whipped around. I could empathize with how chaotic that felt internally for her. Kay would oscillate between focusing on all the challenges outside herself and then jump to challenges that were happening internally. She would interpret internal sensation as something much more serious: she would think being tired meant she was going to faint or a headache meant something was wrong with her brain.

She had a very loving and supportive family and tried to hold most of this catastrophizing in while she was around them, but she let it all out in sessions.

When we talked about revving—giving a word to the action that she was perpetually doing—she immediately recognized that her thoughts were creating much more intense situations. She told me that she would spill something, like a glass of wine, and have to talk about it for hours. We came up with a plan: whenever we noticed her revving, one of us would raise our hand and she would pause, take deep breaths, and settle herself. In the first month or two, we had raised our hand at least a hundred times per session. Over time, it became less and less. She would catch herself beginning to rev and be able to stop it from escalating.

As more space was made, we could focus on what was happening underneath the revving. The more she could take in that I was listening, the less amplified her emotions would be. She started to be able to identify what was a big deal and what was not.

The real breakthrough for Kay came when we started a mindfulness practice that we called "recognizing and marinating in the good." She had spent so much of her life focusing on what was or would be wrong that she essentially became wired that way. Her homework was to look for what was good, enjoyable, pleasurable, and even joyful in her life and within herself. Kay was then to imagine sitting in a bathtub of those feelings, really soaking it in like a sponge.

Within a few weeks, she was able to rewire her nervous system and shift her focus on what felt good and healthy in herself and the world. When painful things came up, Kay was able to process them completely without jumping to something that was wrong. She essentially let go of her attachment to suffering.

She recently described her journey with healing her addiction to drama as breaking free of her life as a horror movie on repeat, and finally living the ups and downs of life.

THE JOURNEY OF SCOTT

Let's end this chapter with the story of Scott. Yes, that's me. I alluded to this in the Preface of this book, but here's a fuller story, which also makes clear just how I got so interested in this phenomenon known as addiction to drama.

Drama is the stirring, the excitement, the exaggeration, the eruption, the unrest, and the battle to feel alive in relation to the numbing of the internal and external world around you.

I know this through my clinical work. But I also know this personally. I spent most of my life chasing the storm, fighting against the calm current, unintentionally dismantling intimacy while trying to create it within myself, with others, and with the world. Even now as I write this, I think, *I hate myself for that time period.* But the reality is, I don't hate myself. That intense statement was just me, reaching for another hit of my drug of choice: drama.

My personal addiction to drama can be summed up as a deep sense of disorganization that suddenly felt soothed and satisfied in more heightened, tense situations. Although I emerged from them frustrated and angry, I would also feel excitement: my own inner chaos had found a container to "justifiably" express itself—which would inevitably lead to an internal experience of satisfaction and sense of reward. In fact, the psychic and emotional energy involved in navigating the event that I perceived as a crisis gave me a brief sense of control.

Reflecting back, I could see that I unintentionally sought or created some of the crisis situations in my life. This need for excitement was reflected in my career choices. I worked as a professional dance choreographer and director, a field in which I was always under stress, with tight deadlines and nonstop challenges; it was a constant resource for drama. Then, in my midtwenties, I met a partner who triggered a deep sense of dysfunction, thereby stirring up an even more intense craving for crisis. While my artistic life flourished from this surge of energy, my socio-emotional well-being quickly deteriorated. My baseline for dysfunction was being tested, and it was soon well beyond my ability, internally and externally, to balance it.

Subsequently, I started developing migraines and transient ischemic attacks (TIAs) due to the pervasive stress. This was the beginning of falling into a deeper shutdown of my emotions and cognitive functioning. My then-partner ended our relationship, and in the aftermath of the separation, I withdrew completely from my career as an artist and isolated myself socially. This was followed by inexplicable health issues that included fainting, blackouts, anxiety, depression, tightness in my chest, a racing heart, and spontaneous hypothyroidism. Although the symptoms were severe, no medical test could explain them.

My hypothesis was that my intense symptoms might be signs of withdrawal from prolonged stress. I noticed that the symptoms were relieved for a brief time after I made contact with my ex-partner. At first, I thought it was relief because of speaking to him directly; however, I also experienced some momentary relief during times when I was involved in other people's crises, listening to gossip, or watching high-action, violent movies. I picked fights with the very people who were supporting me, an action that made no sense. I was creating conditions that you may now recognize after reading this book: it was sensation seeking to bring myself back to a familiar and soothing level of conflict. Finally, at the peak of this malady, I went into cardiac distress and wound up hospitalized for a week.

This crisis served as both a wake-up call and a reset button on my nervous system. In the months after the cardiac distress, I began meditating and practicing yoga every day, reading Buddhism-inspired books, becoming a witness to the desire for drama and chaos, and staying with the discomfort of not giving in to the craving. As I mentioned in this book's Preface, this was both incredibly difficult and mind-numbingly boring. Without drama, it was like the vivid colors of life all faded to monochrome.

In wading through weeks of monotony, however, I opened to a richer and more multidimensional emotional life. I can best describe it as slowly waking up and feeling myself more present and responsive. I began to experience the felt sense of such emotions as gratitude, humility, disappointment, and even happiness—truly for the first time. These were feelings that I had understood cognitively but that had eluded me from an embodied perspective.

When this opening first began, I recall having new bodily sensations, even noticing I had reflexive facial responses that went along with these sensations, without having any recognition of what they meant. After spending some time familiarizing myself with these experiences, I was able to identify them as specific emotional states that developmental psychologists associate with healthier internal "regulation," a word that means the ability to return to balance, with optimal function and adaptability. In other words, the numbness that I knew so well began to be replaced with feelings.

The expansion of my emotional vocabulary gave me a deeper sense of self. With this, I could examine the timeline of my life and extrapolate a deeply layered pattern associated with addiction to drama.

After my own healing journey, as I mentioned, I became deeply interested in addiction to drama but was surprised at the lack of science on the subject. There were no resources to help people understand and work through it. I dedicated myself to research, eventually forging a new career as a researcher, clinical psychologist, and therapy workshop facilitator. I have worked with thousands of individuals like Marty, Suzanne, Lori, Megan, Dean, and Kay and helped guide them on a path to healing. And, over the next three chapters, I hope to do the same for you. But before we move on, here are some powerful suggestions to help heal an addiction to drama from other clients.

TIPS FOR HEALING

I recently asked the many people I have worked with who had an addiction to drama what tools for healing were most effective for their change. The following is a list of these suggestions that generated from their own journeys.

Coin a phrase. Marie finds she can stop the revving by using a phrase (*stop, drop, and roll*) and image she created (the cat relaxing on the couch) that interrupts the pattern and slows her down.

Ask for a signal. Bruce asks his family to give him a signal when his energy starts bulldozing other people.

Counter negative with positive. For Morgan, the most helpful tool was that for every one negative thought she had about herself, someone else, or a situation, she had to come up with three positive thoughts.

Seek acceptance. For Rebecca, a major turning point was finding people who allowed her to make mistakes and express her true feelings and needs without rejection.

Take a break from media. Alan found that turning off social media helped, as did taking a break from the news and anything else that would pull his attention away from himself.

Find ways to harmonize. Andreas found other ways other than crisis to feel in sync with people—she joined a choir and allowed herself to feel vulnerable in literally harmonizing with other voices.

Seek the right therapist. Martina said finding a trauma therapist who could help unravel the deep pain stored in her body was life-affirming.

Heed the code. Rod asked his friends to remind him when he started gossiping or stirring the pot to check in with what he's feeling and what he needs. His code is "Rod, check under the hood!"

Stop seeking attention. Rebecca says she stopped seeking attention so loudly when she let herself actually receive the attention she was already getting.

Choose your words. Erik finds that he can stop some of the drama by changing his language: rather than saying he's so stressed, he will say, "There's a lot going on and there's a lot of people that support me."

Separate past and present. Frances loves the affirmation, "That was the past, and this is the present." She does a lot of journaling to identify what from the past she is projecting into the present.

Care for the inner child. Ashley found that the most powerful tool for her is to catch herself in the creation of stories, and then turn to her inner child and tell her how much she is loved.

Forgive yourself. Frank said that the most significant part of his healing was doing a daily forgiveness meditation. He's learning the power in not holding on to resentment and learning to love and accept himself.

Pursue an interest. Robert has learned to redirect the energy of activation into other sources such as his artwork and swimming.

MYOB. Allison asks her family to remind her to "Mind Your Own Business" when she starts to report about what's happening on her social media or in the news.

Arrange a reality check. Whenever Lexi starts to create unrealistic expectations, project a lack of trust and jealousy, and hyperfocus on perceived mistakes, she has asked her partner to say, "Pause. I know connecting can be vulnerable. I found the real you and I love you."

Consider your contribution. Consider your contribution. Sonny instituted what he calls a 50/50 rule for himself. When he finds himself going into a blaming spiral or chaotic situation, he asks himself how he is partly responsible for this, either the circumstances or his response.

Remove the contributors. Zack did a major purge of friends who were also addicted to drama, or friends who were enabling his drama.

Connect with your body. Kelcie started doing yoga to get more in touch with her body and massages to work on receiving connection.

CHAPTER 11

Milestones of Healing

N OW, LET'S LOOK AT THE ACTUAL PROCESS OF HEALING. WHILE HEALING IS not linear, there are clear milestones along the journey. The process of healing an addiction to drama is a process of reestablishing safety, being present in one's body, expressing the authentic self, growing capacity to be seen and in connection (intimacy), and affirming a sense of belonging.

Since the nervous system of someone addicted to drama has been geared up to expect a threat, disabling the alarm system that seeks, escalates, and creates drama is a threat all unto itself. As you find trusted people, mentors, friends, or therapists that meet you where you are and receive you, little by little you let go of making stories, throwing logs on the fire for intensity, and pulling people in and pushing them away—all the while being met with compassion. This is the foundation that over time reestablishes that you can be safe and feel belonging without the suffering and drama.

The five stages or milestones of healing are:

- ◆ Awareness
- ◆ Action
- ◆ Arrival
- ◆ Letting go
- ◆ Belonging

These stages build upon one another and will offer you a way of tracking your own progress along the healing journey.

STAGE 1: AWARENESS

Before the stage of awareness, you are operating without consciousness of your adaptive survival strategies. These patterns that formed the addiction to drama are in the driver's seat of your life; and the strife and recurring challenges seem to only be coming at you, as opposed to germinating from you. Awareness is the stage that begins to illuminate what has been in the shadows. In the stage of awareness, you are building the capacity to be a compassionate witness without being pulled into your own or someone else's pain and suffering. It takes fortitude to become aware of the addiction and what lies beneath it.

In this first stage, you are beginning to shine light on how the core pain has manifested in the way that you are perceiving and acting in the world. Awareness may rise from asking yourself contemplative questions; looking for patterns in your thoughts, feelings, and behaviors; or perhaps getting feedback from trusted people. It may feel jarring and frustrating for some time as you begin to take notice of how often you are disconnecting from yourself or others or stirring things up. Just know you are not broken, you are not your behavior—you are simply in the stage of recognizing your own survival strategies. One of the most helpful tools for awareness is to bring curiosity to whatever you are attending to—it opens the gateways for discovery.

The following are five ways to bring awareness to primary areas of addiction to drama in this stage.

Pay attention to where and when there is aliveness, connection, and presence to your body—and when there is not. Notice when there is a disconnect to yourself. This may look like being "spaced out" and detached from your body and feelings, being on autopilot, being confused about what is really happening within you or around you, or watching your life from outside of your body as if it were happening on a movie screen (dissociation).

Witness your behaviors and thoughts and begin to take ownership for what is happening around you. Listen closely for the running scripts in your mind that are fueling what you are focusing on and reacting to. Notice how your stories stimulate your exaggerated emotions, and how those emotions fuel the continuation of the story. Recognize how often you are retelling the same story to yourself and others. Observe how much time and energy is being used to justify and validate those thoughts, feelings, and beliefs.

Notice the uneasiness around stillness and ease. There will be cravings to fill or distract from that uneasiness. Recognize all the various ways you personally exacerbate a situation to create more activation and agitation, and less settling, repeatedly throughout the day.

Notice when you allow your emotions to move through you, and when you hold on to them and recycle them as a means of staying activated. Some of the greatest advice I ever received regarding emotions is that emotions are meant to be in motion, and when they are not, they are suppressed. A single wave of an emotion lasts thirty to ninety seconds, and anything after that is a story. Become aware of the emotions you default to and the ones you tend to avoid. This goes for needs (e.g., safety, attention, etc.) as well. You may recognize which of your needs are overshadowed by the intensity of your emotions.

Notice your interactions in different relationships (partners, friends, strangers, community, etc.). Bring your attention to how activation manifests itself, such as when you close off and push people away or as a means to pull people in and feel more connected. You might notice how often you feel conflict or strain in relationships, and how feeling hurt can often escalate to the perception of being harmed. How a small scratch is interpreted as a deep, bloody wound. Observe how often you feel alone or lonely in the presence of others. Become aware of judging, criticizing, and blaming yourself and others as a means of avoiding feelings and needs.

STAGE 2: ACTION

As you become more aware of the patterns around your addiction to drama, and have made the choice for change, the action stage begins. Action is addressing the behavior of an addiction to drama by utilizing the many practices and therapeutic techniques that can support change. These include the following:

- Slowing down
- Meditation and embodiment practices
- Staying present in your body as feelings arise
- Taking pauses and moments of stillness
- Prioritizing rest and recuperation
- Expressing basic feelings and needs
- Receiving connection, validation, feedback, and intimacy
- Flexibly moving between states, such as between activation and settling (also known as sympathetic and parasympathetic nervous systems)
- Discerning fact from fiction in thoughts and stories
- Shifting from narrow thinking to seeing choices, nuances, and optionality

To support you through the action stage, the Appendix of this book shares more than twenty such practices. This stage often feels like wrestling with the compulsion of the addiction so as to make space and address underlying pain and unprocessed trauma. In this stage, you are finding the ability to move into the whirlwind and track your way back out. As you learn to settle, it is normal to find yourself replacing one revving for another. It will take time and repeated practice to remain settled without revving back up.

While confronting your ingrained thought and behavior patterns is hard work, this stage is necessary for healing and deep change to take place.

STAGE 3: ARRIVAL

In the first stage of "awareness," you were building the capacity to witness and watch your own behaviors, needs, impulses, and actions to be able to shift your focus from other people or situations back onto yourself. In the second stage, you have created enough space between revving to begin to address the underlying pain and trauma. Getting to this milestone of "arrival" means you will feel a sense of power from occupying and being present in your body—instead of relying on the false sense of power derived from crisis and chaos.

Life becomes richer and more colorful as you arrive into yourself. Feelings become deeper and more nuanced, as opposed to general, intensified, and exaggerated.

With enough trust, support, and safety, you are able to contact the core hurt underlying the behavior through four phases: explore the benefit, find the missing needs, find the belief, and meet the pain.

Explore the benefit of the addiction to drama. Start with asking yourself the following questions:

- What have been the short-term gains of drama?
- What has it done for you or offered you?
- What role did drama have in your life? Some clients have said, "I felt a sense of control and power," while others said drama kept them energized and feeling young.

Find the missing needs. Take the exploration deeper by asking:

- What in your life has felt absent?
- What have you been searching or looking for? Such as, "I needed to know I was okay and loved" or "I needed to feel found."
- How have you been filling that void or substituting that need?

Find the belief. Alongside the missing need is the underlying script or core negative belief, a belief that got created as a means of attempting to understand why those essential needs weren't met, such as *my emotions are not valid, I'm not worthy of love,* and so on.

- What have you believed about yourself or told yourself because of the absence of these needs?
- What are the things you often say about yourself to yourself?

- What do you believe other people say/think about you?
- What do you believe that you deserve?

Meet the pain. The pain that resides in the body can also be thought of as the part of you that got locked away or exiled when the pain was too much to bear.

Investigate:

- Where does the core pain live in your body?
- How does it want to be contacted, held, met, and provided for in this moment?
- Is there a story or memory that wants to be shared?

Additional practices for meeting this pain can be found in the Appendix.

During this stage emotions that have been suppressed for a long time may be experienced for a sustained amount of time. You might feel sadness for a few weeks. While it may be uncomfortable during this time period, it will pass. As the core pain is understood, felt, and supported, the self-soothing mechanisms creating the addiction to drama lessen. This is preparing you for an even bigger release of an old identity around suffering and pain.

STAGE 4: LETTING GO (RELEASING THE IDENTITY OF SUFFERING)

To live fully, we must let go of who we have been in order to fulfill who we are here to become. The stories we created to justify the sense of victimhood and emotional intensity now begin to feel empty.

Suffering is an incredibly salient thread throughout our human history. As it has become more highlighted through the sensationalism of news, social media, and the stories we tell, our awareness and relationship to suffering has evolved. The familiarity of the narratives and the sensation of pain that we have lived with our entire lives—and even the pain of generations before us—can become our identity. This sense of self in relation to pain and suffering exists on a psychological level, a relationship level, even a cellular level.

The predictable hurt is so ingrained in our identity that letting go of it can feel like a death of sorts. To let go of this identity is disturbing to the way your sense of safety has been wired. And yet the paradox of this stage is that everything you most desire is on the other side of this death of identity.

As you begin to orient yourself away from suffering as an identity, it's important to ask: *Who else am I, without my pain, trauma, or suffering?* When the old stories and reactions begin to feel hollow and lack relevance, turn your focus to what is beginning to grow in that space. Nourish it. As you create the conditions and environment for being seen and heard, your authentic self begins to grow.

Throughout the journey of healing and letting go of this identity, you will question who you are and what you offer to the world without this drama. You will likely experience boredom and a craving for something more.

You may at times return to the old behaviors, slipping back and satisfying the cravings for a hit of drama. This is all part of the journey. When you pause and realign with what is true for you now, you will recognize these are just familiar behaviors that no longer have the need or craving driving them. Then, one day, it will feel right to offer a good-bye to that old system of operating. That farewell might be a memorial service or a letter to that old version of yourself or simply imagining it releasing from your body. Know that there are people in the world waiting to meet this version of you.

STAGE 5: BELONGING

Belonging is our nature; it is fundamental to who we are as humans. In this stage, we are coming back home to ourselves and to one another.

The parts you had to hide away or change so as to be recognized and seen are finally being healed and integrated into who you are becoming. The word *healing* comes from the same etymological roots as the word *whole*. As this journey unfolds, you're no longer operating from a fragmented nervous system doing its best to help feel secure in the world. Rather, connections begin to feel safe.

A sense of belonging, being *a part of* (versus *apart from*), happens over time. If you have been addicted to drama, your first sense of belonging might be the revelation that you belong to yourself. This might appear as compassion, acceptance, and understanding of who you are and what you feel.

Over time, as more of your true self is revealed, there is more for others to see and connect with, to establish an intimacy that validates a sense of worth, purpose, and meaning. As you move through levels of intimacy, there might be brief moments when you start to rev or guard yourself from what you're feeling or what others are feeling. Go slow; connection happens in waves. Trust the process. If you have had an addiction to drama, what you have known for so long is isolation, the absence of belonging.

This is often the time when it's helpful to map out and define what a healthy relationship is—as previous relationships were used as a way to fan the flames of the addiction to drama, stage a reenactment of the trauma, or as a place to deposit the pain and suppressed emotions. *Who are the people in your life who have created a sense of relationship you would like to model?* Define the qualities and features of that relationship. These qualities, that you will embody, become the compass for safe and accepting relationships. As you allow yourself to be found and accepted in these relationships, belonging will naturally emerge.

Here's how we know healing is occurring or has occurred:

- You have a sense of security.
- You feel seen and accepted.
- You feel that you are enough.
- You're less interested in gossiping and more in having deeper connections.
- You're prioritizing your own "business" over other people's.
- You feel a sense of worth.
- Time feels more flexible and less urgent.
- You feel alive in your body.
- Resting feels safe.
- You can receive what other people have to offer.

- Your know your place in the world is inherent to who you are, not what you do.
- Simple is enough.
- You feel in control while adaptable to all the fluctuation of life.
- You are able to enjoy the positive things within your life.
- Your sense of power comes from your ability to find pauses and make choices.
- You are in sync with the world.

CHAPTER 12

Using "Addicted to Drama" Archetypes to Help Yourself Heal

HEALING AN ADDICTION TO DRAMA DOESN'T HAPPEN FROM JUST RECOGNIZ-
ing it or simply taking a pill. The reflex for drama has become embedded in your nervous system and that cycle has worn grooves that are
hard to interrupt. As the pain is deep, you will have to meet it many times.
And before you meet the pain itself, you will meet all the ways in which it
is protected and shielded from your own conscious awareness.

On the following pages, you will find eleven archetypes that are aspects
and traits of an addiction to drama; they apply whether you are dealing with
an addiction to drama yourself or know someone who is. You may recognize
yourself and your healing journey in multiple archetypes. Even if a particular archetype does not resonate with you, the information within that one
can still be a significant support.

For each archetype, you'll find a basic description, questions to ask
yourself, followed by how a therapist might approach this (note that this is
not a substitution for therapy or an invitation for self-diagnosis; rather, it is
a framework for help and healing), and finally, suggested practices that you
can work to help you along on your own journey.

The eleven archetypes are as follows:

- **The External Revver:** *There's just so much going on. I can never get a break!*
- **The Center-Stager:** *I worry that I won't be important and people won't like me if I find stillness.*
- **The Erupter:** *Something just takes over and I explode.*
- **The Victim:** *People always let me down or betray me.*
- **The Drama Bystander:** *They're so dramatic and stressing me out.*
- **The Catastrophizer:** *Bad things just happen to me; things are bad in the world.*
- **The Internal Revver:** *I'm just so stressed out.*
- **The Dramatic Narrator:** *Then he said, then she said . . . can you believe . . .*
- **The Martyr:** *I can't walk away, I'm all they have—they'll be devastated.*
- **The Attachment Seeker:** *Why can't I just find a good man/woman/ partner?*
- **The Storyteller:** *No, let me tell you what actually happened.*

THE EXTERNAL REVVER: THERE'S JUST SO MUCH GOING ON. I CAN NEVER GET A BREAK!

The External Revver finds ways to rev themselves up based on external factors. They are constantly adding too many things to their schedule regardless of capacity, space, and ability to manage. They ignore the signs of overwhelm and stress and continue to pile on more.

The External Revver may demonstrate the following behaviors and thought patterns:

- Constantly telling people how busy they are
- When there is opportunity for rest or stillness—creating stories of disaster, finding things to keep busy or productive, picking fights, etc.
- Equating busyness and productivity with self-worth and validation from others
- Being unable to take a rest: meeting pauses, stops, and idle moments with discomfort, too much emotion, and reaching for distractions
- Finding worth in movement
- Constantly checking phone or refreshing email inbox or social media feed

- Confusing constant movement with momentum; often, they are not even sure what they want with all of this productivity but simply know they do not want to stop moving
- Having a frenetic energy that can bulldoze other people
- Needing things to always be fresh and exciting
- Having an intolerance for boredom or settling
- Talking over and interrupting people
- Experiencing busyness in the mind
- Always wanting to be where the action is
- Stuffing a feeling of emptiness with "stuff" (such as food, video games, social media, relationships, etc.)

Questions to Help

These may interrupt the pattern, add self-awareness, and help in healing:
- What would a break look like? And could you tolerate a break?
- What would being less busy be like?
- Have you ever not been busy? If so, what allowed that? What was that like for you?
- Notice the tempo at which you're speaking: Is there space between your words and sentences? Is there time to hear your own words? What happens when you have an extra pause between your words and sentences? Can you pause a little longer?
- When there is silence in a conversation, what shows up in your body?
- Can you spend less effort and still accomplish the same?
- What are you running away from?

A Therapist Might Suggest . . .

There are often layers of feeling that are masked by a lot of action. There's a sense of "If I'm not busy or productive I'm not necessary" and "Why am I even here on this planet?" Often those who thrive on continuous stress learn to override the internal discomfort and pain by distracting themselves. It's the internalization of "Keep busy and carry on" and "Go faster than you can feel."

If someone grows up in a chaotic or fast-paced environment, that speed of change gets internalized as normal. The person then operates from this tempo—almost as though their nervous system has a limited vocabulary of rhythm and pacing. This causes them to feel out of sync with other people and the world, unless they too are operating in an intensified rhythm and tempo. This perpetuates the pervasive loneliness that those with an addiction experience.

Those with an addiction to drama often confuse collapsing for resting and recuperation. Finding the gradation of energy expenditure and how rest is actualized is a key principle in repatterning an addiction to drama.

Observation and Practice

Constant busyness is a way to generate energy, but it can end up creating more energy than you need to accomplish your goal. On the flip side, that same busyness can cost you your health by spending more energy than you can functionally sustain.

As you begin to create and experience spaciousness, become conscious of when you try to fill it. It will happen over and over again, in more ways than you could imagine. Be gentle on yourself as you start to expose the impulse and craving to distract yourself by stories, work, tension, and what is around you. Slow your breath and connect to a slower tempo of something around you. When you feel your heart and mind racing, remind yourself you deserve to be here in your body with ease and spaciousness. Recognize that in this moment in time it is safe enough to stay with the space. Every time you get pulled back into busyness, pause, name that you are revving, anchor your breath and attention inside your body, and come back to your present.

Journal prompts:

- How else can you get energy without relying on revving?
- What is your relationship to ease?
- What does ease look like?
- What does ease feel like?

Suggested Practices: Grounding Meditation (page 210), Creating Space, Feeling Space, and Resting into Space (page 222), Alternate Nostril Breathing (page 220), and Taking the Time to Taste Your Food (page 221)

Self-Healing Statements

Life is not coming at me, it's coming from me.
My worth is not tied up in my production or productivity.
The space in between is filled with opportunity.

THE CENTER-STAGER: I WORRY THAT I WON'T BE IMPORTANT AND PEOPLE WON'T LIKE ME IF I FIND STILLNESS.

The Center-Stager needs to feel important, special, and recognized, and that need becomes the driving force of all their thoughts, decisions, and actions.

The Center-Stager may demonstrate the following behaviors and thought patterns:

- Oscillating between playing the victim and the hero
- Needing and having a magnetic personality
- Having to be an expert or the best
- Exaggerating the facts to attract attention
- Often misaligning the impact of behavior with intentions
- Seeking validation from those who can't provide it
- Being unable to accept validation from those who do provide it
- Needing to be the life of the party
- Bringing the conversation back to themselves
- Counting likes or followers on social media
- Obsessing over other people's perceptions of them
- Feeling anxious or revving up when there's not much going on
- Posting to be seen as opposed to posting to share
- Needing to be the bearer of bad news so that they can be the healer or hero

Questions to Help

These may interrupt the pattern, add self-awareness, and help in healing:

- Is your own attention enough?
- When was the last time you felt seen, loved, and valued?
- When was the last time you let yourself be seen, loved, and valued?

A Therapist Might Suggest . . .

"False validation" is about the chase for recognition and affirmation. It has very little to do with receiving and absorbing the satisfaction of it. We observe and collect information about what will make a person see us and often end up overriding and betraying our own needs so as to get noticed. In the process of trying to maintain the spotlight we move further from ourselves. The truth is, the further you get from yourself, the harder it is for people to find you.

We get attached to being "important" or "special" because we perceive it as protection from being invisible or abandoned. If you were seen or attended to only in special or heightened moments as a child or adult, you will likely seek and try to reinvent those special and heightened moments as a means to get that same level of attention. Being seen is a reassurance that you are loved and valued, that your existence matters. The problem is that we often bypass the many moments of being truly seen and loved, in search of these heightened special encounters. We may reenact the past by chasing the people who are not going to give us that love. Trying to stay important in the eyes of others is an exhausting full-time job—and some of us have been able to actually make it our job. Try to focus on and receive the love that is there, as opposed to obsessing about the people who won't give it to you.

Observation and Practice

Journal prompt: Write out your judgments, opinions, and fears of these words: *quiet, still, silent,* and *ordinary.* Responses could include things such as *It means the next shoe will drop, I won't be ready, quiet means unproductive, silent people go unnoticed.*

Suggested Practices: Working with the Part of You That Wasn't Seen (page 222), and Social Media Check-In (page 225)

Self-Healing Statements

I am enough as I am.
This moment is enough.
I am seen when I let people see me.

THE ERUPTER: SOMETHING JUST TAKES OVER AND I EXPLODE.

The Erupter is unwilling to take responsibility for emotions and reactions. They perceive their emotions as though they are separate from them. They might say, "There is this frenetic and intense energy that just floods me."

The Erupter may demonstrate the following behaviors and thought patterns:

- Experiencing uncontained catharsis
- Feeling a loss of control
- Blowing things out of proportion
- Spewing words without a recognition of what's being said
- Justifying the intensity of a response with the creation of stories or roping others into it
- Being flooded with feelings and swept away by them
- Feeling rejuvenated, pleased, or energized after an eruption of feelings

Questions to Help

These may interrupt the pattern, add self-awareness, and help in healing:

- What do you imagine you might have been feeling just before something took over?
- How much of that is happening in this moment? On a scale of 1 to 10, how much of that energy is here right now?
- On a scale of 1 to 10, how big does that energy or emotion need to be in order to be seen and acknowledged?
- How much energy or emotion is actually needed for what is happening?

A Therapist Might Suggest . . .

The opposite of frenetic intensity is not calm, it is adaptability and conservation/precision of energy. Going into the cathartic releases can often feel like holding a small glass under a running faucet—it easily overflows. The challenge is that the flooding of feelings (the intensity of the stream of water) is created by that same person who doesn't have the capacity to hold it. In essence, their reaction to their reaction is what is overwhelming them. The task at hand is to increase their tolerance for feelings, recognize their options for responding (as opposed to reacting), and regain their power by acting on those options.

Emotions can be divided into two categories: primary (core) emotions, and secondary (depository) emotions. Primary emotions are our most true experience and reside in our body to help guide us; secondary emotions mask core feelings and are used as a substitute when the core emotions are too much to feel or are suppressed.

For example, when we were growing up, sadness may not have been safe to express or attended to by our caregivers, so in turn we may have defaulted to anger—to be attended to. In this way, we are betraying the expression of our true feelings in order to be seen.

Other examples:

♦ When anger is denied, it becomes rage.
♦ When pain is denied and unprocessed, it becomes numbness, depression, and hopelessness.
♦ When loneliness is denied, it becomes helplessness.
♦ When fear is denied, it becomes panic, mistrust, and paranoia.

We cannot metabolize and heal through secondary emotions. The task is to go beneath secondary emotions and the stories created to reinforce them, connect to the core feelings that are truly present in our bodies, and allow those to be processed.

Observation and Practice

Practice: Talk through the timeline of what happened in a recent event where you were taken over by the bigness of your reaction, and what you were feeling before something took over. Go as slow as you need to so you can start to fill in the blanks.

Practice: With your hand, show the frenetic energy when things get really heated, then pick up a pencil with that intensity. Now, shake it off. Pick up the pencil. How much energy is actually required to pick up that pencil?

Suggested Practices: Identifying How Present Emotions Are in Your Life (page 225), Contacting Feelings (Emotions) in Your Body (page 225), Connecting Feelings and Needs (page 226)

Self-Healing Statements

I am in the driver's seat of my own life.

I can decide how much energy and emotion is needed at this moment.

I can be both anchored in myself and allow emotions to move through me.

THE VICTIM: PEOPLE ALWAYS LET ME DOWN OR BETRAY ME.

The Victim has a sense of loneliness that is confirmed by a self-fulfilled prophecy that no one can be there for them or has their back.

The Victim may demonstrate the following behaviors and thought patterns:

- Rehashing the past—mentally and in conversation
- Overexplaining themselves
- Staying hyperfocused on the past
- Experiencing pervasive loneliness or hypersocializing
- Being unable to let go of the past
- Telling a story over and over again often from the point of the victim
- Holding vengeances, grievances, resentments, and revenge
- Bringing their past forward into every relationship
- Constantly struggling in relationships
- Burning bridges

Questions to Help

These may interrupt the pattern, add self-awareness, and help in healing:

- If you were an outsider looking in, how would you view yourself in relation to what's happening?
- Who's not letting you down right now?
- Who hasn't betrayed you?
- Where have you felt a sense of belonging? And what did that feel like?

A Therapist Might Suggest . . .

When we are hurt, the sting reawakens all the pain of the past. And suddenly the present is flooded by the past. The past skews the present and is projected onto it like an image on a movie screen, leading us to relive (reenact) that pain.

As a means of protection, we create the conditions or the stories that create a confirmation bias and a self-fulfilling prophecy. We simultaneously push people away and ask them to come closer. Hurt always registers as harm, and in turn, we are enraged, deflated, and reaffirmed that no one is here for us.

Try to let go of a victim identity. This is much easier said than done—especially because giving up an aspect of ourselves can be painful and even on some level feel dangerous. Letting go of a victim identity means letting go of what you know (and what's been wired) about being validated, connected with, and seen. Go gently and slowly until you can tolerate and experience being seen in other states besides suffering. Notice when you cling and grip to the circumstances that affirm an identity of suffering.

Observation and Practice

Journal prompt: Sit down with the habit of suffering. Drop the circumstances of why you are suffering and be present with the feeling and the mechanism of it. What is it that the suffering gives you? Familiarity? A sense of life? A sense of being alive?

How has suffering been a form of validation? Who in your past heard or saw you most clearly when there was something wrong? Did suffering come with the reward of being seen?

Observation: Notice if you become competitive with the suffering—comparing woes or upleveling your stories to match the pain of others.

Journal prompt: Float back in your memory and identify the times when you were rightfully victimized, when you didn't have any protection or safety from what was coming at you. How might those be different from recent experiences?

Practice forgiveness. Forgiveness is when we let go of what holds us to the attachment of what happened. It is not saying what happened was okay. If you are continuously recycling the past into the present, please remember anything we can't forgive is revving.

Imagine the lights of the past dimming, and only the light of the present moment is shining. What is happening in the present moment? Discern the past from the present. Remind yourself and repeat, "That was then and this is now."

Suggested Practices: Working with Confirmation Scripts (page 227) and Unpacking the Origins of a Confirmation Script (page 227)

Self-Healing Statements

I can hold my hurt and pain and love it in a way that I desire to be held and loved.

If someone can't show up for me they are revealing their capacity, and it is not a reflection of my worth.

That was then and this is now.

THE DRAMA BYSTANDER: THEY'RE SO DRAMATIC AND STRESSING ME OUT.

In the presence of someone who is addicted to drama, the Drama Bystander gets pulled into their whirlwind and becomes attached to their behavior.

The Drama Bystander may demonstrate the following behaviors and thought patterns:

- Feeling drawn into what others are saying or doing and ending up feeling scattered
- Having difficulty focusing on anything else in their own life
- Being surrounded by people who are constantly in crisis
- Giving up their own needs for other people
- Disconnecting from their feelings and getting stuck in other people's feelings
- Shutting down and having shallow breathing when near intense people
- Putting logs on other people's fires
- Having one's heart in the grip of other people and other things
- Feeling exhausted and tense after interacting with intense people

Questions to Help

These may interrupt the pattern, add self-awareness, and help in healing:

- What are you offering to yourself in other people's intense moments?

- Notice how you respond in these moments: Do you join in and co-rev, engaging and enabling with what they are talking about or doing?
- Does it feel possible to shift your focus away from others and back to yourself?

A Therapist Might Suggest . . .

When in the presence of someone who is addicted to drama, it may feel as if they have pulled you off your axis. It becomes hard to feel grounded in your own body, sensations, and feelings. They have dysregulated the room—nothing is solid or grounding in the environment—and it all feels off kilter, including you. The difficult question is why and how did that happen? It's easy to put the blame and focus back on those who are addicted to drama and more difficult to take responsibility. When you get pulled into their whirlwind, it reflects a loss of your agency. When you realize this, it leads to other difficult questions: When did you give your power up? Are you aware, even though it's hard, that you have a choice? Is it familiar to have your sense of agency taken away? Is this perhaps a way of avoiding yourself by being enmeshed in their whirlwind?

It can be hard to face our own pain, and so we go searching for people who we believe or sense are more broken than we are, and we invest our energy in them. We enable them, and in return, they give us the gift of distraction from what is in our shadow.

Observation and Practice

When you notice yourself caught in the whirlwind of others, be gentle to yourself. The practice is to reclaim your own focus and presence. When you feel pulled toward their chaos, notice the urge to go toward it. Ground yourself with the following practices. And when you lose your grip or let go of your anchor and once again join their whirlwind—forgive yourself, as it's a process.

Suggested Practices: Grounding Meditation (page 210), Anchoring Meditation (page 210), Boundary Practices Parts 1 and 2 (page 211, 212)

Self-Healing Statements

I can focus on me.
I can choose me and my own healing.

They are creating their own storm and I am grounded to the earth and anchored in myself.

I give myself permission not to move into their storm.

THE CATASTROPHIZER: BAD THINGS ALWAYS HAPPEN TO ME; THINGS ARE BAD IN THE WORLD.

The Catastrophizer is always prepared for the worst. It's as though they are wearing glasses with lenses that focus on the negative. It can feel safer, or even life-saving, to perceive the bad before it happens. Knowing all the catastrophic outcomes makes this person feel prepared to survive in crisis.

The Catastrophizer may demonstrate the following behaviors and thought patterns:

- Joy can't be trusted. It won't stay—it feels too fragile, and the fall from joy is too big
- Having a tendency to make globalizing comments, such as "My whole life is falling apart"
- Believing it's easier for things to be difficult than risk being disappointed
- Being unable to see what's working out for you
- Always being prepared for the worst, to see the worst, and to see or create the worst early—before it can happen
- Being challenged to find gratitude, to find the gift in things
- Having a narrowed viewpoint of situations or other people
- Being unable to see and remember the good
- Focusing on what's wrong, who's bad, and bad news
- Secretly wishing for things not to go your way; creating stories or fantasies of life not being easy or working out
- Feeling cursed
- Having a sense of safety in "knowing" how bad things are
- Always countering any acknowledgment of what's going well by returning to what's going wrong

Questions to Help

These may interrupt the pattern, add self-awareness, and help in healing:

- Are you safe right now? Are you safe enough?
- What lets you know you are safe enough (e.g., in your body, environment, relationships, etc.)?
- What in this moment is okay and working for you?

A Therapist Might Suggest . . .

If in childhood no one cared or attended to the good things, then that child, and the adult they become, cannot connect with positive feelings and experiences. This creates the belief that when things are bad or intense, they are seen. When a child grows up in a chaotic or inconsistent environment, it feels like something bad can happen at any moment. Because of this, safety and positive feelings never get wired together. Rather, safety is associated with knowing what is or will be wrong. Those with an addiction to drama will at times create crisis (what is wrong) to be able to feel "safe."

Positive and negative feelings are neither good nor bad—they simply direct us to stay in a situation or change and adapt to it. Positive feelings let us know that we should stay the course and keep doing what we are doing. Negative feelings let us know something needs to change—and energy (activation) is then created to make that change happen. When someone is stuck and only able to attend to negative emotions, they are in a constant cycle of building energy for change. As a result they keep moving, unable to settle into their body or even into the present moment. Finding what is bad or wrong in a situation, themselves, or the world validates a pervasive feeling of discomfort—as though to say, "What I'm feeling makes sense, therefore I make sense." More negative feelings gain more attention and are more contagious, and thus lead to a sense of comradery and potentially being in sync with others.

For those addicted to drama, their senses can get locked into a state of anxiety from pervasive stress and trauma, skewing their view of the world. It's like when someone has a mosquito bite and all they can focus on is the itch; they don't see or feel the 99.99 percent of their skin that does not have a mosquito bite. With someone who is addicted to drama, I will often invite them to notice the 99.99 percent that is not the mosquito bite. Just as they begin to notice or even feel the part of them that is not afflicted, they jump right back in to talking about what is wrong or some other problem that takes them out of comfort. It's a form of both self-sabotage and protection from the vulnerability of letting their guard down and simply being okay.

One significant practice that can counter being locked in negative perceptions is what I call "marinating in the good." This involves connecting to the good inside of oneself, one's relationships, and one's surroundings.

Observation and Practice

Journal prompt: How am I wired toward safety? Danger? Ease? Suffering? Calm? Taking in the good doesn't have to happen all at once, you can take in just a little at a time—like little sips of water. Remember, it's not just a change in mind-set—you are transforming the way in which your senses are oriented toward the world.

Create a Scrapbook of the Good:

- Begin with writing down, drawing, or creating a collage of the good things in your life. If that feels too broad, just take one aspect of your life (such as being a parent or work).
- On the same piece of paper identify some of your personal strengths (such as kindness, empathy, passion, etc.).
- Pick something from your list and keep your attention with it for as long as you can. You might imagine holding it in your hand or letting it be received into your body.
- Connect to the feeling/sensation of the good, as though you could breathe it in.
- Stay with the feeling of the good, also known as marinating in the good.
- Notice when your thoughts or words deviate into something that revs you away from the good. Perhaps raise your hand up in the air as a recognition of moving away from marinating in the good, and then make your way back to focusing on the good. Be patient if you notice it's hard to soak in the good or stay with it for very long—it simply takes time and practice.

Journal prompt: Create a Safety List

Create a list of people, places, smells, colors, objects, and so on that help cultivate a sense of safety.

Suggested Practices: Boundary Practice Part 1: Embodying and Establishing Your Energetic Boundary (page 211) and Exploring Safety (page 217)

Self-Healing Statements

I am safe enough to take in the good.

All emotions are temporary, I release my need to chase positive or negative feelings.

I can tolerate more and more and know what I feel is temporary.

THE INTERNAL REVVER: I'M JUST SO STRESSED OUT.

The Internal Revver uses themselves as a distraction from themselves. Essentially, they are creating more internal stressing from their stress. Negative perceptions of internal sensations, ailments, thoughts, feelings, and external conditions pile up to maintain a sense of constant chaos and crisis, and reacting to it.

The Internal Revver may demonstrate the following behaviors and thought patterns:

- Being unable to be with comfort
- Overanalyzing (paralysis by analysis)
- Experiencing emotional and sensational hypochondria (anxious about body signals)
- Always worrying as a means of avoiding things
- Being unable to recognize progress
- Constantly being in a rush
- Chronically being late
- Leaving things unresolved
- Using avoiding tactics like social media and scrolling
- Comparing themselves to others
- Being unable to relax or let things go
- Focusing on their own issues or challenges
- Speaking to how stressed they are
- Continually thinking about the future and the past
- Worrying about worrying

- ◆ Self-criticizing; as soon as something is easeful, there is a reflex to start focusing on all the bad or wrong things about them

Questions to Help

These may interrupt the pattern, add self-awareness, and help in healing:

- ◆ If you are feeling stressed . . . is it occurring in this moment or in response to the past or perceived future?
- ◆ When was the last time you felt ease and stability? Can you describe what that feels like?
- ◆ What's your relationship with comfort? What brings you comfort? What happens when you place your attention on that comfort? Where do you feel it in your body?

A Therapist Might Suggest . . .

Being chronically stressed out can feel like the world is caving in on you. Those with an addiction to drama are weighted down by the compound stressors in their lives. Being flooded with hormones can feel like a buildup of internal pressure—it's like a time bomb.

It's incredibly difficult for anyone to recognize or acknowledge their contribution to the overwhelm they are experiencing. They may say things like, "No, it's not me; these things are actually happening to me; how could I have created all of these stressors? They are out of my control!" While the stressors might indeed be out of their control, their sensitivity, stories they create and repeat, hyperfocus on the stressors, and their inability to let anything go contributes to the state of being stressed out. Meaning it's not the stressors that are overwhelming; it's the responses to them that are. Being constantly stressed out also signifies an inability to tolerate settling or comfort.

As a person with an addiction to drama starts to settle or relax, they will eventually become distracted by pain/discomfort, self-criticism, dissociation, or stories about other people. It's as though there is a revving reflex that gets activated when a person reaches their nervous system's comfort threshold. I refer to that as "hitting the shelf of settling." As someone with an addiction to drama comes closer to that shelf, their internal alarm signals danger and they begin to rev. If you notice this happening in you, it can be helpful to mobilize the "alarm" energy, through movement, pushing against a wall, stomping your feet—whatever action can release the energy that got stirred as you started to relax. Then, let your attention come back to what has been released (relaxed) and where there is comfort. See if you can stay even a few more seconds with comfort or release.

Settling will bring people closer to the emotions beneath the stress. For those addicted to drama, this stirs a revving response, which is their way of suppressing and avoiding the underlying emotions. The consequence of this suppression, coupled with a hyperfocus on the stressors, produces anxiety. When working with someone who has an addiction to drama who is expressing a high level of anxiety, I often use this perspective: "Anxiousness is the ringing of the telephone from your body, asking you to pick up your phone to connect with what is here . . . Can you let go of focusing on the ringer and pick up the phone and listen?" Essentially, I am suggesting to these individuals that their body signals do not necessarily mean threat or overwhelm—it can be emotions simply needing to be recognized, felt, and metabolized.

Thinking or saying "I'm stressed" or focusing on all the things that could make you stressed is a form of revving. When you recognize this revving occurring, name it, don't shame it. Say to yourself that something has taken you out of the present moment and it's okay to find your way back into the here and now of your body and feelings.

Eventually the goal is to slowly release the identity that has formed around being stressed and habituated to suffering.

Observation and Practice

Three main objectives are:

1. Build more capacity to be in the here and now (presence).
2. Create more space from compound stressors and the attachment to piling them up.
3. Build more tolerance for comfort.

Suggested Practices: Being with Comfort (page 217), Creating Space from Stressors (page 218), and Pandiculation (see page 219)

Self-Healing Statements

It's okay to feel ease and comfort.
I will meet myself one step at a time: slow and steady wins the race.

THE DRAMATIC NARRATOR: THEN HE SAID, THEN SHE SAID . . . CAN YOU BELIEVE . . .

The Dramatic Narrator takes inventory of other people's lives and shares their stories. They use storytelling and dramatization to rev up the room and synchronize with other people. This is done as a means of avoiding internal sensations and feelings.

The Dramatic Narrator may demonstrate the following behaviors and thought patterns:

- Gossiping
- Using exaggerated language
- Employing actions that are not out of pure instinct and response; they are for attention and to shape the way other people see them
- Embellishing stories for the sake of entertainment or the reaction of others
- Sharing stories to validate one's behaviors or big feelings
- Being obsessed with other people's business
- Badmouthing other people
- Retelling and reshaping stories to boost and boast your sense of power
- Hyperfocusing on doing things/having experiences so you share a story about it later or post a photo of it on social media
- Being the judge, jury, and executioner of everyone else
- Overanalyzing or chasing the "why" of someone's behavior
- Reporting to others what you saw on social media

Questions to Help

These may interrupt the pattern, add self-awareness, and help in healing:

- When the focus is strongly on other people, how is that focus being pulled from you?

- What are you not able to attend to when you are focusing on other people's lives?
- Notice, if you're talking a lot about other people, where are you in relation to this story?
- Notice, as you describe other people's faults and actions, what is this doing for you? To you?
- How are you making yourself feel superior or inferior as you replay a story?
- By painting the people in this story in a certain light, how is that adding to the excitement, entertainment, or intensity of the story? Do you feel you need this to pull people into the story and to give you attention?

A Therapist Might Suggest . . .

When a person who is addicted to drama speaks about others without locating themselves through using a first-person perspective and owning their feelings, this is a way of avoiding connection with oneself or allowing others to really see them. It is also a reflection of an inability to feel solid in yourself and be in the open vulnerability of connection with others. The lack of a solid sense of self is replaced with a self-critic.

The self-critic is almost always in the driver's seat, saying, "I am not enough to be interesting or wanted—but other people and stories are." The draw of being a dramatic narrator is that it captures other people's attention and overrides the pain of having to hear the critic.

Healing occurs when this person can shift from telling stories to expressing their feelings, needs, and authentic self.

Observation and Practice

Next time you find yourself in a conversation where somebody is gossiping or dramatically narrating, observe:

- How do you feel?
- How do you want to engage?
- Does it pull you or keep your attention?
- Do you believe them?
- Do you feel safe in their presence?

- What thoughts does it elicit about you?

Next time you find yourself in a conversation where you are gossiping or dramatically narrating, observe:

- How do I feel?
- Does this story feel true?
- Do I feel like I can stop?
- What do I want or need from sharing?

Suggested Practices: Choosing Your Style of Narration (page 228), and Reflective Narrative Practice (page 229)

Self-Healing Statements

I no longer need to hide myself in stories and other people's lives.
It does not make me feel better to take other people down.
My story and the truth will be accepted and received.

THE MARTYR: I CAN'T WALK AWAY, I'M ALL THEY HAVE—THEY'LL BE DEVASTATED.

Enabling others is a way of attaining control and stability.

The Martyr may demonstrate the following behaviors and thought patterns:

- Finding self-importance in being the rescuer
- Playing the referee between other people's chaos
- Needing to control the situation
- Maintaining stability by way of engaging in other people's drama
- Doing things to be able to share what they did
- Confusing sympathy for pity
- Running around trying to extinguish the fires other people have lit
- Feeling like the world is out of control and there is something only they can do about it
- Needing to be acknowledged for how generous they are with their care, time, and self
- Creating conditions and scenarios in which they are needed—usually manipulated

- Making themselves invaluable to people in need, which keeps them in control of when people can and cannot leave them
- Offering their help and then resenting those who take it
- Waiting for others to dismantle the relationship to be able to get out of it
- Being unable to control their own experience, they attempt to control someone else's
- Cleaning up after other people's catharsis
- Enabling other people's intensity

Questions to Help

These may interrupt the pattern, add self-awareness, and help in healing:

- Who would you be if you weren't needed by someone else?
- When you are meeting other people's needs, who is tending to yours?
- What do you feel you gain from being invaluable to another in their time of pain, chaos, stress?
- How are you contributing to others' chaos and addiction to drama?
- Is it possible to feel people want to connect with you even if you are not needed at their time of distress?

A Therapist Might Suggest . . .

This archetype of addiction to drama is usually created when one has had to be the middle person between order and chaos for relationships in their past. Underneath the facade of being a good person is a deep anxiousness, fear, and need for control. Making themselves needed and wanted is a way to exert that control. They will often feel their own needs don't matter; they feel that they only have value if they are helping someone, thus making themselves indispensable to the person in trouble. They seek worth, power, validation, and a sense of identity by what they are to other people rather than from an intrinsic sense of self from inside.

This is something to watch for in people who have chosen or naturally been drawn into professions that fix, attend to, and heal others. The actions people take in response to their deep desire for belonging are often at the direct expense of maintaining their boundaries.

Healing an addiction to drama will reduce exhaustion and burnout and make therapeutic work truly centered on the client's process, as opposed to a means to distract from one's own life or get a hit of drama.

Observation and Practice

Journal prompts:

- What are the things I have control over in my life?
- What are the things I don't have control of in my life?
- When I am tending to everyone else's life, what in my life isn't being tended to?
- When I am not trying to control or fix other situations, what in me is unhealed/unmet?

Suggested Practices: Boundaries and Agency with Your Personal Space (page 212) and Controlling Chaos (page 213)

Self-Healing Statements

I am able to ground while allowing chaos and crisis to happen around me.
Other people are capable of handling their own lives.
I am more than I offer in a relationship.

THE ATTACHMENT SEEKER: WHY CAN'T I JUST FIND A GOOD MAN/WOMAN/PARTNER?

The Attachment Seeker is constantly in the cycle of "not finding the right person." They may be attracted to the wrong person (such as the "bad boy" or someone who is not stable, consistent, or safe). They find themselves in a perpetual loop of the same experience in relationships without learning, growing, or changing.

The Attachment-Seeker may demonstrate the following behaviors and thought patterns:

- Spacing out and dissociating while there is intimacy or connection
- Big love = big fights
- Being turned off by the "nice guy"
- Repeating the same patterns with different partners

- Being unable to trust or receive intimacy
- Starting fights just to feel some connection
- Magnifying the wound of previous relationships
- Mistaking a red flag for excitement, and excitement for passion/connection
- Feeling the most "love" for your partner during or after a fight
- Using trauma as the bonding agent or glue of the relationship
- Focusing on what's wrong in the relationship and other person, as opposed to what's right
- A grounded and stable partner will make them feel out of sync, bored, like there is always something better for them.

Questions to Help

These may interrupt the pattern, add self-awareness, and help in healing:

- Do you know your red flags? What do you do when you see them? How do you attempt to ignore them when they are arising?
- What is the pattern you continually see emerging in every attempt or actual relationship?
- What do you imagine they might see your role here as?
- What was your relationship like to your parents?
- What was love and connection like as a child?
- How would each person in your family define love? What were the tools they used to attain and maintain it?

A Therapist Might Suggest . . .

Those with an addiction to drama often act out their early attachment wounds in relationships. They seek big excitement and experience bigger disappointments. Fights, mistrust, and walling off to intimacy are recurring themes.

There is often a victim mentality to love and intimacy without a willingness to see how we are contributing to the pattern playing out. Intensity is often confused with attraction and connection.

If we grew up with caregivers that primarily showed attention when things were heightened, bad, or intense, we likely began to adapt that as our love language. Our love language is the way we express love, and also the way in which we can receive it. This might look like starting fights for no apparent reason, feeling closeness when the other person is pulling away, or co-revving rather than coregulating with your partner, and so on.

A substantial part of healing an addiction to drama is about reestablishing safe connection. This includes a connection to yourself and others. This often involves finding those in life who will see you and love you unconditionally and slowly allowing yourself to be seen and connected with.

Observation and Practice

Journal prompt: Make a list of nonnegotiables in a relationship so you are better able to observe the pattern and provide your own needs rather than playing it out through a repetitive experience.

Journal prompt: List all the needs that were not met when you were a child. Now, list all the needs that have not been met in previous relationships. Then, go through each of those needs and identify how you might offer those to yourself, or how you might allow others to offer those to you.

Contemplation: Notice your own anxiety around the deepening stages of intimacy. How can you care for yourself at each stage without disconnecting from the other person?

Suggested Practices: Hugging Meditation (pages 214) and Letting Yourself Feel and Be Felt (page 216)

Self-Healing Statements

I am becoming the person I truly seek.
It is safe to be vulnerable.
I am reclaiming intimacy by allowing myself to be seen and recognized.

THE STORYTELLER: NO, LET ME TELL YOU WHAT ACTUALLY HAPPENED.

The Storyteller creates stories in their mind, fills in the blanks by creating imaginative scenarios, and projects them onto reality as though that were the truth. Even though the scenario is manufactured, the physiological response is real.

The Storyteller may demonstrate the following behaviors and thought patterns:

- Everything is being played out internally in the imagination and then responded to externally
- Superimposing the past onto the present with no ability to access a new reality
- Finding evidence/inventing evidence to support their point of view
- Having a vivid imagination where they repeatedly play out every part in a story
- Perpetually doubting and mistrusting others as a form of protection
- Using overgeneralizations or globalizing a feeling or belief (such as feeling sad in the moment and then saying they're always sad, or someone always does something, etc.)
- Diagnosing someone with some psychological disorder and then creating stories that fit that diagnosis
- Being unable to decipher what actually happened vs what they believe has happened
- Having a conflict between realities (their reality will always be ensured to win out)
- Desiring to prelive/prefeel conflict and confrontation in their mind first
- Saying common phrases, such as "How could you?" "How dare you?" "Can you believe he/she/they . . . ?"
- Having beliefs and perceptions that are rigid and inflexible
- Imagining themselves playing out the stories that actually get their needs met
- Life has nothing new, mysterious, or wondrous for them, because they've been living it out in their head
- Having a full emotional life only in the imagined relationship with others
- Being unable to connect with another person in real life because they have been relating to the imagined version of that person in their mind. They will often expect the person to be up-to-date with the

conversation that has been happening in their mind alone. This creates even more distance in the relationship

◆ Imagining tragedy or their own funeral and playing out what they think/hope people will say about them

Questions to Help

These may interrupt the pattern, add self-awareness, and help in healing:

◆ If you put the story to the side, what is it that you are sensing and feeling in this moment? What do you need?

◆ What are you hoping for the outcome of this imagined story? Can you provide that outcome to and for yourself?

◆ What was the feeling before you went into the active imagination that you were unable to tolerate? What was the feeling just previous to the active imagination that you felt you needed to leave?

A Therapist Might Suggest . . .

Often one will imagine a scenario or reason why something is happening, and then will create and act out that scene in their mind. The body cannot tell the difference between reality and the active imagination, which creates confusion and further disconnection from reality. For example, my client Recce recently shared that as he was preparing for a dinner party, his boyfriend texted and said he needed a nap. Recce immediately jumped into a story that his partner was saying he was not going to come help and—even worse—was going to be late to the dinner party. He felt utterly abandoned and subsequently shut down. He started ruminating about how his partner was not the right person for him and this was a perfect example of how he could never truly show up. He was angry at himself for choosing his partner and was furious and resentful at his partner for abandoning him. Even though his partner sent several texts stating that regardless of wanting a nap, he was on his way, Recce couldn't accept them. Recce found himself stuck in his story, like his body was frozen in time with that false truth. There was nothing Recce or anyone else could do to get him out of it.

Simply expressing how one is feeling and their true needs is so diffi-cult to communicate that the only safe place for this to happen is in their active imagination. Because they never express these sentiments in real life, feelings of resentment toward others begin to emerge. This also results in creating internal fantasies whereby they can play out victimhood, revenge, and abandonment.

The stories you create to rev yourself are shields to protect your heart. Nothing can come in or out, and the person addicted to drama becomes walled off from reality, and imprisoned within their imagination. We must be willing to forgo our imagination and heal the past to meet what is truly happening in the present.

Observation and Practice

Journal prompt: When you find yourself in an unpleasant experience, go back and identify the story you told yourself about what was happening or was going to happen before the unpleasant experience. Notice the difference between your inner story and the actual experience.

Suggested Practices: Reflective Narrative Practice (page 229), Stop Creating Stories from the Past (page 230), Stop Creating Stories from the Imagined Future (page 230), and Stepping Away from Stories (page 229)

Self-Healing Statements

When I ground myself in my feelings and needs and accept that at times they can't always be met, I can stay with myself and not my stories.
Life has more for me in the future than I may know.
I can trust what is unfolding in this process.

CHAPTER 13

A Bird in the Storm: How to Thrive in Relation to Those with an Addiction to Drama

A S SHARED IN EARLIER CHAPTERS, THERE ARE MANY COMMON RESPONSES to an encounter with someone who is addicted to drama. These can include feeling frustrated, exhausted, disoriented, ungrounded, and even at times excited.

Engaging with those who have an addiction to drama demands a lot of internal and external resources and will certainly require additional attention to your own care. Self-care means attending to physical, psychological, and emotional needs to preserve your health and thrive. Here is a collection of practices for optimizing your self-care around those who are addicted to drama.

IDENTIFYING WITHOUT JUDGMENT

Perhaps before reading this book you had encounters with someone who was addicted to drama, but you did not understand what was happening or didn't quite have a term to anchor the experience. Simply being able to identify to yourself what is happening—such as "I recognize this as addiction to drama"—can release a significant amount of tension and anxiety.

When the term "addicted to drama" becomes a derogatory label, however, it can mean that you're having some underlying feelings about the encounter that need to be acknowledged and supported. Attending to those is an important part of your self-care.

Also, when you can identify the situation and the common patterns of that person it can empower you by giving context to your experience, help you orient yourself to what is happening and why, and bring more awareness to what you need for yourself in the situation. Understanding and "labeling" without judgment is a sign that you are supporting yourself with more clarity, and not holding on to any unprocessed emotion from the encounter.

EMPATHIC UNDERSTANDING AND STEPPING BACK

Hopefully, throughout this book, you'll have realized that no matter how much you try or wish for someone who is addicted to drama to just change their behavior and make better choices, it's not that easy. This can stir your own frustration, disappointment, exhaustion, and even possibly a sense of failure. If you hear yourself saying things like "If they could just know what they're doing" or "If I stand up to them they will stop," then turn your attention back to yourself. Give yourself a hug, letting yourself know that what's most important is your health and well-being. You are not responsible for fixing someone who has an addiction to drama: their healing is in their hands.

One particular practice I would recommend is called a reframe. It means changing your orientation to the behavior to help shift and soften your response. When you see someone start to engage in the drama cycle, offer statements to yourself that allow you to step back and get space, such as these:

- They are again being pulled into the craving of drama.
- I see that they are revving.
- Something very painful in them is trying to be avoided right now.
- What they are truly seeking is outside their awareness.

- This is the only way right now they know how to connect.
- This is the best way they know right now how to navigate their trauma.
- They are needing to be this big and intense because they are asking to be seen.
- This is how they remind themselves they are alive.
- It may be really scary for them to be seen.
- This is a reflection of them feeling a sense of worthlessness.
- Gossiping and sharing bad news is how they can feel important and needed.
- If they could stop themselves, they would.

This "reframing" is not making excuses; it is to help you avoid being pulled into the drama and instead be a compassionate witness. Often, when we can show grace to others in this way, we can soften from our own armoring and find compassion for ourselves in this situation.

CLARIFYING YOUR BOUNDARIES

Many people feel they have to harden up and become" armored" around those with an addiction to drama. The challenge is that when those we care about feel someone armoring up, they interpret that as a form of abandonment. Perhaps we can redefine boundaries as creating the right amount of space that allows you to care for yourself while still being in a relationship to them. While sometimes that might mean not speaking or being in their presence for some time, there are also ways of creating space and safety while in proximity to that person.

> **Check the space.** When you are around someone who is addicted to drama, bring your attention to the actual space between you. Imagine that space as a buffer between the two of you, and use the actual space as a support to maintaining boundaries.
> **Set a time.** Set the amount of time you have available for them. You might say things like, "You're important to me and I have ten minutes

before my next meeting." Or "I'm sorry you're hurting and I can be present for fifteen minutes right now."

Clarify what you can hear. Clarify what you're open to hearing and not open to hearing, such as

» "I'm having a difficult time and can't hold space for this right now."

» "I'm open to hearing how you're feeling right now and what you need for support. I don't have the space to hear the details of the story."

» "I can be present to listen to what happened, but I don't have the capacity to hear any blaming as to why it happened."

» "Now is not a good time; what's your availability like later?"

Keep it short. Keep reflections short, such as *I'm sorry. I hear you. That sounds difficult. I can't imagine. Ouch.* Avoid asking questions about the stories.

One thing at a time. Be clear you can only be with one topic at a time. "I hear that there's a lot to share, and the best way I can listen is by staying with one topic at a time."

Don't get hemmed in. Don't let yourself get stuck in a small space. If possible, find places to talk that are spacious. You might say, "I'm open to listening, but I need to do it while walking through nature."

Take a break. You can ask for pauses in the conversation. "There's a lot being shared; I just need a pause/break to reflect and even just refresh."

Orient to now. If you feel like you're getting pulled into the person's past, orient into the present moment, noticing what colors and objects are around you. You might say, "There's a lot of the past that's being shared; I need to take a moment to focus on the present moment," or ask, "Do you feel safe in this moment?"

Ask what is needed. Invite a resolution, such as "What do you feel like you need?" or "What might you need to find a resolution?"

GROUNDING IN THE MIDST OF A WHIRLWIND

One of the more difficult and prevalent experiences in the presence of someone in an active cycle of drama is the whirlwind that gets created. Without warning, it can suddenly feel like the room is spinning and there's less air to breathe; you may become disoriented, confused, ungrounded, and disconnected from yourself. It can suddenly feel as if you're on a roller-coaster ride that you didn't choose to be on. No matter how clear your boundaries are, sometimes the force of the whirlwind can dislodge you with a dramatic impact. The following are some suggestions in supporting yourself during a whirlwind.

Identify It

When you recognize that you are being pulled into someone's whirlwind, name it. Say to yourself, "This is their whirlwind," then remind yourself why this is happening and what choices you have:

- "They are trying to pull me in as a way to feel connection. I can say no to connecting in this way."
- "This is the only way their unprocessed trauma can show up right now. As the trauma is being deposited onto me and into the environment, I won't be able to make sense of it and I won't try."
- "This situation has become the stage of their pain. I can choose not to be part of this reenactment."

Stay Present and Come into the Here and Now

When entrapped in a drama whirlwind it can be difficult to orient to what's happening in the moment; it can feel like a warped sense of time and space. Orient yourself to the present by doing the following:

- Take ten slow, deep breaths and feel the heat of the breath as it moves in and out of your nose. Just focus on your breath. Remind yourself what is truly happening in this present moment is your breath, as it's moving in and out.

- Build up some saliva in your mouth and bring your awareness to how it moves through your mouth and down your throat.
- Unlock your eyes by looking around the space and seeing and naming some of the colors that are in that space.
- Listen and name five things you can hear.

Find Grounding

Often, those who were in a drama whirlwind report feeling pulled into a chaos where it becomes difficult to find their own physical and emotional stability. The main focus is to reclaim your sense of anchor and recalibrate from that sense of stability.

- Plant your feet into the floor. Push them down and notice the floor beneath you, supporting you.
- Plant your hands down into the ground or supporting surface. Feel the engagement of your muscles as you press down.
- Press your back and pelvis into a wall or chair. Notice the support behind you, supporting you.
- Place your hands on top of your head, feeling the gentle compression and sense of gravity flowing down through your head, spine, legs, and into your feet.
- Reexamine the situation from a sense of being more anchored and grounded.

Bring Yourself Back to You

Once you have anchored yourself, focus on bringing your attention back to you. Often those who are in this situation feel like the whirlwind is pulling them out of themselves, similar to how people feel like they lost themselves in a job or relationship. Here's what to do:

1. Reclaim your attention and focus back to you.
2. Turn your attention to how you are feeling.
3. Then, turn your focus to what you need and how to get it.

Stay Focused on What's Real

Being pulled into a whirlwind can seem like reality as you know it is spinning out of control. What you knew as up is down, and what was right and true is now warped and unclear. For now:

- Avoid making any new conclusion or understandings of yourself or the world in this state.
- Keep focused on what you know is true, simple things like the world is round, apples come from trees, the grass is green, and the sky is blue.
- Stay with facts that are absolute and not open to interpretation.

SHAKING IT OFF

Remember that all that activation circulating through the person addicted to drama is contagious. And if you have spent time with someone while they are in the active phase of the addiction, you will have some secondhand drama in you. It's important that you connect to that activation in yourself and mobilize it. You might do some gentle shaking, a workout, or yoga, whatever activity most allows you to discharge that energy.

One simple practice is to notice where in your body that activation or residual charge is. Tap on it to bring it to the surface, or imagine spreading it so it's more dispersed through your body. Then, mobilize that activation by any of the methods suggested earlier.

Identify What Restores and Recuperates You

Often people who have interactions with those who are addicted to drama report feeling a residue of the drama and exhaustion. Here are some suggestions to support you in those times:

These might include being in nature, listening to music, doing some exercise or movement, eating something nourishing, or creating art. Make a list and refer to it after an interaction, and make sure you take the time to replenish yourself. It wasn't a conscious choice for you to have given up so much of your energy (just as it wasn't a conscious choice for the person with the drama addiction to have drained your energy), so be gentle with why it happened and focus on caring for yourself.

Use Cleansing Rituals

Plan a ritual that will help remove the residue of the interaction or exposure to a whirlwind of drama. These could include the following:

- **Hand washing:** You can literally wash your hands or just imagine doing so. As you wash your hands, visualize all the residue being washed away.
- **Showering:** Similar to washing your hands, sometimes you may feel like you need to be immersed in running water as a way to cleanse yourself of any entanglement or residue from the interaction.
- **Zooming out:** You might feel "stuck to" that person or what they were saying or how they were behaving. Zoom out to a bird's-eye view and see how much space is now between you and them. Try imagining a refreshing gust of air moving through the space between you and them.
- **Affirmation:** Repeating an affirmation for cleansing can be helpful, such as: "What's mine is mine and what's yours is yours." Try this affirmation as you place one hand on your chest and the other hand in front of you with your palm facing out. You might imagine that the hand facing out is giving back any of the residue you took on from them.
- **Smudging with sage:** Burning dried sage, known as smudging, is a purification ritual emerging from Indigenous traditions that helps cleanse the space and change the composition of the air. As you move the burning sage around your body, picture any energy or activation that is not yours moving out and away along with the smoke.
- **Naming your experience:** It can be helpful to simply acknowledge for yourself or share that it was a difficult or heavy experience to be with them while they were in a drama cycle.
- **Purifying light:** You can imagine a powerful purifying light moving through you. As the light moves completely through you, allow whatever energies or feelings that you picked up from your encounter to move out.

- ◆ **Cutting the cords:** Draw an infinity symbol on a piece of paper. Put your name in one loop and theirs in the other. Then, take scissors and cut the "cord" link between the circles.
- ◆ **Body brushing:** Brush your whole body from head to toe with your hands, brushing off the entanglements that you are carrying along with you.

BREAKING UP WITH SOMEONE WHO IS ADDICTED TO DRAMA

While the tools mentioned so far will allow you to be more grounded and strengthen your boundaries in relation to someone who is addicted to drama, the truth is sometimes that is not enough to maintain or sustain the relationship. Sometimes, you will just have to walk away and end the relationship (for now) with a lover, friend, or family member for your own preservation. While the terms "break up," "walk away from someone," or "leave the relationship" are often used, the reality is that you are making the conscious choice to return your energy and attention back to yourself. You are walking away from the behaviors of the addiction, and for now that also means walking away from the person who has the addiction.

There are several stages in this process of leaving the relationship and returning to yourself.

1. **Acknowledging change is needed.** In this stage, we are acknowledging that the conditions and the environment with someone who is addicted to drama are not allowing you to feel stable, secure, balanced, empowered, or healthy. It is not your job to fix them or make everything right; it is your job to attend to yourself. The truth is, if you're not able to be present for yourself in this relationship, you end up just being part of their trauma reenactment of their feeling abandoned. Cycling through their trauma reenactment, where you are not able to support your own well-being, is a major signifier things have to change; specifically, by a significant pause or ending the relationship.

2. **Setting up your support system.** In any major change of relationship, it's helpful to shift your attention from what you are moving away from and redirect it to what you are moving toward. This includes setting up the structures of what or who you will focus on during this transition. A healthy transition will include feeling safe and secure to transition out of this relationship—which will require support. We all need someone to catch us as we fall from the familiarity that we have known. This support can include friends, family, a therapist, or even a support group. Create a list of supports and begin to bring them more into the foreground of your life.

3. **Caring for yourself.** If you have been in any type of relationship with someone who is addicted to drama, a good amount of your energy, attention, and resources have been focused on and pulled into their whirlwinds. Any type of big change takes energy, and in fact it's easier to stay in our ruts because it requires less initial energy than the change. That being said, it's important that you begin to recuperate your energy and resources to initiate this transition. This can include reconnecting to hobbies, visiting special places, eating healthy food, getting a significant amount of sleep, and engaging in activities that feel recuperative and enlivening to you.

4. **Clarifying and setting your boundaries.** At this stage, you are clarifying what leaving will look like during and after it is complete. Because boundaries are often not created or kept in these relationships, it's helpful to lean into your support systems to help you create a clear exit plan that doesn't result in you falling back into the relationship. You can always reconnect with the person later, but the priority at this point is your well-being.

5. **Leaving.** As part of your action plan to leave, decide how much you will communicate with them, what you wish to communicate, and where it feels safest to communicate what is happening (e.g., in front of other people or at a park, etc.). While what you decide to communicate is up to you, I do recommend sharing only what you need to.

As you enact the separation, focus on this transition or change being about your well-being.

Additional things to keep in mind:

- **Walking away will trigger them.** As you enact your boundaries and say no to this relationship in this way, at this time, it will activate their sense of being abandoned and harmed. You will likely see an escalation of intensity and action. This may include anger, denial, blame, and/or big tears. It may also include gossiping about you or even trying to enact weaponized empathy. Whatever their reaction, and there will be one, focus on the people and things that give you a sense of support. Attend to the reason that you are choosing to create more boundaries and moving away from them at this time. Notice if you have created an armoring to do so, and when possible see if you can set the armor down so that you're not carrying it into other relationships or aspects of your life.
- **Keep your sense of safety at the fore.** If they respond in a way that you feel might be harmful to you or themselves, it's important to seek the advice and support of a licensed professional or authority. Please do not further compromise your well-being when there are trained professionals to assist.
- **Acknowledge your own withdrawal.** Remember, unlike most other addictions, drama is contagious. As you move away from someone with an addiction to drama, you will experience both relief and withdrawal. That withdrawal might show up as feeling fatigued or collapsed or even as finding yourself thinking about them or coming up with excuses as to why you should go back. You might even find yourself stirring things up in other places of your life to get a refresh of the hit you experienced while you were in that relationship. It's helpful to acknowledge the withdrawal and be honest with yourself if you have found substitute ways of getting the hit. Over time, acknowledging and choosing not to participate in revving will

help reduce the withdrawal, at which point you will begin to recuperate your energy.

As you heal from your own secondary drama exposure, just remember that you have the choice and power to preserve your energy and well-being. As you reestablish a sense of grounding and repair your boundaries, know that you are not alone: there are many people on a similar path of bringing peace and stability back to their lives after engaging with drama.

Epilogue: Saying Good-Bye

I'T'S THE END OF THE WORLD AS WE KNOW IT. NO, OF COURSE IT'S NOT—BUT saying good-bye is hard. For those of us who have been or are addicted to drama, good-byes were usually done in the blazing heat of a fire. And then the all-too-familiar feeling of absence sets in, and the stirring of drama begins to take us far away from the pain.

Sometimes it's helpful to end where we began. An addiction to drama is far more complex, layered, and pervasive than simply an extravagantly loud cry for attention. It's a way of trying to exist in a world you are constantly out of sync with—chasing sensation to feel alive and seeking crisis as a way of validating an unidentifiable and insatiable discomfort. Being addicted to drama is like a living, breathing storm, searching for a grounding rod, and consequently pulling everything into its vortex yet destroying the ground on which it so desperately wishes to land. This nuanced phenomenon, which many of us are caught in, is no different than a drug that you might ingest, inhale, or shoot up. Except the "drug" isn't something that you can tangibly hold: you can only seek it or manufacture it.

Drama is the stirring, the excitement, the exaggeration, the eruption, the unrest, and the battle to feel alive in relation to the numbing of the internal and external world around you. And it's not just incredibly addictive, it is also contagious.

To some degree, each of us has been exposed to or is addicted to drama. But we are not broken. We are not problems waiting to be solved. We are human beings unraveling the deep binds that have caused us to chase or be chased by the dips and the hits of our stress response. We are just trying to make our way back home. For some, home means to be surrounded by those who don't pull us into their vortex of chaos, who can sit next to us in silence or at play and feel at ease. For others, coming home means it's safe to be in our bodies, to feel what we are feeling and express our needs—and to know those feelings and needs are okay. It also means that our truest and most authentic self is neither too much nor not enough—but rather, it is just right. To come home means that we can finally exhale and dial down the pervasive holding of tension—so that we can finally be held.

We are all human beings, just trying to make our way back home.

Appendix:
Practices and Prompts for Healing

A S THE PATTERNS OF AN ADDICTION TO DRAMA ARE DEEPLY WIRED INTO the body, it can be profoundly helpful to explore practices that can directly change the nervous system. This Appendix contains a sampling of practices that I used in my own healing journey, as well as in my practice with those who are addicted to drama. Many of these practices were also helpful for those in relation to people addicted to drama—to ground and reset themselves.

These practices are sorted into two sections. The first is a collection of physical exercises and guided meditations/visualizations. The second are prompts for journaling and guided reflection to explore and build self-awareness. While most of these practices can be done on your own, it is always advised to have a licensed therapist to process your experiences with and explore them more deeply. A therapist who is versed in somatic stress or trauma therapies might be very helpful.

I suggest you read through the practices, and then make a recording of them on your phone so you can easily access the practice, reflection, or prompt.

PHYSICAL PRACTICES AND GUIDED MEDITATIONS

ANCHORING MEDITATION

The practice is to reclaim your own focus and presence. This practice will help to bring you back to yourself when you are being pulled toward chaos.

1. Come into a comfortable position, seated, standing, or lying down. If it feels comfortable, close your eyes.
2. Imagine that your whole body is a candle.
3. Inside the middle of the candle is a wick—imagine that wick moving down the center of your body from top to bottom.
4. You might even imagine lighting the top of the wick.
5. At the bottom of the wick is an anchor, something that helps the wick ground down and maintain stability.
6. Stay with the feeling of being anchored in your body for several minutes.
7. As the whirlwind of someone else tries to pull the flame, bring your attention back to the wick and the anchor that grounds it.

GROUNDING MEDITATION

If you grew up in a chaotic environment or are pulled into a whirlwind of drama, grounding can help you regain a sense of inner stability.

1. Come to a comfortable position, seated or standing against a wall, or lying down.
2. Bring your attention to where your body is making contact with the supporting surface.
3. Imagine your breath moving into the space between you and the supportive surface. Let your attention and breath be on where you are supported.
4. Imagine that the supportive surfaces are coming up to receive the weight of your body.
5. See where you can say yes to receiving that support and allowing the weight of your body to rest into it. (You can always add a weighted blanket or sandbag on your body.)

6. Name those places out loud where you feel both supported and can rest into that support.

7. Finally, bring your attention to where your body is contacting the ground. Imagine that you could begin to grow roots down into the earth from that point of contact. Feel the rootedness of your whole body.

8. If you notice at times that your thoughts begin to pull you away from that groundedness, just note it, and see if you can bring attention back to where you are supported and rooted.

BOUNDARY PRACTICE PART 1: EMBODYING AND ESTABLISHING YOUR ENERGETIC BOUNDARY

Boundaries are essentially our personal guidelines and limits, giving us a clear sense of where we begin and end. They can be physical borders or symbolic limits. Emotional/energetic boundaries are arguably our most primal way of discerning between "I," "you," and "we." They are all about respecting feelings. To support yourself in building and upholding boundaries, try the following.

1. Come into a comfortable position, seated, standing, or lying down.

2. Bring your awareness to where your body is making contact with the supporting surface beneath you.

3. See where you can say yes to being received by the supporting surface. Bring your attention to where you feel a sense of groundedness and anchor.

4. From that sense of anchor extend both of your arms out, touching the edge of space where they can reach. If your arms get tired at any point during the practice, you can rest them and resume when you're ready.

5. At the end of where you can reach in the space, imagine a bubble or membrane that fully surrounds you. Use your hands to trace the edge of this bubble/membrane all the way around you.

6. Once you have traced it, you might even imagine your hands coloring in the lining of the membrane: the sides of the bubble, the front and

back, the top and bottom. You might wish to breathe into the edges of the bubble, as though your breath could also paint/fill in the inner lining of it.

7. Notice just how grounded and anchored you can feel inside of this three-dimensional bubble.

8. Now, bring your attention and hands to the part of the bubble that feels the strongest, and more clear and secure. Notice the response in you as you make contact with this place of strength in your boundary.

9. Next, identify the next strongest and clearest place along that membrane. When you've found it, let your attention, hands, and breath rest in that place. Connect into that felt sense of strength, security, and clarity. Notice the response in your body as you make contact with this.

You may wish to pause here, or you can continue on with this next part.

BOUNDARY PRACTICE PART 2: RECLAIMING YOUR SPACE

1. As you connect to the three-dimensional bubble around you, take a few moments to notice how that feels.

2. In your mind's eye, consciously move everyone from inside of this bubble to the outside of the bubble. That includes everyone and everything that has made its way inside of your boundary. Move them as far or as close as feels supportive to you.

3. Notice the response in your body, thoughts, and breath as you create this space.

4. If you notice you are pulling people back in or leaving your bubble to attend to other people or crises—reground your body, recuperate your boundary, and care for yourself and what you are feeling that hasn't been previously attended to.

BOUNDARIES AND AGENCY WITH YOUR PERSONAL SPACE

This is a partner practice; I suggest you explore this practice with someone you trust, as a way to repair boundary ruptures. Boundary ruptures occur when our choices and consent have been violated. Being able to make decisions about what or who you say yes or no to can help regain a sense of power and repair ruptures. Choose who will be Partner A and who will be Partner B.

1. Partner A stands about 20 feet away from Partner B.
2. Partner A will close their eyes if that feels safe to do so. Partner A will also lift their hand up in the air and show Partner B the signals for

   Stop

   Come closer

   Move away

3. *Partner B:* It's important that you listen and respond exactly to Partner A.
4. *Partner A:* Keep your hand up the whole time, listening to your intuition of what you need. Use your hand signals to clarify just how close or far away you want your partner to be and at what speed feels right for you.
5. After five minutes of exploring, pause, and notice how it feels in your body to be recognized (seen and heard) in this way.

CONTROLLING CHAOS

This practice allows chaos and crisis to exist without jumping in, and to know that your sense of being needed may not fill the whole of feeling unseen, unheard, and unrecognized. Know that you are worthy of being loved beyond what you can offer.

In the same way as you would watch a train go by or sit back in a theater and watch a movie, this exercise will help you observe someone having an experience while tempering any desire of wanting it to be different or to control another's experience or the outcome.

1. Sit in a loud or crowded area—it can be in a public space or in a well-trafficked area in your home. Bring your awareness inward, following the movement of your breath.
2. Each time a sound takes you out of presence—notice it. For example, if you hear traffic or someone in your household, or the sound of a siren, watch how your mind pulls you into it, creates a story about what's happening or why, and adds images to accompany the story. This is the act of being pulled out of presence.

3. Upon noticing that you have been pulled out of presence—name it, perhaps saying, "I have left myself in the pursuit of something or someone else."

4. Come back in. Shift your attention back to your breath, to the sensations of your body. You may wish to tap gently on your body as a place to direct your focus.

5. Keep practicing noticing, naming, and coming back into presence. You will learn to stay longer in presence and be able to bring yourself back sooner upon noticing it.

6. Let yourself watch in your mind's eye a recent event of someone or something that felt challenging or chaotic. Engage in the same practice of noticing, naming, and coming back until you can observe what's happening in your surroundings while simultaneously being in connection to what is happening within you. Each time you get pulled into the chaos, notice it, name it, and bring yourself back to you.

7. When you can stay present with yourself, you are ready to try this with people and situations you cannot control. Be there for yourself, with whatever emerges in you, in ways that perhaps others in the past could not be present with you.

HUGGING MEDITATION (REESTABLISHING SELF-REGULATION)

A substantial part of healing an addiction to drama is about reestablishing safe connection to oneself and others. This meditation provides a physical way to rebuild connection.

1. Get a large pillow and place it on your lap.

2. Come to a comfortable position sitting or lying down. If you're sitting, sit against a wall or chair with an additional pillow behind your back.

3. If it feels right, let your eyes close. Bring your attention to where your body is contacting the supporting surfaces (e.g., the chair or the earth).

4. Notice how the supportive surface is coming up to meet the edges of your body, as though the earth is coming upward to hold you.

See where you can say yes to allow yourself to be held and supported. Where you can say yes to your whole body (weight and presence) being received. And where the supportive surface in turn receives you.

5. Bring the pillow (from your lap) to the front of your body, hugging the pillow as much or as little as you wish. Notice just how much the pillow is holding and supporting your front body. Take some time to receive that sense of being held and supported.

6. Bring your awareness to the pillow behind you. Lean into the pillow as it receives and holds you.

7. Bring your awareness to the sense of being hugged from the front and back. Take some time to receive that sense of being held and received. It's as though the hug from the pillows is saying, "I'm here with you."

8. [If you're sitting] Take one hand and place it on the top of your head. Give a little compression downward, so that you feel that gentle containment and hug between the top and the bottom of your body. Take some time to receive that sense of being held and received. It's as though the compression from your hand and the ground is saying, "I'm here with you." Rest your hand down whenever you need.

9. Take two pillows or imagine two pillows hugging the sides of your body. You might also imagine the hands of someone you trust giving a gentle hug to the sides of your body as if to say, "I'm here with you." Take some time to receive that sense of being held and supported.

10. Take some time for a full-body hug, hugging from front to back, side to side, and top to bottom. See where you can say yes to receiving the hug and being held in support. Perhaps repeat the words "I am here with you." Take all the time you need to slowly absorb and internalize the experience of being held and received.

11. As you are being held, turn your focus inward to whatever sensation or feelings are present.

12. You can also ask yourself what in you wants to be recognized or acknowledged (from your day, week, or about a particular event or

situation). Allow for whatever sensations, feelings, images, or memories to emerge into your awareness.

13. Stay present with what you're feeling. If you notice yourself disconnecting from the sensations and feelings in your body—reconnect by attuning to the ground, tightening the hug from the pillows.

14. As you allow yourself to be present with the sensations and feelings, expand your awareness to the sense of being hugged and supported, as though the hug from the pillows is saying, "I'm here with you."

15. Take your time with this practice as you are rewiring the experience, so that you can be held and received with whatever you are feeling and expressing.

16. After practicing this with yourself, you may wish to find someone you trust to replace the pillows, to whom you can say, "I'm here with you."

LETTING YOURSELF FEEL AND BE FELT

For those with an addiction to drama, intimacy can feel dangerous. This practice is intended to make you more familiar with openness and intimacy.

1. Come to a comfortable sitting or lying position.

2. Place your hands on your heart.

3. Let your breath flow into your hands and the space around your heart.

4. Bring your awareness to where your hands are touching your heart.

5. If possible (let your heart) receive the touch and heat from your hands.

6. You might imagine opening little air vents in your skin and heart to let the temperature and touch of your hands in. If you notice you close off or are not yet receiving—just stay with it and build the trust.

7. Notice how it feels for your heart to be felt.

8. Explore this same practice on different parts of your body.

After some practice of feeling yourself and allowing yourself to be felt, you may wish to try this with someone who you feel safe with. Go slow and pause when you feel yourself close off to feeling or being felt. You can ask for more space or whatever you need in those moments to reconnect with yourself, and then possibly the other person.

EXPLORING SAFETY

Those with an addiction to drama will at times create crisis (what is wrong) to feel "safe." When a child grows up in a chaotic or inconsistent environment, it feels like something bad can happen at any moment. Because of this, safety and positive feelings never get wired together. Rather, safety is associated with knowing what is or will be wrong. This practice can help you to explore what safety truly is and get used to a healthy feeling of security.

1. Come into a comfortable position, sitting, standing, or lying down.
2. Take a moment to observe the space (room) you're in. Notice all the things in the room that bring you comfort (e.g., objects, colors, smells, etc.) in that space.
3. Take time to receive the presence of those things that bring you comfort.
4. Then, turn your focus inward and notice where that sense of comfort is present in your body.
5. As you feel the sense of comfort in your body, ask yourself, "Am I safe here?" Notice the response in your body.
6. Gently let your eyes open—bring your focus back out to the space (room), and back to the things in the room that are comforting. Once again, connect with those things that bring you comfort. Ask yourself, "Am I safe here?" Notice the response in your body.
7. Then, once again, close your eyes, asking yourself, "Am I safe here?"
8. If the answer is yes, notice what in your body lets you know you're safe. Describe the felt sense of safety (e.g., warm, sturdy, secure, etc.).
9. If the answer is no, just stay with connecting to the comforting things in the room. Sometimes we need to spend a longer amount of time with comfort before a sense of safety can emerge.

BEING WITH COMFORT

As a person with an addiction to drama starts to settle or relax, they will eventually become distracted by pain/discomfort, self-criticism, dissociation, or stories about other people. It's as though there is a revving reflex that gets activated when a person reaches their nervous system's comfort threshold. This practice will help you habituate to a sense of stillness and ease.

1. Come into a comfortable seated, standing, or lying position.
2. Take your time to really set yourself up for comfort.
3. Can you make yourself even more comfortable? And even a little more?
4. Describe the comfort. Where is it? How does it show up in your body?
5. Can you settle yourself into that comfort like settling into a bath?
6. Notice what allows you to stay in comfort or what might take you out of it.

CREATING SPACE FROM STRESSORS

Thinking or saying "I'm stressed," or focusing on all the things that could make you stressed, is a form of revving. This practice will help you to take your foot off the pedal and give you some mental distance from perceived stressors.

1. Gather five to ten pillows and stack them on top of one another.
2. This stack represents all the stressors in your life that are stacked on top of one another and create compound stress that often gives us a sense of feeling heavy and immobile.
3. You might place that stack of pillows on your lap to feel the metaphorical weight of those stressors.
4. Starting at the top of the stack, assign that pillow the name of one of the stressors. And then throw or place it somewhere in the room.
5. Take a moment to notice how it feels to have that much less weight.
6. Go through and assign a stressor to each remaining pillow and place or throw it somewhere in the room.
7. As you separate out each stressor, take some time to feel that much less weight from the pileup of the pillows and perhaps reflected as less pressure and weight in your own body. Can you stay with the lack of weight and pressure?
8. Also, bring your attention to the literal space between each of the pillows (stressors).

9. As you recognize the space between them, notice how that feels in your body.

10. Notice if there is a part of you that tries to pull back any of the stressors into your awareness. Return to seeing and breathing into the space between you and the stressors, and between the stressors.

11. The intention is to build up more capacity, not to pile up or pull the stressors back in.

12. As you create more space for yourself, notice what sensations and feelings are present in that space.

PANDICULATION

Pandiculation is a simple practice that helps identify the current level of tension in the neuromuscular system and can help reduce tension. When tension becomes integrated into everyday life, we stop attending to it consciously. Even without awareness, the tone and tension can still have a significant impact on our posture, attention, and an overreadiness to respond to stimuli.

Pandiculation is purposefully contracting and releasing tension in specific body areas in succession, working with each area in isolation. At the end, you'll pause to notice the change in sensation; the goal is to become aware of our subconscious tendency to hold on to tension so that we can choose to let it go.

If you notice as you engage in one area, another area tightens—what is called a coupled tension—pause and try to relax that area. We want to be able to separate out these coupled areas. If you notice that relaxing one area causes another part to tense—then you have become aware of a reflexive response to maintain a certain level of tension in the body. This will be addressed later in the section on hitting a shelf.

1. Come into a comfortable position, seated, standing, or lying down.

2. Begin with closing your hands into a fist—a strong engagement—then a slow release. Repeat once more.

3. Contract your forearms with a strong engagement. And then a slow release.

4. Contract your upper arms with a strong engagement. And then a slow release.

5. Contract your shoulders with a strong engagement. And then a slow release.

6. Contract your neck with a strong engagement. And then a slow release.

7. Contract your head and face with a strong engagement. And then a slow release.

8. Contract your chest with a strong engagement. And then a slow release.

9. Contract your upper back with a strong engagement. And then a slow release.

10. Contract your abdomen with a strong engagement. And then a slow release.

11. Contract your mid/low back with a strong engagement. And then a slow release.

12. Contract your pelvis with a strong engagement. And then a slow release.

13. Contract your upper legs with a strong engagement. And then a slow release.

14. Contract your lower legs with a strong engagement. And then a slow release.

15. Contract your feet with a strong engagement. And then a slow release.

16. Pause at the end of your release to register and absorb the change in tone/engagement.

The pandiculation practice can sometimes release an area that has been holding and the result is a flood of that stored energy in the tissues. You might wish to do some type of mobilization work, such as shaking or moving, however that energy wants to be moved.

ALTERNATE NOSTRIL BREATHING

In this breath practice, you will explore what it feels like to be in a pause with a slight retention of the breath. You might imagine your body like a sponge taking the breath fully in, absorbing. Or perhaps more the sense of the breath diffusing into the blood and being moved through the whole body, where it's distributed and taken in by every cell. The practice of pausing and absorbing creates a sense of space and also helps you feel into a sense of space. Slow down, and take a deeper pause between inhale and exhale with each round.

1. Find a comfortable position whether seated, standing, or lying down.
2. Bring your right hand up toward your nose.
3. Exhale completely out of both nostrils.
4. Place your thumb on the outside of your right nostril, closing the passage of breath through the right nostril.
5. Inhale through your left nostril. Then, close your left nostril off with one of your other fingers.
6. Pause in the space between your inhale and exhale.
7. Open the right nostril (by lifting your thumb off) and exhale.
8. Extend the pause between the exhale and the next inhale.
9. Inhale through the right nostril. Then, close your right nostril off with your thumb.
10. Pause in the space between your inhale and exhale.
11. Open the left nostril (by lifting your finger off) and exhale.
12. Extend the pause between the exhale and the next inhale.
13. This is one complete cycle.
14. Repeat for 10 cycles or for 5 minutes.

TAKING THE TIME TO TASTE YOUR FOOD

This simple mindfulness practice can help to slow down and reconnect to inner sensations.

1. Pick a few simple items—with one to two ingredients.
2. Slowly bring the food to your lips. Slow down the processes between the first contact of the food to your mouth to placing it inside of your mouth.
3. Spend several minutes tasting and connecting with a single piece of the food. Take the time to feel the textures, the weight and density, the layers of flavors.

4. Notice how your whole body responds to slowing down and immersing yourself in what you're eating.

REFLECTIONS AND JOURNAL PROMPTS

CREATING SPACE, FEELING SPACE, AND RESTING INTO SPACE

The tendency to fill any empty space with thoughts or busyness has been identified and worked on with mindfulness practices for thousands of years in various Eastern philosophies. For example, the practice of finding Madhya (meaning "center"), originated from nondual tantric philosophy. The intention of the practice is to find the gap (space) at the end of a thought or breath, notice the craving to fill that space, and build tolerance for being present with the space and the unknown. Victor Frankel once said, "Between stimulus and response there is a space. In that space is our power to choose our response. In our response lies our growth and our freedom." In this way, developing a practice to be able to find and embrace space ultimately leads to agency and a sense of power in the world, feelings that are ultimately stripped away by the nature of a reflexive survival strategy and an addiction toward staying activated.

Where might we find these moments of space?

- In the space between the inhale and the exhale
- In the silence between sounds
- In the synapses between impulse
- In the space between thoughts
- In the time between dusk and dawn

In your journal, start to identify moments or situations where you can create space and allow yourself to feel and rest into that space.

WORKING WITH THE PART OF YOU THAT WASN'T SEEN

The part of you that wasn't seen is often a part that holds a fair amount of pain and trauma. It is as though that part that was unseen and unheard at a young age became frozen in time with the pain of it all. This can be part of the internalization of not being seen or heard, or because trauma or other childhood events made it not safe enough to be present with and metabolize these experiences. At the core of this part that doesn't want to be seen is indeed a desire to be seen and connected with, so it's important to go slow and not rush a process. It will take some time to uncouple being seen and being exposed or building the trust that you are worthy of being seen and that there is space, time, permission, and support to be seen and heard. The following exercise may be done with someone you trust, or you can record it so that you are able to visit what you find with time. Move slowly, be patient, and revisit this exercise as much as you need to feel seen and heard.

1. Come into a comfortable position, in a comfortable environment. Take a few minutes to arrive into your body, finding the support of the ground and your breath.

2. Call forth the part that hasn't been seen. You may experience its presence as sensation in your body, an inner child, image, or inner voice.

3. If this part doesn't feel accessible or even if it does, state your highest intention for wanting to connect with this part.

4. Where and how do you feel the presence of this part in your body?

5. What does it look like?

6. We get to know our parts by asking them questions and listening to their response. A part may give us information in the form of words, images, body sensations, emotions, or a sense of direct knowing. Invite this protector to come sit on the cushion in front of you. Once again, let it know that you want to hear its feelings and experiences as a witness and as a support.

7. Once you have an image or a sense of it there, perhaps see if there is a way to make consensual contact with this part: move closer to it, speak directly to it, send love, physical contact, eye contact, sing a song together, or even move and breathe in rhythm with it.

8. Once in contact with this part, begin to ask these questions out loud. Let your imagination be unfiltered as you open to any response.

   » What would you like me to call you? A name?

   » What is your role in my system/what do you do?

» What do you feel?

» What makes you feel that way?

» How long have you been here (doing that role)?

» What do you want and need?

» What would you like me to know about you?

9. As you receive the responses, what would you like to say to this part, out loud? And how does it respond to you?

10. Next, ask this part to share with you when it first started feeling unseen and unheard. Ask it to share with you an image or a memory of this experience. (Note: Memories may show as sensation or nonlinear images—respect anything that comes as part of the healing process.)

11. Invite the part to share as much detail as it would like about this image or memory. Ask how it made this part feel when this happened. Let this part know that you are here with it.

12. Ask if there is anything more that it wants you to know or understand.

13. If it feels right for this part, ask if you can join it in this memory or image to provide support and any help.

14. Ask how this part would like you, the adult, to be with it in this experience. What can you do differently than what was possible then? Provide what is needed through your own imagery and imagination.

15. Take the time to offer the support or requests from this part. Notice how it feels in your body as you do. Invite the part to really marinade in the good of being supported, seen, and heard.

16. Gently let this part know it has been living in the past, and you would like it to come to the present where things will be different. You may wish to invite it to go for a walk with you at this time.

17. As you spend time together in the present, you might create a ritual to relieve this part of any weight or pain that is here. Perhaps it can let it be released into the wind, or earth, or sun, something that can receive it and transform it.

18. Thank this part for letting you connect with it, to see and be seen. Once this is complete, see what this part would like to do now.

19. Notice what feels different in you.

SOCIAL MEDIA CHECK-IN

Our social media avatars (see page 137) can create distance between us and our inner truth. Use this practice to get in touch with deeper needs.

1. For one week, every time you want to share something online, pause and ask yourself:
    » What do I need in this moment?
    » What is the goal of this post?
    » What am I really hungry for? (e.g., *attention, connection, for my sadness to be seen and felt, to know I'm not forgotten, etc.*)
2. Pause before posting and stay with the feeling and need that you discovered by slowing down and asking yourself the previous questions.
3. Notice what happens when these feelings and needs are acknowledged.
4. If you decide to post, notice what happens in relation to those needs you identified—do they get met?

IDENTIFYING HOW PRESENT EMOTIONS ARE IN YOUR LIFE

Using the following questions as a guide for your journaling, be as honest as possible.

1. Go through a list of emotions:
    Anger, Sadness, Disgust, Excitement, Disappointment, Despair, Joy, Sensuality, Pleasure, Loneliness, Hope, Worry, Anxiousness, Empowerment, Heartbreak, Shock, Tenderness, Peacefulness
2. Check in with yourself about each of these emotions:
    » Which of these emotions is okay for me to feel?
    » Which of these emotions do I connect with and feel?
    » Which of these emotions is it okay for me to express?
    » Which of these emotions do I express?

CONTACTING FEELINGS (EMOTIONS) IN YOUR BODY

Emotions can be divided into two categories: primary (core) emotions, and secondary (depository) emotions. Primary emotions are our most true experience and reside in our body to help guide us; secondary emotions mask core feelings and are used as a substitute when the core emotions are too much to feel or are suppressed. Use this practice to get in touch with primary emotions.

1. Identify a feeling/emotion that is present.
2. Check in with your body by scanning to see if that feeling is present at this moment. If the feeling word is not the right fit—then go back to find the right fit.
3. On a scale of 1 to 10, how present does the feeling feel right now?
4. Where does that feeling reside in your body?
5. Can you turn toward that feeling, reading your body, making gentle contact with it, like dipping the tip of your finger into a lake or pond?
6. As you contact the feeling (emotion), perhaps notice how it can be described. What are the qualities of the feeling (e.g., big, warm, sharp, heavy, frozen, light, bright, etc.)?
7. Stay with it, perhaps noticing if the contact allows it to move. As a true emotion is in motion, can you give it permission to let it move through your body?

CONNECTING FEELINGS AND NEEDS

This is a fill-in-the-blank practice intended to bring more awareness to your feelings and needs.

1. When _____ happened,
2. I felt/feel _____ [it can be more than one feeling: e.g., affectionate, hopeful, happy, confident, excited, grateful, inspired, refreshed, admiration, love, satisfaction, scared, annoyed, frustrated, guilty, embarrassed, angry, disgusted, pain, vulnerable, confused, aversion, longing, sad, tense, etc.].
3. It reminds me of_____ [a memory and recognition of associated experiences].
4. And what I need is_____ [there can be more than one need: e.g., meaning, connection, trust, support, empathy, being seen/heard, security, play, belonging, ease, trust, action, compassion, etc.).

WORKING WITH CONFIRMATION SCRIPTS

Confirmation scripts are the internal monologue of beliefs that we repeat to ourselves. They are like a broken record that just keeps playing on the turntable: "No one loves me," "They have a better life than I do," "I am going to be alone," and so on.

When we slow down, connect into the body in the present moment, we can begin to recognize we are feeding off these confirmation scripts: revving ourselves up as opposed to responding to what feels present in our body. Confirmation scripts are the beliefs that justify the addiction to drama and the behaviors that emerge from it, such as "I have to fight for my voice to be heard, because no one sees me" or "I have to stay vigilant because I'm the only one that can protect my family."

The confirmation scripts often become our identity, and we find the situations or view the situations that confirm that script. When you catch yourself saying familiar lines over many situations, these are often a confirmation script.

When you recognize a confirmation script, label it as such: "This statement is a script I use to justify the reflex of moving away from myself . . . this is a part of revving" or "I am not these thoughts, I am not these conditions." You can also imagine putting a name tag on the statement that says "confirmation script" so it is clearly labeled every time it comes up.

UNPACKING THE ORIGINS OF A CONFIRMATION SCRIPT

A common key feature in people with an addiction to drama is a lack of confidence in themselves (can be seen as underlying busyness), their self-worth, or the ability to trust others. Lack of confidence appears in the stories/confirmation scripts we tell ourselves that emerge from the times when someone didn't see, hear, or meet us. Use the following prompts for your journaling practice:

1. Where does lack of confidence show up in your life?
2. When were the times that someone didn't see you or hear you?
3. What story did you create about yourself to explain why they didn't see or hear you?

4. To counter the negative confirmation scripts, write down a time that you experienced someone seeing and hearing you in a way that felt safe. Describe that experience. What did that feel like? What is a positive script you can create from this experience?

CHOOSING YOUR STYLE OF NARRATION

Here is an experiential practice going through three variations of narration. Notice for yourself after each one if it feels familiar and unfamiliar.

1. Pick a story from your life that has a moderate level of activation or intensity to it. On a scale of 1 to 10, something more like a 4 or 5.
2. Set a timer for four minutes.
3. For this first round, you're going to share what happened out loud, including what others did or said.
4. At the end of the four minutes, pause and notice how you feel after sharing the story in that way. Does it feel familiar? Unfamiliar?
5. Once again, set the timer for four minutes.

1. For this round, you are going to focus on what's happening in you. You can spend a maximum of 20 percent of the time on what happened (just under a minute), and the rest of the time is focused on how you're feeling in the moment in response to the event. You'll use such language as "In this moment I'm feeling" and then describe the qualities of that feeling in your body. You might wish to even close your eyes.
2. At the end of the four minutes, pause and notice how you feel after sharing the story in that way. Does it feel familiar? Unfamiliar?
3. Set a timer for four minutes.
4. For this third round, share the same story from the perspective of you as the hero. The hero's story talks about how you made it through this challenge and how you are able to be here now speaking about it. It may also allude to what you learned and how you grew through this experience.
5. At the end of the four minutes, pause and notice how you feel after sharing the story in that way. Does it feel familiar? Unfamiliar?

Observe and write down in your journal how each style of narrative felt in relation to the others. The first style is called dramatic narrative; its focus is on the narrative, cause and effect, and linear progression of the story (he did this, and then she did that, etc.). The second style of narration is called reflective narrative, as it focuses more on the internal individual experience in the here and now. The third style is called the hero's narrative and focuses on the growth and learning of the experience. The intention here is to be able to catch yourself in a dramatic narrative in which you're focusing on the action and behavior of others, embellishing, and creating more intensity. When you identify yourself in that dramatic narrative, pause, ground, and check in with what is underneath the excitement of sharing it from a dramatic expression— what are you feeling? Place yourself in relation to what you want to share. What feels important to be recognized and acknowledged? What is it that you need? And then see what of that can be shared in a reflective narrative.

REFLECTIVE NARRATIVE PRACTICE

Speak a story you have about yourself or someone else out loud. After every sentence that you speak, pause and ask yourself, "How am I feeling at this moment?" As you're sharing, can you feel your breath, the weight of your body, or a sense of being anchored (connected) to the ground? If you feel disconnected from yourself in the story, pause and come back to connecting to yourself.

STEPPING AWAY FROM STORIES

When you find yourself falling into a story in your mind, use your senses and your breath to pull yourself out of the imagination and back into the present moment. Additional presencing tools include the following:

- ◆ Notice the colors in your room.
- ◆ Listen to the sounds around you.
- ◆ Feel your skin against the floor.
- ◆ Notice the quality of the air and temperature.
- ◆ Begin to list facts of what is occurring, what you know as absolute truth. What lets you know it's true at this moment?

- List all the facts that are story, speculation, or imagination.
- Ask yourself how this story you are telling yourself or others is familiar to past stories you've told.

STOP CREATING STORIES FROM THE PAST

A common revving tactic is to relive and replay stories of the past. The intention of this practice is to notice when you are being engulfed in a memory that activates you, and to then step back from that memory.

1. Notice when you are cycling in a memory of the past. Recognize if you are doing one of the 3 R's: replaying it, reenacting it, or re-creating it.
2. You might imagine temporarily placing the memory in a box. Next, you're going to set poles around the box. Then, see yourself setting yellow "caution" tape around the poles. Section off this box and space that are holding this memory. This is not to say that the memory is bad or dangerous; rather, we are hypnotically cautioning ourselves from using the memory as a device to rev ourselves. If there is an attempt to use this memory to fuel, then you will have to go through the caution tape, which will make the action more conscious.
3. After setting the caution tape, notice the amount of space between you and the memory. You might wish to allow your breath to fill the space.
4. At this point bring your awareness attention back to you. What is present in you?

STOP CREATING STORIES FROM THE IMAGINED FUTURE

Another common revving tactic is to project yourself into potential future scenarios. It's like taking a yoga or meditation class and suddenly, you're in the fantasy of yelling at a past lover or the customer service representative you feel wronged by. This exercise will help you deconstruct the future "memory" and put it away.

1. Notice yourself creating a story about other people or something that is about the future. Again, notice if you are creating something that is not happening in the present moment and if you begin to replay it, reenact it, or re-create different versions of it.

2. Step back. I often use the statement "I'm setting the placemat for someone who's not coming to dinner," "I'm buying a tool for a project I'm not constructing," or "I'm purchasing a motorcycle when I don't even drive"—some version of this.

3. After repeating the statement, take action to deconstruct the future memory. For example, if you are using the first statement about dinner, see yourself starting to put all the dishes back: the cup, plate, glass, silverware, and placemat. Put them back in their respective drawers. And come sit at the table with what and who is actually here. In other words, come back to what is happening in the present moment, such as the yoga or meditation class.

Acknowledgments

EVEN THOUGH THERE WERE MANY, MANY HOURS SPENT ALONE IN A ROOM researching and writing, it truly took a village of support and incredibly expressive and honest human beings to make this book. I am very grateful for each person who contributed to the research and the formation of this manuscript. My dear friends Rae Johnson, Nkem Ndefo, Arielle Schwartz, Caitlin Cady, Heather Lord, and Lailey Wallace for the late-night conversations, honest feedback, and infinite cheerleading. To my Embody Lab family, for always being such a pillar of support and helping me actualize so many of my dreams. Ally Bogard, for sitting with me for many hours deconstructing every sentence and offering your encouragement and beautiful ideas for the development of the book. My incredible family: Mom, Dad, and Nikki, who never faltered on providing their unconditional excitement and love through every step of the way. Luann Fortune, who gently guided me through the processes of being both a researcher and a writer. Theopia Jackson, who believed in me and the pursuit of this work. Elizabeth Osgood Campbell, for all the wonderful development conversations and guiding me through the processes of how to write a book. To Steven Porges, for the many conversations that stimulated the growth of the book.

The staff at Hachette, especially Renée Sedliar, who took a chance on me and so steadfastly believed in getting *Addicted to Drama* out into the world.

Notes

CHAPTER 3: COMMON SYMPTOMS AND IMPACTS
OF ADDICTION TO DRAMA

1. Shelley E. Taylor and Fuschia M. Sirois, *Health Psychology*, 2nd ed. (Toronto, ON: McGraw Hill, 2012); Robert Pearl, "Stress in America: The Causes and Costs," *Forbes*, October 9, 2014, https://www.forbes.com/sites/robertpearl/2014/10/09/stress-in-america-the-causes-and-costs/; E. Kozora et al., "Major Life Stress, Coping Styles, and Social Support in Relation to Psychological Distress in Patients with Systemic Lupus Erythematosus," *Lupus* 14, no. 5 (2005): 363–372, https://doi.org/10.1191/096120330 5lu2094oa.

2. Bessel van der Kolk et al., "Inescapable Shock, Neurotransmitters, and Addiction to Trauma: Toward a Psychobiology of Post-Traumatic Stress," *Biological Psychiatry* 20, no. 3 (1985): 314–325, https://doi.org/10.1016/0006-3223(85)90061-7.

3. Delana Marie Parker, "In Sync: Daily Mood and Diurnal Cortisol Synchronization Between Pre-adolescents and Their Mothers and Fathers," UCLA Electronic Theses and Dissertations, 2017, https://escholarship.org/uc/item/1vb60880; S. J. Dimitroff et al., "Physiological Dynamics of Stress Contagion," *Scientific Reports* 7, no. 1: 1–8 (2017); B. B. Gump and J. A. Kulik, "Stress, Affiliation, and Emotional Contagion," *Journal of Personality and Social Psychology* 72, no. 2 (1997): 305–319, https://doi .org/10.1037/0022-3514.72.2.305.

CHAPTER 5: BUILDING THE PERFECT STORM:
THE BASELINE OF AN ADDICTION TO DRAMA

1. Urie Bronfenbrenner, "Ecological Models of Human Development," in *Readings on the Development of Children*, ed. Mary Gauvain and Michael Cole (New York: Freeman, 1994), 37–43.

2. John A. Astin, "Mind-Body Therapies for the Management of Pain," *Clinical Journal of Pain* 20, no. 1 (2004): 27–32, https://doi.org/10.1097/00002508-200401000 -00006; Robert Kugelmann, "Pain in the Vernacular: Psychological and Physical," *Journal of Health Psychology* 5, no. 3 (2000): 305–313; Naomi I. Eisenberger, "Broken Hearts and Broken Bones: A Neural Perspective on the Similarities Between Social and Physical Pain," *Current Directions in Psychological Science* 21, no. 1 (2012): 42–47, https://doi .org/10.1177/0963721411429455.

3. Kelly A. Davies et al., "Insecure Attachment Style Is Associated with Chronic Widespread Pain," *Pain* 143, no. 3 (2009): 200–205.

4. Alessia Passanisi et al., "Attachment, Self-Esteem and Shame in Emerging Adulthood," *Procedia—Social and Behavioral Sciences* 191, no. 2 (2015): 342–346, https://doi.org/10.1016/j.sbspro.2015.04.552; David R. Cook, "Shame, Attachment, and Addictions: Implications for Family Therapists," *Contemporary Family Therapy* 13 (1991): 405–419, https://doi.org/10.1007/BF00890495; David S. Bennett, Margaret Wolan Sullivan, and Michael Lewis, "Neglected Children, Shame-Proneness, and Depressive Symptoms," *Child Maltreatment* 15, no. 4 (2010): 305–314, https://doi.org /10.1177/1077559510379634.

5. Louis Leung, "Leisure Boredom, Sensation Seeking, Self-Esteem, and Addiction," in *Mediated Interpersonal Communication*, ed. Elly A. Konijn et al. (New York: Routledge, 2008), 359–381.

6. Laura MacPherson et al., "Changes in Sensation Seeking and Risk-Taking Propensity Predict Increases in Alcohol Use Among Early Adolescents," *Alcoholism: Clinical and Experimental Research* 34, no. 8 (2010): 1400–1408, https://doi.org /10.1111/j.1530-0277.2010.01223.x.

CHAPTER 6: WIRED FOR DRAMA: THE ROLE OF STRESS

1. Johannes Klacki and Eva Jones, "Effects of Mortality Salience on Physiological Arousal," *Frontiers in Psychology* 10 (2019): 1893, https://doi.org/10.3389/fpsyg .2019.01893.

2. Hans Selye, "The Evolution of the Stress Concept: The Originator of the Concept Traces Its Development from the Discovery in 1936 of the Alarm Reaction to Modern Therapeutic Applications of Syntoxic and Catatoxic Hormones," *American Scientist* 61, no. 6 (1973): 692–699.

3. Selye, "The Evolution of the Stress Concept."

4. Hans Selye, *The Stress of Life* (New York: McGraw-Hill, 1956).

5. L. Harper, "Epigenetic Inheritance and the Intergenerational Transfer of Experience," *Psychological Bulletin* 131, no. 3 (2005): 340–360, https://doi.org/10.1037 /0033-2909.131.3.340; Teresa I. Sivilli and Thaddeus W. W. Pace, "The Human Dimensions of Resilience: A Theory of Contemplative Practices and Resilience," Garrison Institute, 2014, https://www.garrisoninstitute.org/wp-content/uploads/2016/03

/The_Human_Dimensions_of_Resilience.pdf; D. S. Goldstein and I. J. Kopin, "Evolution of Concepts of Stress," *Stress* 10 (2007): 109–120.

6. Annina Seiler et al., "Adverse Childhood Experiences, Mental Health, and Quality of Life of Chilean Girls Placed in Foster Care: An Exploratory Study," *Psychological Trauma: Theory, Practice, Research, and Policy* 8, no. 2 (2016): 180–187, https://doi .org/10.1037/tra0000037.

7. Vincent J. Felitti et al., "Relationship of Childhood Abuse and Household Dysfunction to Many of the Leading Causes of Death in Adults: The Adverse Childhood Experiences (ACE) Study," *American Journal of Preventive Medicine* 14, no. 4 (1998): 245–258, https://doi.org/10.1016/S0749-3797(98)00017-8.

8. Shanta R. Dube et al., "Childhood Abuse, Household Dysfunction, and the Risk of Attempted Suicide Throughout the Life Span: Findings from the Adverse Childhood Experiences Study," *JAMA* 286, no. 24 (2001): 3089–3096, https://doi.org/10.1001 /jama.286.24.3089.

9. Felitti et al., "Relationship of Childhood Abuse and Household Dysfunction"; Tamara B. Franklin et al., "Epigenetic Transmission of the Impact of Early Stress Across Generations," *Biological Psychiatry* 68, no. 5 (2010): 408–415, https://doi.org/10.1016/j .biopsych.2010.05.036.

10. Ann Louise Hunter, Helen Minnis, and Philip Wilson, "Altered Stress Responses in Children Exposed to Early Adversity: A Systematic Review of Salivary Cortisol Studies," *Stress* 14, no. 6 (2011): 614–626, https://doi.org/10.3109/10253890.2011.577848.

11. L. Harper, "Epigenetic Inheritance and the Intergenerational Transfer of Experience," *Psychological Bulletin* 131, no. 3 (2005): 340–360, https://doi .org/10.1037/0033-2909.131.3.340.

12. T. Canli, "Toward a 'Molecular Psychology' of Personality," in *Handbook of Personality: Theory and Research*, ed. Oliver P. John, Richard W. Robins, and Lawrence A. Pervin (New York: Guilford, 2008), 311–327; R. F. Krueger and W. Johnson, "Behavioral Genetics and Personality," in *Handbook of Personality: Theory and Research*, ed. Oliver P. John, Richard W. Robins, and Lawrence A. Pervin (New York: Guilford, 2008), 287–310.

13. Natan P. Kellermann, "Epigenetic Transmission of Holocaust Trauma: Can Nightmares Be Inherited?" *Israel Journal of Psychiatry and Related Sciences* 50, no. 1 (2013): 33.

14. Hunter, Minnis, and Wilson, "Altered Stress Responses in Children Exposed to Early Adversity."

15. Urie Bronfenbrenner, "Ecological Models of Human Development," in *Readings on the Development of Children*, ed. Mary Gauvain and Michael Cole (New York: Freeman, 1994), 37–43.

16. Sara R. Jaffee et al., "Chaotic Homes and Children's Disruptive Behavior: A Longitudinal Cross-Lagged Twin Study," *Psychological Science* 23, no. 6 (2012): 643–650, https://doi.org/10.1177/0956797611431693.

17. Bernard J. Baars, *In the Theater of Consciousness: The Workspace of the Mind* (New York: Oxford University Press, 1997).

18. Elaine N. Aron, Arthur Aron, and Jadzia Jagiellowicz, "Sensory Processing Sensitivity: A Review in the Light of the Evolution of Biological Responsivity," *Personality and Social Psychology Review* 16, no. 3 (2012): 262–282, https://doi .org/10.1177/1088868311434213.

19. Aron, Aron, and Jagiellowicz, "Sensory Processing Sensitivity"; John E. Richters and Everett Waters, "Attachment and Socialization: The Positive Side of Social Influence," in *Social Influences and Socialization in Infancy*, ed. Saul Feinman and Michael Lewis (Cleveland: Plenum Press, 1991), 185–213.

20. Richters and Waters, "Attachment and Socialization."

21. Antonia Bifulco et al., "Adult Attachment Style as Mediator Between Childhood Neglect/Abuse and Adult Depression and Anxiety," *Social Psychiatry and Psychiatric Epidemiology* 41, no. 10 (2006): 796–805, https://doi.org/10.1007/s00127-006-0101-z; K. A. Davies et al., "Insecure Attachment Style Is Associated with Chronic Widespread Pain," *Pain* 143, no. 3 (2009): 200–2005, https://doi.org/10.1016/j.pain.2009.02.013.

22. E. Waters, D. Hay, and J. Richters, "Infant-Parent Attachment and the Origins of Prosocial and Antisocial Behavior," in *Development of Antisocial and Prosocial Behavior: Research, Theories, and Issues*, ed. Dan Olweus, Jack Block, and Marian Radke Yarrow (New York: Academic Press, 1986), 97–125.

CHAPTER 7: CAUGHT IN THE GRIP: WHEN A SURVIVAL STRATEGY BECOMES AN ADDICTION

1. Bruce E. Compas et al., "Coping with Stress During Childhood and Adolescence: Problems, Progress, and Potential in Theory and Research," *Psychological Bulletin* 127, no. 1 (2001): 87–127, https://doi.org/10.1037/0033-2909.127.1.87.

2. Compas et al., "Coping with Stress During Childhood and Adolescence."

3. Alan I. Leshner, "Addiction Is a Brain Disease, and It Matters," *Science* 278, no. 5335 (1997): 45–47, https://doi.org/10.1126/science.278.5335.45; A. Thomas McLellan et al., "Drug Dependence, a Chronic Medical Illness: Implications for Treatment, Insurance, and Outcomes Evaluation," *JAMA* 284, no. 13 (2000): 1689–1695, https:// doi.org/10.1001/jama.284.13.1689.

4. Mark Griffiths, "A 'Components' Model of Addiction Within a Biopsychosocial Framework," *Journal of Substance Use* 10, no. 4 (2005): 191–197, https://doi.org/10.1080 /14659890500114359.

5. J. D. Kruschwitz et al., "High Thrill and Adventure Seeking Is Associated with Reduced Interoceptive Sensitivity: Evidence for an Altered Sex–Specific Homeostatic Processing in High–Sensation Seekers," *European Journal of Personality* 28, no. 5 (2014), 472–481, https://doi.org/10.1002%2Fper.1946.

6. Johann Hari, *Chasing the Scream: The First and Last Days of the War on Drugs* (New York: Bloomsbury Publishing USA, 2015).

7. Bruce K. Alexander, Patricia Hadaway, and Robert Coambs, "Rat Park Chronicle," *British Columbia Medical Journal* 22, no. 2 (1980): 32–45; Bruce K. Alexander, "The Disease and Adaptive Models of Addiction: A Framework Evaluation," *Journal of Drug Issues* 17, no. 1 (1987): 47–66, https://doi.org/10.1177/002204268701700104.

8. R. Gurung, B. Sarason, and I. Sarason, "Close Personal Relationships and Health Outcomes: A Key to the Role of Social Support," in *Handbook of Personal Relationships: Theory, Research and Interventions*, 2nd ed., ed. Steve Duck et al., (Chichester, UK: Wiley, 1997): 547–573; John F. Kelly and Rudolf Moos, "Dropout from 12-Step Self-Help Groups: Prevalence, Predictors, and Counteracting Treatment Influences," *Journal of Substance Abuse Treatment* 24, no. 3 (2003): 241–250.

9. Gabor Maté, "Addiction: Childhood Trauma, Stress and the Biology of Addiction," *Journal of Restorative Medicine* 1, no. 1 (2012): 56–63.

10. Gabor Maté, *In the Realm of Hungry Ghosts: Close Encounters with Addiction* (Berkeley: North Atlantic Books, 2010).

11. Andreas von Leupoldt et al., "Dyspnea and Pain Share Emotion-Related Brain Network," *NeuroImage* 48, no. 1 (2009): 200–206, https://doi.org/10.1016/j.neuroimage.2009.06.015.

12. Shelley E. Taylor and Fuschia M. Sirois, *Health Psychology*, 2nd ed. (Toronto, ON: McGraw Hill, 2012).

13. Francis J. Keefe et al., "Coping with Rheumatoid Arthritis Pain: Catastrophizing as a Maladaptive Strategy," *Pain* 37, no. 1 (1989): 51–56, https://doi.org/10.1016/0304-3959(89)90152-8; Steven Stosny, *Treating Attachment Abuse: A Compassionate Approach* (New York: Springer, 1995); Michael J. Sullivan et al., "Theoretical Perspectives on the Relation Between Catastrophizing and Pain," *Clinical Journal of Pain* 17, no. 1 (2001): 52–64, https://doi.org/10.1097/00002508-200103000-00008.

14. Hillel Glover, "Emotional Numbing: A Possible Endorphin-Mediated Phenomenon Associated with Post-Traumatic Stress Disorders and Other Allied Psychopathologic States," *Journal of Traumatic Stress* 5, no. 4 (1992): 643–675, https://doi.org/10.1002/jts.2490050413; Billi Gordon, "Excessive Attention-Seeking and Drama Addiction: Portrait of Neglect," *Obesely Speaking* (blog), *Psychology Today*, November 4, 2014, https://www.psychologytoday.com/us/blog/obesely-speaking/201411/excessive-attention-seeking-and-drama-addiction; Bessel van der Kolk et al., "Inescapable Shock, Neurotransmitters, and Addiction to Trauma: Toward a Psychobiology of Post-Traumatic Stress," *Biological Psychiatry* 20, no. 3 (1985): 314–325, https://doi.org/10.1016/0006-3223(85)90061-7.

15. Maté, *In the Realm of Hungry Ghosts*.

16. Martin P. Paulus, "Decision-Making Dysfunctions in Psychiatry—Altered Homeostatic Processing?" *Science* 218, no. 5850 (2007): 602–606, https://doi.org/10.1126/science.1142997.

17. Caroline Durlik and Manos Tsakiris, "Decreased Interoceptive Accuracy Following Social Exclusion," *International Journal of Psychophysiology* 96, no. 1 (2015):

57–63; Lori Haase et al., "When the Brain Does Not Adequately Feel the Body: Links Between Low Resilience and Interoception," *Biological Psychology* 113 (2016): 37–45; J. D. Kruschwitz et al., "High Thrill and Adventure Seeking Is Associated with Reduced Interoceptive Sensitivity: Evidence for an Altered Sex–Specific Homeostatic Processing in High–Sensation Seekers," *European Journal of Personality* 28, no. 5 (2014): 472–481.

18. Ali Cheetham et al., "The Role of Affective Dysregulation in Drug Addiction," *Clinical Psychology Review* 30, no. 6 (2010): 621–634; William W. Stoops and David N. Kearns, "Decision-Making in Addiction: Current Knowledge, Clinical Implications and Future Directions," *Pharmacology Biochemistry and Behavior* 164 (2018): 1–3.

19. Jean M. Williams, Phyllis Tonymon, and Mark B. Andersen, "Effects of Life-Event Stress on Anxiety and Peripheral Narrowing," *Behavioral Medicine* 16, no. 4 (1990): 174–181; Tracie J., Rogers and Daniel M. Landers., "Mediating Effects of Peripheral Vision in the Life Event Stress/Athletic Injury Relationship," *Journal of Sport and Exercise Psychology* 27, no. 3 (2005): 271–288.

20. Jacek Kolacz, Katja K. Kovacic, and Stephen W. Porges, "Traumatic Stress and the Autonomic Brain-Gut Connection in Development: Polyvagal Theory as an Integrative Framework for Psychosocial and Gastrointestinal Pathology," *Developmental Psychobiology* 61, no. 5 (2019): 796–809, https://doi.org/10.1002/dev.21852.

21. Jacek Kolacz, Gregory F. Lewis, and Stephen W. Porges, "The Integration of Vocal Communication and Biobehavioral State Regulation in Mammals: A Polyvagal Hypothesis," in *Handbook of Behavioral Neuroscience*, ed. Stefan M. Brudzynski (London: Elsevier, 2018), 23–34, https://doi.org/10.1016/B978-0-12-809600-0.00003-2.

22. Elizabeth A. Krusemark et al., "When the Sense of Smell Meets Emotion: Anxiety-State-Dependent Olfactory Processing and Neural Circuitry Adaptation," *Journal of Neuroscience* 33, no. 39 (2013): 15324–15332; https://doi.org/10.1523/JNEUROSCI.1835-13.2013.

23. Nancy K. Dess and David Edelheit, "The Bitter with the Sweet: The Taste/Stress/Temperament Nexus," *Biological Psychology* 48, no. 2 (1998): 103–119.

24. F. Ozel, "Time Pressure and Stress as a Factor During Emergency Egress," *Safety Science* 38. no. 2 (2001): 95–107.

25. John H. Riskind and Carolyn C. Gotay, "Physical Posture: Could It Have Regulatory or Feedback Effects on Motivation and Emotion?" *Motivation and Emotion* 6, no. 3 (1982): 273–298, https://doi.org/10.1007/BF00992249.

26. Susan M. Andersen, Inga Reznik, and Lenora M. Manzella, "Eliciting Facial Affect, Motivation, and Expectancies in Transference: Significant-Other Representations in Social Relations," *Journal of Personality and Social Psychology* 71, no. 6 (1996): 1108, https://doi.org/10.1037/0022-3514.71.6.1108; Susan. M. Andersen et al., "Transference in Social Perception: The Role of Chronic Accessibility in Significant-Other Representations," *Journal of Personality and Social Psychology* 69, no. 1 (1995): 41–57, https://doi.org/10.1037/0022-3514.69.1.41; Serena Chen, Susan M. Andersen, and

Katrina Hinkley, "Triggering Transference: Examining the Role of Applicability in the Activation and Use of Significant-Other Representations in Social Perception," *Social Cognition* 17, no. 3 (1999): 332–365, https://doi.org/10.1521/soco.1999.17.3.332.

27. Robert Soussignan, "Duchenne Smile, Emotional Experience, and Autonomic Reactivity: A Test of the Facial Feedback Hypothesis," *Emotion* 2, no. 1 (2002): 52.

28. Sally Goddard Blythe, *Attention, Balance and Coordination: The A.B.C. of Learning Success* (West Sussex, UK; John Wiley & Sons, 2009).

CHAPTER 8: THE DRAMA CYCLE: CHAOS IN THE BLINK OF AN EYE

1. George F. Koob, "The Dark Side of Emotion: The Addiction Perspective," *European Journal of Pharmacology* 753 (2015): 73–87, https://doi.org/10.1016/j.ejphar.2014.11.044.

2. Lauren M. Bylsma, Ad J. J. M. Vingerhoets, and Jonathan Rottenberg, "When Is Crying Cathartic? An International Study," *Journal of Social and Clinical Psychology* 27, no. 10 (2008): 1165–1187.

3. Arielle Tambini et al., "Emotional Brain States Carry Over and Enhance Future Memory Formation," *Nature Neuroscience* 20 (2017): 271–278, https://doi.org/10.1038/nn.4468.

4. Jeremy Adams and Robert J. Kirkby, "Excessive Exercise as an Addiction: A Review," *Addiction Research & Theory* 10, no. 5 (2002): 415–437; Falk Kiefer et al., "Is Withdrawal-Induced Anxiety in Alcoholism Based on β-Endorphin Deficiency?" *Psychopharmacology* 162, no. 4 (2002): 433–437; Joseph Volpicelli et al., "The Role of Uncontrollable Trauma in the Development of PTSD and Alcohol Addiction," *Alcohol Research & Health* 23, no. 4 (1999): 256.

CHAPTER 9: OVERSTIMULATED AND UNDERCONNECTED: THE GLOBAL DRUG OF DRAMA

1. Brian Resnick, Julia Belluz, and Eliza Barclay, "Is Our Constant Use of Digital Technologies Affecting Our Brain Health? We Asked 11 Experts," Vox, February 26, 2019, https://www.vox.com/science-and-health/2018/11/28/18102745/cellphone-distraction-brain-health-screens-kids.

2. Annette Hill, *Reality TV: Audiences and Popular Factual Television* (New York: Routledge, 2005); Julia Stoll, "Most Popular TV Genres in the U.S. 2017," Statista, January 13, 2021, https://www.statista.com/statistics/201565/most-popular-genres-in-us-primetime-tv/.

3. John McDonough and Karen Egolf, *The Advertising Age Encyclopedia of Advertising* (New York: Routledge, 2015); Daniel Romer, Kathleen Hall Jamieson, and Sean Aday, "Television News and the Cultivation of Fear of Crime," *Journal of Communication* 53, no. 1 (2003): 88–104, https://doi.org/10.1111/j.1460-2466.2003.tb03007.x.

4. Ted Chiricos, Kathy Padgett, and Marc Gertz, "Fear, TV News, and the Reality of Crime," *Criminology* 38, no. 3 (2000): 755–786, https://doi.org/10.1111/j.1745 -9125.2000.tb00905.x; Dennis T. Lowry, Tarn Ching Josephine Nio, and Dennis W. Leitner, "Setting the Public Fear Agenda: A Longitudinal Analysis of Network TV Crime Reporting, Public Perceptions of Crime, and FBI Crime Statistics," *Journal of Communication* 53, no. 1 (2003): 61–73, https://doi.org/10.1111/j.1460-2466.2003 .tb03005.x; Romer, Jamieson, and Aday, "Television News and the Cultivation of Fear of Crime."

5. Amrisha Vaish, Tobias Grossman, and Amanda Woodward, "Not All Emotions Are Created Equal: The Negativity Bias in Social-Emotional Development," *Psychological Bulletin* 134, no. 3 (2008): 383–403, https://doi.org/10.1037/0033-2909 .134.3.383.

6. Cristina M. Alberini, "Long-Term Memories: The Good, the Bad, and the Ugly," *Cerebrum* 2010 (2010): 21, https://www.ncbi.nlm.nih.gov/pmc/articles/PMC3574792/.

7. Benjamin E. Hilbig, "Good Things Don't Come Easy (to Mind)," *Experimental Psychology* (2011), https://doi.org/10.1027/1618-3169/a000124.

8. John R. Hibbing, Kevin B. Smith, and John R. Alford, "Differences in Negativity Bias Underlie Variations in Political Ideology," *Behavioral and Brain Sciences* 37 (2014): 297–307; Scott O. Lilienfeld and Robert D. Latzman, "Threat Bias, Not Negativity Bias, Underpins Differences in Political Ideology," *Behavioral and Brain Sciences* 37, no. 3 (2014): 318.

9. Christine Liebrecht, Lettica Hustinx, and Margot van Mulken, "The Relative Power of Negativity: The Influence of Language Intensity on Perceived Strength," *Journal of Language and Social Psychology* 38, no. 2 (2019): 170–193; Paul Rozin and Edward B. Royzman, "Negativity Bias, Negativity Dominance, and Contagion," *Personality and Social Psychology Review* 5, no. 4 (2001): 296–320.

10. Gloria Mark et al., "Email Duration, Batching and Self-Interruption: Patterns of Email Use on Productivity and Stress," *CHI '16L Proceedings of the 2016 CHI Conference on Human Factors in Computing Systems* (2016): 1717–1728, https://doi .org/10.1145/2858036.2858262.

11. Jonathan Spira and Joshua Feintuch, "The Cost of Not Paying Attention: How Interruptions Impact Knowledge Worker Productivity," Information Overload Research Group, January 1, 2015, https://iorgforum.org/wp-content/uploads/2011/06 /CostOfNotPayingAttention.BasexReport1.pdf.

12. E. Alison Holman, Dana Rose Garfin, and Roxane Cohen Silver, "Media's Role in Broadcasting Acute Stress Following the Boston Marathon Bombings," *Proceedings of the National Academy of Sciences* 111, no. 1 (2014): 93–98.

13. Stephanie J. Dimitroff et al., "Physiological Dynamics of Stress Contagion," *Scientific Reports* 7, no. 1 (2017): 1–8.

14. Christian Collet et al., "Autonomic Nervous System Correlates in Movement Observation and Motor Imagery," *Frontiers in Human Neuroscience* 7 (2013): 415.

15. Brock Bastian, Jolanda Jetten, and Laura J. Ferris, "Pain as Social Glue: Shared Pain Increases Cooperation," *Psychological Science* 25, no. 11 (2014): 2079–2085, https://doi.org/10.1177/0956797614545886.

16. Juan Herrero et al., "Socially Connected but Still Isolated: Smartphone Addiction Decreases Social Support over Time," *Social Science Computer Review* 37, no. 1 (2019): 73–88.

Bibliography

Adams, Jeremy, and Robert J. Kirkby. "Excessive Exercise as an Addiction: A Review." *Addiction Research & Theory* 10, no. 5 (2002): 415–437.

Alberini, Cristina M. "Long-Term Memories: The Good, the Bad, and the Ugly." *Cerebrum* 2010 (2010): 21. https://www.ncbi.nlm.nih.gov/pmc/articles/PMC3574792.

Alexander, Bruce K. "The Disease and Adaptive Models of Addiction: A Framework Evaluation," *Journal of Drug Issues* 17, no. 1 (1987): 47–66. https://doi.org/10.1177/002204268701700104.

Alexander, Bruce K., Patricia Hadaway, and Robert Coambs. "Rat Park Chronicle." *British Columbia Medical Journal* 22, no. 2 (1980): 32–45.

Andersen, Susan M., Noah S. Glassman, Serena Chen, and Steve W. Cole. "Transference in Social Perception: The Role of Chronic Accessibility in Significant-Other Representations." *Journal of Personality and Social Psychology* 69, no. 1 (1995): 41–57. https://doi.org/10.1037/0022-3514.69.1.41.

Andersen, Susan M., Inga Reznik, and Lenora M. Manzella. "Eliciting Facial Affect, Motivation, and Expectancies in Transference: Significant-Other Representations in Social Relations." *Journal of Personality and Social Psychology* 71, no. 6 (1996): 1108. https://doi.org/10.1037/0022-3514.71.6.1108.

Aron, Elaine N., Arthur Aron, and Jadzia Jagiellowicz. "Sensory Processing Sensitivity: A Review in the Light of the Evolution of Biological Responsivity." *Personality and Social Psychology Review* 16, no. 3 (2012): 262–282. https://doi.org/10.1177/1088868311434213.

Astin, John A. "Mind-Body Therapies for the Management of Pain." *Clinical Journal of Pain* 20, no. 1 (2004): 27–32. https://doi.org/10.1097/00002508-200401000-00006.

Baars, Bernard J. *In the Theater of Consciousness: The Workspace of the Mind.* New York: Oxford University Press, 1997.

Bastian, Brock, Jolanda Jetten, and Laura J. Ferris. "Pain as Social Glue: Shared Pain Increases Cooperation." *Psychological Science* 25, no. 11 (2014): 2079–2085. https://doi.org/10.1177/0956797614545886.

Bennett, David S., Margaret Wolan Sullivan, and Michael Lewis. "Neglected Children, Shame-Proneness, and Depressive Symptoms," *Child Maltreatment* 15, no. 4 (2010): 305–314. https://doi.org/10.1177/1077559510379634.

Bifulco, Antonia, Junghye Kwon, Catherine Jacobs, Patricia M. Moran, Amanda Bunn, and Nils Beer. "Adult Attachment Style as Mediator Between Childhood Neglect/Abuse and Adult Depression and Anxiety." *Social Psychiatry and Psychiatric Epidemiology* 41, no. 10 (2006): 796–805. https://doi.org/10.1007/s00127-006-0101-z.

Blackburn-Munro, G., and R. E. Blackburn-Munro. "Chronic Pain, Chronic Stress and Depression: Coincidence or Consequence?" *Journal of Neuroendocrinology* 13, no. 12 (2001): 1009–1023. https://doi.org/10.1046/j.0007-1331.2001.00727.x.

Blythe, Sally Goddard. *Attention, Balance and Coordination: The A.B.C. of Learning Success.* West Sussex, UK; John Wiley & Sons, 2009.

Bronfenbrenner, Urie. "Ecological Models of Human Development." *In Readings on the Development of Children*, edited by Mary Gauvain and Michael Cole, 37–43. New York: Freeman, 1994.

Bylsma, Lauren M., Ad J. J. M. Vingerhoets, and Jonathan Rottenberg. "When Is Crying Cathartic? An International Study." *Journal of Social and Clinical Psychology* 27, no. 10 (2008): 1165–1187.

Canli, T. "Toward a 'Molecular Psychology' of Personality." In *Handbook of Personality: Theory and Research*, edited by Oliver P. John, Richard W. Robins, and Lawrence A. Pervin, 311–327. New York: Guilford, 2008.

Carlson, Neil R. *Foundations of Behavioral Neuroscience.* New York: Pearson Education, 2014.

Chapman, Gary D. *The 5 Love Languages.* Farmington Hills, MI: Walker Large Print, 2010.

Cheetham, Ali, Nicholas B. Allen, Murat Yücel, and Dan I. Lubman. "The Role of Affective Dysregulation in Drug Addiction." *Clinical Psychology Review* 30, no. 6 (2010): 621–634.

Chen, Serena, Susan M. Andersen, and Katrina Hinkley. "Triggering Transference: Examining the Role of Applicability in the Activation and Use of Significant-Other Representations in Social Perception." *Social Cognition* 17, no. 3 (1999): 332–365. https://doi.org/10.1521/soco.1999.17.3.332.

Chiricos, Ted, Kathy Padgett, and Marc Gertz. "Fear, TV News, and the Reality of Crime." *Criminology* 38, no. 3 (2000): 755–786. https://doi.org/10.1111/j.1745-9125.2000.tb00905.x.

Collet, Christian, Franck Di Rienzo, N. El Hoyek, and Aymeric Guillot. "Autonomic Nervous System Correlates in Movement Observation and Motor Imagery." *Frontiers in Human Neuroscience* 7 (2013): 415.

Compas, Bruce E., Jennifer K. Connor-Smith, Heidi Saltzman, Alexandria Harding Thomsen, and Martha E. Wadsworth. "Coping with Stress During Childhood and Adolescence: Problems, Progress, and Potential in Theory and Research." *Psychological Bulletin* 127, no. 1 (2001): 87–127. https://doi.org/10.1037/0033-2909.127.1.87.

Cook, David R., "Shame, Attachment, and Addictions: Implications for Family Therapists." *Contemporary Family Therapy* 13 (1991): 405–419, https://doi.org/10.1007/BF00890495.

Davies, Kelly A., G. J. Macfarlane, J. McBeth, Richard K. Morriss, and Chris Dickens. "Insecure Attachment Style Is Associated with Chronic Widespread Pain." *Pain* 143, no. 3 (2009): 200–205. https://doi.org/10.1016/j.pain.2009.02.013.

Dess, Nancy K., and David Edelheit. "The Bitter with the Sweet: The Taste/Stress/Temperament Nexus." *Biological Psychology* 48, no. 2 (1998): 103–119.

Dimitroff, Stephanie J., Omid Kardan, Elizabeth A. Necka, Jean Decety, Marc G. Berman, and Greg J. Norman. "Physiological Dynamics of Stress Contagion." *Scientific Reports* 7, no. 1 (2017): 1–8.

Dube, Shanta R., Robert F. Anda, Vincent J. Felitti, Daniel P. Chapman, David F. Williamson, and Wayne H. Giles. "Childhood Abuse, Household Dysfunction, and the Risk of Attempted Suicide Throughout the Life Span: Findings from the Adverse Childhood Experiences Study." *JAMA* 286, no. 24 (2001): 3089–3096. https://doi.org/10.1001/jama.286.24.3089.

Durlik, Caroline, and Manos Tsakiris. "Decreased Interoceptive Accuracy Following Social Exclusion." *International Journal of Psychophysiology* 96, no. 1 (2015): 57–63.

Eisenberger, Naomi I. "Broken Hearts and Broken Bones: A Neural Perspective on the Similarities Between Social and Physical Pain." *Current Directions in Psychological Science* 21, no. 1 (2012): 42–47. https://doi.org/10.1177/0963721411429455.

Felitti, Vincent J., Robert F Anda, Dale Nordenberg, David F. Williamson, Alison M. Spitz, Valerie Edwards, Mary P. Koss, and James S. Marks. "Relationship of Childhood Abuse and Household Dysfunction to Many of the Leading Causes of Death in Adults: The Adverse Childhood Experiences (ACE) Study." *American Journal of Preventive Medicine* 14, no. 4 (1998): 245–258. https://doi.org/10.1016/S0749-3797(98)00017-8.

Fogel, Alan. *Body Sense: The Science and Practice of Embodied Self-Awareness* (Norton Series on Interpersonal Neurobiology). New York: W. W. Norton & Company, 2013.

Franklin, Tamara B., Holger Russig, Isabelle C. Weiss, Johannes Gräff, Natacha Linder, Aubin Michalon, Sandor Vizi, and Isabelle M. Mansuy. "Epigenetic Transmission of the Impact of Early Stress Across Generations." *Biological Psychiatry* 68, no. 5 (2010): 408–415. https://doi.org/10.1016/j.biopsych.2010.05.036.

Gardiner, Harry W., Jay D. Mutter, and Corinne Kosmitzki. *Lives Across Cultures: Cross-Cultural Human Development.* Boston: Allyn & Bacon, 1998.

Glover, Hillel. "Emotional Numbing: A Possible Endorphin-Mediated Phenomenon Associated with Post-Traumatic Stress Disorders and Other Allied

Psychopathologic States." *Journal of Traumatic Stress* 5, no. 4 (1992): 643–675. https://doi.org/10.1002/jts.2490050413.

Goldstein, D. S., and I. J. Kopin." Evolution of Concepts of Stress. *Stress* 10 (2007): 109–120.

Gordon, Billi. "Excessive Attention-Seeking and Drama Addiction: Portrait of Neglect." *Obesely Speaking* (blog), *Psychology Today*, November 4, 2014. https://www.psychologytoday.com/us/blog/obesely-speaking/201411/excessive-attention-seeking-and-drama-addiction.

Griffiths, Mark. "A 'Components' Model of Addiction Within a Biopsychosocial Framework." *Journal of Substance Use* 10, no. 4 (2005): 191–197. https://doi.org/10.1080/14659890500114359.

Gump, B. B., and J. A. Kulik. "Stress, Affiliation, and Emotional Contagion." *Journal of Personality and Social Psychology* 72, no. 2 (1997): 305–319. https://doi.org/10.1037/0022-3514.72.2.305.

Gurung, R., B. Sarason, and I. Sarason. "Close Personal Relationships and Health Outcomes: A Key to the Role of Social Support." In *Handbook of Personal Relationships: Theory, Research and Interventions*, 2nd ed., edited by Steve Duck et al. Chichester, UK: Wiley (1997): 547–573.

Haase, Lori, Jennifer L. Stewart, Brittany Youssef, April C. May, Sara Isakovic, Alan N. Simmons, Douglas C. Johnson, Eric G. Potterat, and Martin P. Paulus. "When the Brain Does Not Adequately Feel the Body: Links Between Low Resilience and Interoception." *Biological Psychology* 113 (2016): 37–45.

Hari, Johann. *Chasing the Scream: The First and Last Days of the War on Drugs*. New York: Bloomsbury Publishing USA, 2015.

Harper, L. "Epigenetic Inheritance and the Intergenerational Transfer of Experience." *Psychological Bulletin* 131, no. 3 (2005): 340–360. https://doi.org/10.1037/0033-2909.131.3.340.

Herrero, Juan, Alberto Urueña, Andrea Torres, and Antonio Hidalgo. "Socially Connected but Still Isolated: Smartphone Addiction Decreases Social Support over Time." *Social Science Computer Review* 37, no. 1 (2019): 73–88.

Hibbing, John R., Kevin B. Smith, and John R. Alford. "Differences in Negativity Bias Underlie Variations in Political Ideology." *Behavioral and Brain Sciences* 37 (2014): 297–307.

Hilbig, Benjamin E. "Good Things Don't Come Easy (to Mind)." *Experimental Psychology* 59, no. 1 (2011): 38–46.

Hill, Annette. *Reality TV: Audiences and Popular Factual Television*. New York: Routledge, 2005.

Holman, E. Alison, Dana Rose Garfin, and Roxane Cohen Silver. "Media's Role in Broadcasting Acute Stress Following the Boston Marathon Bombings." *Proceedings of the National Academy of Sciences* 111, no. 1 (2014): 93–98.

Horvath, Paula, and Marvin Zuckerman. "Sensation Seeking, Risk Appraisal, and Risky Behavior." *Personality and Individual Differences* 14, no. 1 (1993): 41–52. https://doi.org/10.1016/0191-8869(93)90173-Z.

Hunter, Ann Louise, Helen Minnis, and Philip Wilson. "Altered Stress Responses in Children Exposed to Early Adversity: A Systematic Review of Salivary Cortisol Studies." *Stress* 14, no. 6 (2011): 614–626. https://doi.org/10.3109/10253890.2011.577848.

Jaffee, Sara R., Ken B. Hanscombe, Claire M. A. Haworth, Oliver S. P. Davis, and Robert Plomin, "Chaotic Homes and Children's Disruptive Behavior: A Longitudinal Cross-Lagged Twin Study," *Psychological Science* 23, no. 6 (2012): 643–650, https://doi.org/10.1177/0956797611431693.

Keefe, Francis J., Gregory K. Brown, Kenneth A. Wallston, and David S. Caldwell. "Coping with Rheumatoid Arthritis Pain: Catastrophizing as a Maladaptive Strategy." *Pain* 37, no. 1 (1989): 51–56. https://doi.org/10.1016/0304-3959(89)90152-8.

Kellermann, Natan P. "Epigenetic Transmission of Holocaust Trauma: Can Nightmares Be Inherited?" *Israel Journal of Psychiatry and Related Sciences* 50, no. 1 (2013): 33.

Kelly, John F., and Rudolf Moos. "Dropout from 12-Step Self-Help Groups: Prevalence, Predictors, and Counteracting Treatment Influences." *Journal of Substance Abuse Treatment* 24, no. 3 (2003): 241–250.

Kiefer, Falk, Mirko Horntrich, Holger Jahn, and Klaus Wiedemann. "Is Withdrawal-Induced Anxiety in Alcoholism Based on β-Endorphin Deficiency?" *Psychopharmacology* 162, no. 4 (2002): 433–437.

Klacki, Johannes, and Eva Jones, "Effects of Mortality Salience on Physiological Arousal," *Frontiers in Psychology* 10 (2019): 1893. https://doi.org/10.3389/fpsyg.2019.01893.

Kolacz, Jacek, Katja K. Kovacic, and Stephen W. Porges. "Traumatic Stress and the Autonomic Brain-Gut Connection in Development: Polyvagal Theory as an Integrative Framework for Psychosocial and Gastrointestinal Pathology." *Developmental Psychobiology* 61, no. 5 (2019): 796–809. https://doi.org/10.1002/dev.21852.

Kolacz, Jacek, Gregory F. Lewis, and Stephen W. Porges. "The Integration of Vocal Communication and Biobehavioral State Regulation in Mammals: A Polyvagal Hypothesis." In *Handbook of Behavioral Neuroscience*, edited by Stefan M. Brudzynski, 23–34. London: Elsevier, 2018. https://doi.org/10.1016/B978-0-12-809600-0.00003-2.

Koob, George F. "The Dark Side of Emotion: The Addiction Perspective." *European Journal of Pharmacology* 753 (2015): 73–87. doi:10.1016/j.ejphar.2014.11.044.

Kozora, E., M. C. Ellison, J. A. Waxmonsky, F. S. Wamboldt, and T. L. Patterson. "Major Life Stress, Coping Styles, and Social Support in Relation to Psychological Distress in Patients with Systemic Lupus Erythematosus." *Lupus* 14, no. 5 (2005): 363–372. https://doi.org/10.1191/0961203305lu2094oa.

Krueger, R. F., and W. Johnson. "Behavioral Genetics and Personality." In *Handbook of Personality: Theory and Research*, edited by Oliver P. John, Richard W. Robins, and Lawrence A. Pervin, 287–310. New York: Guilford, 2008.

Kruschwitz, J. D., U. Lueken, A. Wold, H. Walter, and M. P. Paulus. "High Thrill and Adventure Seeking Is Associated with Reduced Interoceptive Sensitivity: Evidence for an Altered Sex–Specific Homeostatic Processing in High–Sensation Seekers." *European Journal of Personality* 28, no. 5 (2014), 472–481. https://doi .org/10.1002%2Fper.1946.

Krusemark, Elizabeth A., Lucas R. Novak, Darren R. Gitelman, and Wen Li. "When the Sense of Smell Meets Emotion: Anxiety-State-Dependent Olfactory Processing and Neural Circuitry Adaptation." *Journal of Neuroscience* 33, no. 39 (2013): 15324–15332. https://doi.org/10.1523/JNEUROSCI.1835-13.2013.

Kugelmann, Robert. "Pain in the Vernacular: Psychological and Physical." *Journal of Health Psychology* 5, no. 3 (2000): 305–313.

Leshner, Alan I. "Addiction Is a Brain Disease, and It Matters." *Science* 278, no. 5335 (1997): 45–47. https://doi.org/10.1126/science.278.5335.45.

Leung, Lewis, "Leisure Boredom, Sensation Seeking, Self-Esteem, and Addiction," in *Mediated Interpersonal Communication*, edited by Elly A. Konijn, Sonja Utz, Martin Tanis, and Susan B. Barnes, 359–381. New York: Routledge, 2008.

Liebrecht, Christine, Lettica Hustinx, and Margot van Mulken. "The Relative Power of Negativity: The Influence of Language Intensity on Perceived Strength." *Journal of Language and Social Psychology* 38, no. 2 (2019): 170–193.

Lilienfeld, Scott O., and Robert D. Latzman. "Threat Bias, Not Negativity Bias, Underpins Differences in Political Ideology." *Behavioral and Brain Sciences* 37, no. 3 (2014): 318.

Lowry, Dennis T., Tarn Ching Josephine Nio, and Dennis W. Leitner. "Setting the Public Fear Agenda: A Longitudinal Analysis of Network TV Crime Reporting, Public Perceptions of Crime, and FBI Crime Statistics." *Journal of Communication* 53, no. 1 (2003): 61–73. https://doi.org/10.1111/j.1460-2466.2003.tb03005.x.

MacPherson, Laura, Jessica F. Magidson, Elizabeth K. Reynolds, Christopher W. Kahler, and C. W. Lejuez. "Changes in Sensation Seeking and Risk-Taking Propensity Predict Increases in Alcohol Use Among Early Adolescents." *Alcoholism: Clinical and Experimental Research* 34, no. 8 (2010): 1400–1408. https://doi.org /10.1111/j.1530-0277.2010.01223.x.

Mark, Gloria, Shamsi T. Iqbal, Mary Czerwinski, Paul Johns, Akane Sano, and Yuliya Lutchyn. "Email Duration, Batching and Self-Interruption: Patterns of Email Use on Productivity and Stress." *CHI '16L Proceedings of the 2016 CHI Conference on Human Factors in Computing Systems* (2016): 1717–1728. https://doi .org/10.1145/2858036.2858262.

Maté, Gabor. "Addiction: Childhood Trauma, Stress and the Biology of Addiction." *Journal of Restorative Medicine* 1, no. 1 (2012): 56–63.

————. *In the Realm of Hungry Ghosts: Close Encounters with Addiction.* Berkeley: North Atlantic Books, 2010.

McDonough, John, and Karen Egolf. *The Advertising Age Encyclopedia of Advertising.* New York: Routledge, 2015.

McLellan, A. Thomas, David C. Lewis, Charles P. O'Brien, and Herbert D. Kleber. "Drug Dependence, a Chronic Medical Illness: Implications for Treatment, Insurance, and Outcomes Evaluation." *JAMA* 284, no. 13 (2000): 1689–1695. https://doi.org/10.1001/jama.284.13.1689.

Ozel, F. "Time Pressure and Stress as a Factor During Emergency Egress." *Safety Science* 38, no. 2 (2001): 95–107.

Parker, Delana Marie. "In Sync: Daily Mood and Diurnal Cortisol Synchronization Between Pre-adolescents and Their Mothers and Fathers." UCLA Electronic Theses and Dissertations, 2017. https://escholarship.org/uc/item/1vb60880.

Passanisi, Alessia, Carmela Madonia, Giovanni Guzzo, and Davide Greco, "Attachment, Self-Esteem and Shame in Emerging Adulthood," *Procedia—Social and Behavioral Sciences* 191, no. 2 (2015): 342–346, https://doi.org/10.1016/j.sbspro.2015.04.552.

Paulus, Martin P. "Decision-Making Dysfunctions in Psychiatry—Altered Homeostatic Processing?" *Science* 218, no. 5850 (2007): 602–606. https://doi.org/10.1126/science.1142997.

Pearl, Robert. "Stress in America: The Causes and Costs." *Forbes*, October 9, 2014. https://www.forbes.com/sites/robertpearl/2014/10/09/stress-in-america-the-causes-and-costs/.

Porges, Stephen W. *The Polyvagal Theory: Neurophysiological Foundations of Emotions, Attachment, Communication, and Self-Regulation* (Norton Series on Interpersonal Neurobiology). New York: W. W. Norton & Company, 2011.

Resnick, Brian, Julia Belluz, and Eliza Barclay. "Is Our Constant Use of Digital Technologies Affecting Our Brain Health? We Asked 11 Experts." Vox, February 26, 2019. https://www.vox.com/science-and-health/2018/11/28/18102745/cellphone-distraction-brain-health-screens-kids.

Richters, John E., and Everett Waters. "Attachment and Socialization: The Positive Side of Social Influence." In *Social Influences and Socialization in Infancy,* edited by Saul Feinman and Michael Lewis, 185–213. Cleveland: Plenum Press, 1991.

Riskind, John H., and Carolyn C. Gotay. "Physical Posture: Could It Have Regulatory or Feedback Effects on Motivation and Emotion?" *Motivation and Emotion* 6, no. 3 (1982): 273–298. https://doi.org/10.1007/BF00992249.

Rogers, Tracie J., and Daniel M. Landers. "Mediating Effects of Peripheral Vision in the Life Event Stress/Athletic Injury Relationship." *Journal of Sport and Exercise Psychology* 27, no. 3 (2005): 271–288.

Romer, Daniel, Kathleen Hall Jamieson, and Sean Aday. "Television News and the Cultivation of Fear of Crime." *Journal of Communication* 53, no. 1 (2003): 88–104. https://doi.org/10.1111/j.1460-2466.2003.tb03007.x.

Rozin, Paul, and Edward B. Royzman. "Negativity Bias, Negativity Dominance, and Contagion." *Personality and Social Psychology Review* 5, no. 4 (2001): 296–320.

Ryan, Richard M., and Edward L. Deci. "Self-Determination Theory and the Facilitation of Intrinsic Motivation, Social Development, and Well-Being." *American Psychologist* 55, no. 1 (2000): 68–78. https://doi.org/10.1037/0003-066X.55.1.68.

Seiler, Annina, Stefanie Kohler, Martina Ruf-Leuschner, and Markus A. Landolt. "Adverse Childhood Experiences, Mental Health, and Quality of Life of Chilean Girls Placed in Foster Care: An Exploratory Study." *Psychological Trauma: Theory, Practice, Research, and Policy* 8, no. 2 (2016): 180–187. https://doi.org/10.1037/tra0000037.

Selye, Hans. "The Evolution of the Stress Concept: The Originator of the Concept Traces Its Development from the Discovery in 1936 of the Alarm Reaction to Modern Therapeutic Applications of Syntoxic and Catatoxic Hormones." *American Scientist* 61, no 6 (1973): 692–699.

————. *The Stress of Life.* New York: McGraw-Hill, 1956.

Sivilli, Teresa I., and Thaddeus W. W. Pace. "The Human Dimensions of Resilience: A Theory of Contemplative Practices and Resilience." Garrison Institute, 2014. https://www.garrisoninstitute.org/wp-content/uploads/2016/03/The_Human_Dimensions_of_Resilience.pdf.

Soussignan, Robert. "Duchenne Smile, Emotional Experience, and Autonomic Reactivity: A Test of the Facial Feedback Hypothesis." *Emotion* 2, no. 1 (2002): 52.

Spira, Jonathan, and Joshua Feintuch. "The Cost of Not Paying Attention: How Interruptions Impact Knowledge Worker Productivity." Information Overload Research Group, January 1, 2015. https://iorgforum.org/wp-content/uploads/2011/06/CostOfNotPayingAttention.BasexReport1.pdf.

Stoll, Julia. "Most Popular TV Genres in the U.S. 2017." Statista, January 13, 2021. https://www.statista.com/statistics/201565/most-popular-genres-in-us-primetime-tv/.

Stoops, William W., and David N. Kearns. "Decision-Making in Addiction: Current Knowledge, Clinical Implications and Future Directions." *Pharmacology Biochemistry and Behavior* 164 (2018): 1–3.

Stosny, Steven. *Treating Attachment Abuse: A Compassionate Approach.* New York: Springer, 1995.

Sullivan, Michael J., Beverly Thorn, Jennifer A. Haythornthwaite, Francis Keefe, Michelle Martin, Laurence A. Bradley, and John C. Lefebvre. "Theoretical Perspectives on the Relation Between Catastrophizing and Pain." *Clinical Journal of Pain* 17, no.1 (2001): 52–64. https://doi.org/10.1097/00002508-200103000-00008.

Tambini, Arielle, Ulrike Rimmele, Elizabeth A. Phelps, and Lila Davachi. "Emotional Brain States Carry Over and Enhance Future Memory Formation." *Nature Neuroscience* 20 (2017): 271–278. https://doi.org/10.1038/nn.4468.

Taylor, Shelley E., and Fuschia M. Sirois. *Health Psychology*, 2nd ed. Toronto, ON: McGraw-Hill Ryerson, Ltd., 2012.

Vaish, Amrisha, Tobias Grossman, and Amanda Woodward. "Not All Emotions Are Created Equal: The Negativity Bias in Social-Emotional Development." *Psychological Bulletin* 134, no. 3 (2008): 383–403. https://doi.org/10.1037/0033-2909.134.3.383.

van der Kolk, Bessel, Mark Greenberg, Helene Boyd, and John Krystal. "Inescapable Shock, Neurotransmitters, and Addiction to Trauma: Toward a Psychobiology of Post-Traumatic Stress." *Biological Psychiatry* 20, no. 3 (1985): 314–325. https://doi.org/10.1016/0006-3223(85)90061-7.

Volpicelli, Joseph, Geetha Balaraman, Julie Hahn, Heather Wallace, and Donald Bux. "The Role of Uncontrollable Trauma in the Development of PTSD and Alcohol Addiction." *Alcohol Research & Health* 23, no. 4 (1999): 256.

von Leupoldt, Andreas, Tobias Sommer, Sarah Kegat, Hans Jörg Baumann, Hans Klose, Bernhard Dahme, and Christian Büchel. "Dyspnea and Pain Share Emotion-Related Brain Network." *NeuroImage* 48, no. 1 (2009): 200–206. https://doi.org/10.1016/j.neuroimage.2009.06.015.

Waters, E., D. Hay, and J. Richters. "Infant-Parent Attachment and the Origins of Prosocial and Antisocial Behavior." In *Development of Antisocial and Prosocial Behavior: Research, Theories, and Issues*, edited by Dan Olweus, Jack Block, and Marian Radke Yarrow, 97–125. New York: Academic Press, 1986.

Williams, Jean M., Phyllis Tonymon, and Mark B. Andersen. "Effects of Life-Event Stress on Anxiety and Peripheral Narrowing." *Behavioral Medicine* 16, no. 4 (1990): 174–181.

Zuckerman, Marvin. "Sensation Seeking: The Balance Between Risk and Reward." In *Self-Regulatory Behavior and Risk Taking: Causes and Consequences*, edited by Lewis P. Lipitt and Leonard L. Mitnick, 143–152. Norwood, NJ: Alex Publishing Co., 1991.

Index

About the Author

Dr. Scott Lyons is a licensed clinical psychologist, doctor of osteopathy (Spain), and mind-body medicine practitioner who specializes in therapies for infants, youth, and adults. Scott is the creator of The Embody Lab—a hub for embodied education, self-discovery, and healing—and developer of Somatic Stress Release™—a process of restoring our biological adaptation system. Scott is also founder of Omala—wellness tools for transformation.

www.TheEmbodyLab.com
www.DrScottLyons.com
IG @DrScottLyons